One Mississippi, Two Mississippi

AJP/MDP062103-6/22/65—PHILADELPHIA, MS: Three memorial march-
ers sit on the steps at the burned ruins of the Mt. Zion Methodist Church after
completing a 12-mile-long march to commemorate the deaths a year ago of three
civil rights workers. Some 70 persons marched from downtown Philadelphia to
the rural church, the burning of which was being investigated by the three when
they were slain. United Press International Telephoto (also shown on the cover).
© Bettmann/CORBIS

One Mississippi, Two Mississippi

*Methodists, Murder, and the Struggle
for Racial Justice in Neshoba County*

— ◦)◦(—

CAROL V. R. GEORGE

OXFORD
UNIVERSITY PRESS

OXFORD

UNIVERSITY PRESS

Oxford University Press is a department of the University of
Oxford. It furthers the University's objective of excellence in research,
scholarship, and education by publishing worldwide.

Oxford   New York

Auckland   Cape Town   Dar es Salaam   Hong Kong   Karachi
Kuala Lumpur   Madrid   Melbourne   Mexico City   Nairobi
New Delhi   Shanghai   Taipei   Toronto

With offices in

Argentina   Austria   Brazil   Chile   Czech Republic   France   Greece
Guatemala   Hungary   Italy   Japan   Poland   Portugal   Singapore
South Korea   Switzerland   Thailand   Turkey   Ukraine   Vietnam

Oxford is a registered trademark of Oxford University Press
in the UK and certain other countries.

Published in the United States of America by
Oxford University Press
198 Madison Avenue, New York, NY 10016

Library of Congress Cataloging-in-Publication Data
George, Carol V. R.
One Mississippi, two Mississippi : Methodists, murder, and the struggle for racial justice in
Neshoba County / Carol V.R. George.
pages cm
Includes bibliographical references.
ISBN 978-0-19-023108-8 (cloth : alk. paper)   1. Methodists—Mississippi—Neshoba
County—History.   2. Neshoba County (Miss.)—Race relations—History.   3. African
Americans—Crimes against—Mississippi—Neshoba County—History.   I. Title.
BX8249.N46G46 2015
305.896'0730762685—dc23
2014034000

1 3 5 7 9 8 6 4 2
Printed in the United States of America
on acid-free paper

Dedicated to the people of Mt. Zion United Methodist Church

Whose house is this? . . . why does its lock fit my key?
TONI MORRISON, Home

Contents

Preface

IN THE EARLY summer of 2001, I made my initial research trip to Mississippi, after learning that the state was to release the files of the Mississippi State Sovereignty Commission to a limited public. The Sovereignty Commission was the state's spy agency during the civil rights era, tasked with looking into anything connected with Mississippi movement activity. My companion at the only two viewing machines in the state archives in Jackson was Jenny Irons, at that time completing a dissertation in sociology on the Sovereignty Commission, and whose family lived in Philadelphia, Mississippi. When she learned of my work in American religious history, she suggested I might want to visit Mt. Zion United Methodist Church in Longdale, just outside Philadelphia, which had been burned by the Ku Klux Klan in a conspiracy to murder three young civil rights workers in 1964. The three men killed, Michael Schwerner and Andrew Goodman of New York, and James Chaney of Meridian, Mississippi, have come to occupy a special place in the American historical record, their courage and commitment well known. However, little has been written about the contributions of Mt. Zion Church to that same civil rights project. Its formative role was attested to by a speaker at its fiftieth commemoration service, who said that if ever one's courage flagged, a walk around Mt. Zion Church and its cemetery would restore it.[1] Mt. Zion's people are as the three young men were; courageous, committed, historically embattled and threatened, yet through it all they remain fixed on a better future.

I left my reading of the Sovereignty Commission files behind in Jackson, more than a little eager to escape their stories from the crypt, and so with New York license plates on my car, I drove two hours east to Philadelphia, and then on to Longdale. I found the country road that posted a sign to Mt. Zion United Methodist Church, though after traveling some

distance down the road I failed to find the church. I stopped to ask directions from two people who were washing their car. Jennifer Riley Hathorn
and Freddie Grady put their work aside, offered directions to the church,
and suggested I stop by on the way back. After walking around the neat
brick church and its grounds, I returned to the front yard where Jennifer
and Freddie waited. They were very proud of their church and their community, but they said they had been troubled for a long time by the image
of Longdale community that had been portrayed in the 1989 Hollywood
movie *Mississippi Burning*. They believed the movie dealt only in stereotypes, caricaturing the black residents of Longdale as victimized, powerless
recipients of white violence, while portraying the FBI agents working the
1964 murder case as the true heroes of the Neshoba conspiracy. From the
perspective of Jennifer and Freddie, Mt. Zion Church members had been
soldiers in the battle against segregation for a long time, with their constant goal an inclusive society in the church and in the community.

Like many black veterans of the civil rights movement, Jennifer and
Freddie believed the movie distorted the black Southern experience, and
conveyed that distortion to a large public audience. Mt. Zion's members
did not think they were powerless or victimized, the two agreed, and were
people who nurtured a keen appetite for education for their children.
Jennifer was a nurse, then working as the director of the local day-care
center, Freddie a lineman for Neshoba County, and like many others in
Longdale, they could claim relatives who had worked in the civil rights
movement and had represented the church in the Methodist conference.
It was hardly a new revelation to them that the media typically misrep-
resented the lives of black people, but *Mississippi Burning* was different.
A controversial film, it reached new audiences, and although a work of
fiction, it managed to convey the sense that it was *the* master narrative of
Mississippi black life. For Jennifer and Freddie, the depiction was not only
wrong, but damaging to the present interests of the community, whose
most urgent needs were jobs and schools, not service at restaurants or
Walmart.

It was also important to Jennifer and Freddie, and then later to me,
that Mt. Zion was a Methodist church, part of the predominantly white
denomination then known as the United Methodist Church. The denomination boasted that it was an "inclusive" church, welcoming to everyone,
although most Methodists knew that local congregations were racially
exclusive. The nearby city of Philadelphia was home to the white First
United Methodist Church, and Longdale, out in the country, to the black

Mt. Zion United Methodist church, a separation replicated in most congregations around the country. So between research trips to Philadelphia, Jackson, and Longdale, I scoured Methodist historical records in the official Methodist Archives in Madison, New Jersey, by then determined to learn more about Mt. Zion Church. In the Methodist Archives I learned about the Central Jurisdiction, the racially separate administrative unit the denomination created in 1939 in order to heal the North-South breach in the church. As I examined the records, I became convinced that the Central Jurisdiction represented far more than a bureaucratic move, but was an important symbolic statement by America's largest Protestant denomination about its attitude toward all the loyal black members who struggled to pay their church assessment from very limited resources. At a crucial time in America's cultural development, the Methodist Church had given its stamp of approval to separation based on race. Denominational records also showed the differing responses to the Central Jurisdiction in the black community of Methodists and the white. White Southerners were convinced that the new segregated unit was an inspired compromise that would end regional separation. The differing responses of the two communities of Methodists seemed profound, incorporating matters of perception, values, even time: white Methodists in the South found their references in the past; and black Methodists, while hardly heedless of their brutal history, consistently looked toward the future for promise of change.

The differences in racial perceptions that were exposed in the conflict over the Central Jurisdiction addressed directly the problem Gunnar Myrdal described in his two-volume work *The American Dilemma*. Americans aspire to be known for their democratic ideals, their equality of opportunity, their access to equal justice, although in the recesses of their souls they recognize that they fall short of those values in their dealings with black Americans. It is as if they confess, "the good that I would do, that I do not." The dilemma is like the can that gets kicked down the road for someone else to deal with.

In the case of Mt. Zion Church in Neshoba County, the failure of the Methodist Church and the state of Mississippi to come to terms with the constituent parts of the American Dilemma led in the 1960s and 1970s to a racial conflagration in the area. Mt. Zion was entrapped in the Klan conspiracy that led to the lynching of the three young men. Their church was burned, some of its members beaten, and hopes for the precious right to vote postponed. The ashes of that fire continue to smolder, in the state and in the nation.

It is possible that, as historian Joseph Crespino has written, Mississippi has for so long been *In Search of Another Country* that significant social change is unlikely.[2] Yet as I researched this work, I discovered forces of transformation in communities quietly working toward a distant goal of reconciliation. Some of these efforts are quite local, with the Philadelphia Coalition in Neshoba County as one example, while others are statewide, such as the parent organization known as the Winter Institute for Racial Reconciliation in Oxford. And there are impassioned individuals who bring energy and resources to the task of healing the brokenness of the past. These advocates of change remain a small, dedicated, and under-funded coalition of groups and individuals, who understand that the damaged past must be acknowledged before authentic reconciliation can occur in the future. In April 2014, the *New Yorker* magazine, in comments about a Harlem art show, observed, "the South is ever with us, stirring bitter and sweet associations."[3] The statement is a commentary on the duality of Mississippi culture, though it is the sweet associations that the advocates of reconciliation aim to cultivate.

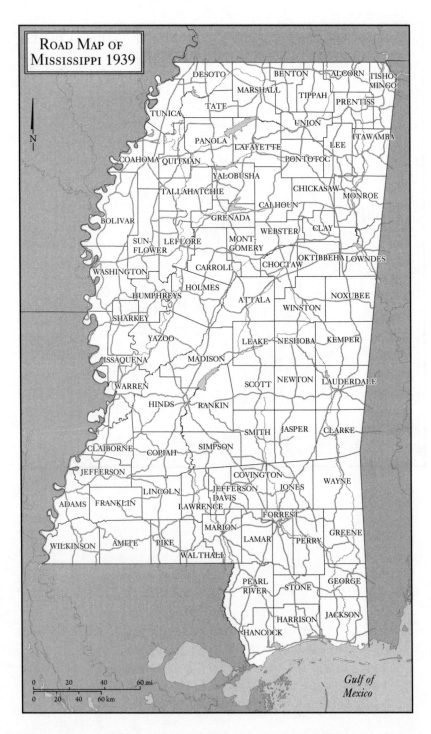

ROAD MAP OF
MISSISSIPPI 1939

N

DESOTO
MARSHALL
BENTON
ALCORN
TISHO-
MINGO
TIPPAH
PRENTISS
TATE
TUNICA
UNION
PANOLA
LAFAYETTE
LEE
ITAWAMBA
COAHOMA QUITMAN
PONTOTOC
YALOBUSHA
CHICKASAW
MONROE
TALLAHATCHIE
CALHOUN
GRENADA
WEBSTER
CLAY
BOLIVAR
SUN-
FLOWER
LEFLORE
MONT-
GOMERY
WASHINGTON
CARROLL
CHOCTAW
OKTIBBEHA
LOWNDES
HOLMES
HUMPHREYS
ATTALA
NOXUBEE
SHARKEY
WINSTON
YAZOO
ISSAQUENA
MADISON
LEAKE
NESHOBA
KEMPER
WARREN
HINDS
RANKIN
SCOTT
NEWTON
LAUDERDALE
SMITH
JASPER
CLARKE
CLAIBORNE
COPIAH
SIMPSON
JEFFERSON
COVINGTON
WAYNE
LINCOLN
JEFFERSON
DAVIS
JONES
ADAMS
FRANKLIN
LAWRENCE
FORREST
GREENE
MARION
LAMAR
PERRY
WILKINSON
AMITE
PIKE
WALTHALL
PEARL
RIVER
STONE
GEORGE
HARRISON
JACKSON
HANCOCK

0   20   40   60 mi
0   20   40   60 km

*Gulf of
Mexico*

Source: After an original map held by the Mississippi Department of Archives and History.

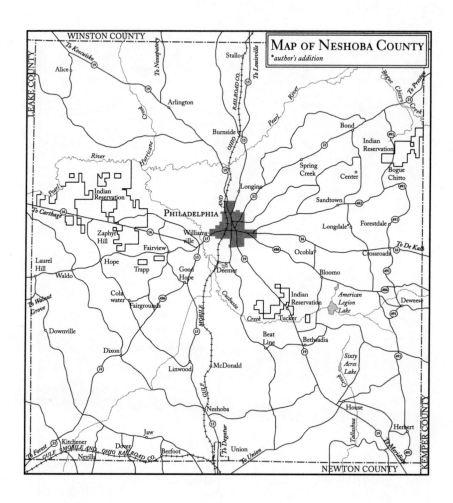

MAP OF NESHOBA COUNTY
author's addition

WINSTON COUNTY

LEAKE COUNTY

To Koscutsko
Alice
Arlington
River
Hurricane Creek
Pearl
Indian Reservation
To Cartbage
Zaphyr Hill
Fairview
Laurel Hill
Hope
Trapp
Waldo
Cola water
Fairgrounds
Downville
Dixon
Linwood
McDonald
Neshoba
Jaw
To Forest
Kitchener
Dover
Berfoot
Nevilla
To Decatur
Union
To Union

Stallo
To Louisville
Burnside
Longino
PHILADELPHIA
Williams-ville
Goon Hope
Deemar
RAILROAD CO.
OHIO
MOBILE AND
GULF
MOBILE AND OHIO RAILROAD CO.
Cushushba Creek

To Prestor
Bogue Chitto Creek
Pearl River
Bond
Indian Reservation
Spring Creek
Center
Bogue Chitto
Sandtown
Longdale
Forestdale
To De Kalb
Ocobla
Bloomo
Crossroads
Indian Reservation
American Legion Lake
Deweese
Tucker
Beat Line
Bethsadia
Sixty Acres Lake
House
Herbert
To Meridian

KEMPER COUNTY

NEWTON COUNTY

One Mississippi, Two Mississippi

Introduction

IN THE COURSE of writing this book, I have tried to stay mindful of the advice of Flannery O'Connor about the value of "reading a small history in a universal light," an insight that has influenced my thinking about how a country church of black Methodists can serve as a prism for examining America's perplexing problem of race, what Gunnar Myrdal called the "American Dilemma." Mt. Zion United Methodist Church in Longdale, Mississippi, in the hilly east central part of the state, was founded by freed people who accepted the hopes for social revolution that Reconstruction promised, and the words of missionaries of the Methodist denomination who said equal treatment was the right of all God's children. That revolution was short-lived, the racial gains of Reconstruction quickly replaced with a white supremacist social code and legalized discriminatory Jim Crow. The account here deals with Mt. Zion and its Neshoba County environment largely during the twentieth century and some years after, when church and state in Mississippi congealed in a "totalistic society" so fundamental it often seemed like a police state. Yet Mt. Zion Church, like many other congregations of black Methodists in the South, embraced the beliefs of the founders, confident that in the struggles over race, they held the moral high ground. Even during the vast exodus of migrants during the Great Migration, relatively few black Methodists left the Magnolia State. These Methodists called themselves the "faithful Black Remnant."

Mt. Zion is not an ordinary country church. Its internet address is http://www.historicmtzion.org, a designation that acknowledges its role in the memorable Freedom School project to expand the black vote during the summer of 1964. By that time, Mt. Zion was already experienced in the struggle with the white supremacist forces that controlled the state and permeated the Methodist Church, both locally and nationally.

Its members remember the stories from that tragic past and are eager to tell them. In the telling of their memories, as well as in the recall of the experiences of their ancestors, they always somehow double back to the human rights issue of "how they were treated," by whites and their institutions. Ever mindful of the history of slavery and Jim Crow, people speak most feelingly of the pain of public humiliation and social invisibility—an issue barely touched on in the American historical record. Archbishop Desmond Tutu of South Africa proposed a remedy: before racial healing can truly begin in any broken society, he said it is necessary for oppressors and oppressed to excise the wounds of the past. Relying on a recurrent metaphor of "healing," Archbishop Tutu noted, "However painful the experience, the wounds of the past must not be allowed to fester. They must be opened. They must be cleansed. And balm must be poured on them so they can heal."[1] Like many others inside and outside Mississippi, I have wondered how realistic is the possibility for communities that have long battled each other to come to terms with a past once controlled by conditions of inequality and oppression, and learn to live in peace. The first requirement for the process of reconciliation is a commitment to learning about the reality of each other's past, to engage in radical and painful truth-telling.

In 1965, Mt. Zion initiated an annual commemorative service to honor the three men who died and their mission to extend the black vote, to tell the truth in historical context. Or, as veteran civil rights activist David Dennis said, "This [commemoration service in 2014] is not just about them; it is about all of them," the ones who died, the ones who struggled past glaring sheriffs to try to vote, and the ones who, like the residents of Longdale, supported movement workers with food and shelter.[2] They were constant witnesses to the "Second Reconstruction" of the 1960s, confident that unlike its predecessor, this one would not go backwards. The annual service, a time for not just truth telling but also bridge building and creating public history, transformed Mt. Zion from a small, hard-to-find country church, into a magnet for other racial egalitarians in the state, and even in the nation. Church members participated in organizations like the interracial Philadelphia Coalition and the statewide Winter Institute for Racial Reconciliation, collective efforts to make justice available to all citizens of the state. Participants in this triracial "other Mississippi" know they are a minority in the state, but they are convinced their work will produce results, and extend the options available to the next generation.

Reading material about Mississippi's racial conflicts during the period this work covers—from 1879 to 2005—can feel like participating in a battle in "another country." The language is inevitably charged: it speaks of struggles, battles, sieges, even conflict. It recalls images of a state that was an even greater threat to slaves than other places, when slaves were warned their punishment could be to be "sold down the river" to Mississippi. It had a reputation for being able to tame the most recalcitrant slave. It was the first of the Confederate states to undo the gains of Reconstruction with ever more restrictive Jim Crow laws. The Magnolia State welcomed the Klan and used state funds to pay for the spying operations of the Mississippi State Sovereignty Commission. It memorialized the *Lost Cause* and perpetuated the "Plantation Myth" of the Old South. This is "one" Mississippi, the Mississippi of the Old South: it has deep roots, and continues to grow new branches. Many black people speak of losing children "to the streets" because of the continuing barriers of second-generation Jim Crow.

Those whose goal is to bring change and an inclusive society to Mississippi espy quite different characteristics in the state. Nicknamed the "Hospitality State," Mississippi, these advocates of change contend, is also home to people who are caring, literate, welcoming, and tolerant. Their work is to help such qualities flourish, primarily by focusing on education reform, young people, the next generation, and mobilizing the vote. The "haters and bitter enders," according to former Governor William Winter, represent the old massive resistance crowd of the 1950s and 1960s, and they are people over sixty years old.[3] Their day is passing, he is convinced, with a new day on the horizon. When that day comes, the "other Mississippi" that argues for compassion and tolerance will become the dominant Mississippi.

Finally, "one Mississippi, two Mississippi" is sometimes taken as a way of measuring time. Repeated at a moderate pace to "ten Mississippi" should take ten seconds. Time moves forward and change occurs. Nevertheless, and quite paradoxically, a persistent problem throughout this work has been the differing meanings applied to words that connote time. What does "all deliberate speed" mean? Or "speedy implementation"? Did the federal government and the Methodist denomination mean to convey a sense of immediacy by those terms, or were the meanings as Mississippi Methodist John Satterfield said they were: "eventually," or "when you get around to it?" Mandated change is meant to occur at the measured rate of "one Mississippi, two Mississippi," while voluntary change can proceed at a much more leisurely pace, more in keeping with the honeyed accents of white Southerners.

In researching this work, the primary evidence has come from the recollections of members of Mt. Zion, from their colleagues within the "other Mississippi," both black and white, while including a few representatives of the "Old South" Mississippi. I am aware that oral history can be as fallible as documentary history. There is actually little documentary material relating to Mt. Zion, except in select records of land transactions, tax rolls, and voting registers. Since 1980, *The Neshoba Democrat* has given fuller and more accurate coverage to the various black communities in its circulation area. One of the most useful resources has been Methodist conference Minutes, General Conference Records, and reports of the various commissions delegated to resolve the vexing issues raised by the Central Jurisdiction. I have also used material from the COFO (Council of Federated Organizations) Collection in the possession of Jan Hillegas. Much of the basic narrative of the Neshoba tragedy in 1964 was shaped by journalists who covered the story, most of them white, and all of them aware of the dramatic appeal of a story recounting the brutal murders of three idealistic young men on a mission to advance the rights of others. That storyline did not require much context, which meant the experience of the black community intimately involved in the tragedy was left out. Mt. Zion's context is presented here.

This work is intended not only to provide that previously overlooked perspective, but to recount the efforts of a community of black Methodists to survive in a racist environment that extended beyond "the closed society." Their struggle was with the then largest Protestant denomination in the country, with a federal government that preferred benign neglect to active involvement, and with a state bureaucracy that ignored the ill treatment visited on a majority of its citizens. It is a story that, at Mt. Zion at least, ends as always with hope for the future, combined with the lessons learned through historical experience: the need to be ever-watchful of those who envy your optimism and faith. There is much work yet to be done.

PART ONE

History and Memory

Settling Longdale, Mississippi,
and Mt. Zion Methodist Church

I

As We Remembered Zion, 1833–1890

Waller asked prospective juror W. E. Greer: Do you think it is a crime for a white man to kill a nigger in Mississippi? Judge Hendrick: What was his answer? Waller: He's thinking it over.
NASH AND TAGGART, Mississippi Politics

The emancipation of four million of slaves had opened at our very door a wide field calling alike for mission and educational work. It has developed upon the Church a fearful responsibility.
FREEDMAN'S AID SOCIETY REPORT, 1866[1]

The Role of Memory in Neshoba History

Whereas no place in America has escaped the burden of race initiated by seventeenth-century slave traders, few have been remembered as a regimen so harsh on its black residents as Mississippi. It's an image that emerges in Diane McWhorter's allusion to the state: "In the landscape of the national imagination, Mississippi was once the heart of darkness, a faraway jungle where exploitation and evil coexisted under a ground cover of flowers as well as poisonous bramble."[2] The description continues to resonate with many in twenty-first-century America, who still think of Mississippi as far away, "another country" even, where the mysterious beauty of the state has helped contribute to a plenitude of gifted writers, but where tangled brambles still hide extreme forms of the old racism, including its having the record for the greatest number of lynchings. National media representations contribute little toward creating anything resembling a more conciliatory spirit emerging through the racial thicket, though plans circulating for a new civil rights museum in Jackson would suggest there are important actors in the state who believe the time for change has come. The tenacity of old memories—of the *Lost Cause* and the "Plantation Myth"—has been damaging to both whites and blacks, and has resisted the pull of more recent history.

There is a need, therefore, for Mississippians, perhaps Americans generally, to "come to terms with the past," an effort that involves retracing the state's "dark journey." There has always been a third racial grouping in Mississippi, the Choctaw Indians, whose own dark experience began in 1833 when the majority of their ancestors were driven out, but who in contemporary Neshoba County contribute much to the growth of the local economy. The focus here, however, is on the living testimony of those who endured Mississippi's cruel Jim Crow era, people who knew personally the indignities of the white supremacist social code, yet often found ways to evade it and soldier on. They are individuals who through membership or friendship or kinship have ties to Mt. Zion United Methodist Church in Longdale.

Their recall provides one context for understanding the history of the area and the collective memories of local residents, black and white. The pioneering sociologist on the subject of collective memory, Maurice Halbwachs, has said that collective memory must be understood in context, and Neshoba County in east central Mississippi provides the living landscape for interpreting the experience of both Methodist Mt. Zion and the nearby, mostly white, city of Philadelphia.[3] Memory, like history, has subjective limitations, but it is an important vehicle used by individuals and groups to encode their past. White Neshoba County, compact and segregated for most of its existence, has demonstrated a nearly intractable hold on its remembered past, making it a useful area for studying racial dynamics over a long period of time, and the hold of memory on the process. For most of its life, Neshoba County's racial proportions have been constant, with two-thirds of the population white, about a third black, and a scattering of Choctaws.

The county is mostly rural with no large cities, and was never part of the fabulously wealthy society of nineteenth-century cotton planters in the Delta. Its residents reveal a sense of place, with great fondness for the area, the topography helping to foster an intimacy among neighbors. The region and the land have had a formative effect on Mt. Zion Church and its local community of Longdale, whose earliest settlers were drawn there by talk of available land. The hamlet of Longdale, a hollow in the country, provided protection at a time when it was needed, but also access to a city only eight miles away.

The first black settlers were also pioneering Methodists, likely familiar with the evangelizing social witness of the church, who were formally introduced to the denomination by traveling missionaries. There were many varieties of Methodism in the South, some exclusively black, or "African." But Mt. Zion's people chose to align with the large, predominantly white, national body, an alternative to what was becoming a "closed society." From the very beginning enthusiastic, Mt. Zion members were loyal Methodists who regarded it their moral responsibility to support a church that announced itself as racially inclusive. Racial inclusiveness, received as a moral imperative, remained its mission and its witness thereafter.

Early Neshoba: The Setting

Neshoba County was founded in 1833 by whites and their slaves shortly after most of the Indian residents were driven out. The Choctaws had ceded their land to the government, although some remained behind. Ironically, it was their descendants, many decades later, who sparked the economic revitalization of the region with gambling casinos and other entrepreneurial skills. Mississippi's racial history has neglected the Choctaw presence primarily because the fundamental racial contest was between whites and blacks. The battles over race are startling, yet racial conflict was not unique to Neshoba or to the rest of the nation. The racial history of Neshoba County is synonymous in the public mind with the brutal murders of movement activists Michael Schwerner, James Chaney, and Andrew Goodman in 1964. Thus, while racism has been manifest everywhere in the nation, it is the extremity in scale and in kind in Mississippi, which has usually gone unchecked, that contributes to its iconic image. The underlying themes in this work—hope and fear, alienation and community, death and reconciliation, faith and despair—have perplexed all people at various times, not just in Neshoba. But it is the starkness of the struggle there, of which the cold-blooded murders of three young men is just one example, that contributes to a singularly stark interpretation of the area.

Despite its relatively small black population, Neshoba has been notable in the state's racially troubled past. Its topography, so different from the rich Delta region, has permitted Neshoba County to cultivate a pattern of race relations in harmony with its landscape. From first settlement, white supremacy was the controlling ideology here as elsewhere in the state, but because of the configuration of the land, plantation-style farming was never an option. The heavily timbered hills and the sticky red clay soil were not hospitable to large-scale farming. So the area never became home to the kind of large black labor force found in the major cotton-growing areas. The scrubby, treed land was good for cattle, timber, some cotton and other agriculture, but not plantation farming. Its black population was therefore smaller than in the Delta, and there was more land that whites seemed not to want.

Mt. Zion's early settlers, recently freed, were likely drawn to Neshoba because of the rumors of available land. The county's hilly geography meant that few of its white residents would be able to compete with the ostentatious lifestyles of Delta planters, who for a time presented the largest concentration of millionaires in the country. There were a few pockets of exceptional wealth in Neshoba to be sure, mostly among the timber magnates, but the county never gave the appearance of having anything similar to the super-rich "class" that existed in the Delta. Neshoba's black population became farmers, sharecroppers, and some teachers, and it was consistently about one-third of the total. One result of this sort of racial distribution is that the white majority could have few misgivings about shaping policy to its advantage, unlike the Delta area where it was sometimes necessary for white planters and other employers dependent on black labor to make concessions to the black workforce. But both on Delta plantations and small farms elsewhere, blacks were counted on to be the unpaid labor for white farmers, first as slaves, then as indebted sharecroppers, though occasionally in Neshoba as paid timber workers and domestics.

A Détente between Methodism and Slaveholding

An important memory, often forgotten, is that Mississippi once presented an alternate racial picture. The state was triracial until the 1830 Treaty of Dancing Rabbit drove out most Choctaws.[4] There was also a short but notable period of interracial cooperation between whites and blacks in the earliest years of settlement, much of it due to the efforts of Methodist circuit riders. Beginning with the work of an itinerant minister, the Reverend Tobias Gibson in 1799, there was a sprinkling of biracial congregations of followers of John Wesley located around a base Gibson laid down in Natchez. By the time of Gibson's death in 1804 there were 132 whites and 72 blacks enrolled in the denomination. Methodism seemed suited to frontier Mississippi; the white settlers liked its enthusiastic outdoor camp meetings and its fervent preaching, and blacks were especially drawn to its antislavery message, historically associated in the state with the arrival in 1810 of William Winans, though the work was known among black Methodists since the denomination's famous Christmas Conference of 1784. By 1816, Methodist membership had grown to 1,551 whites and 410 blacks, an increase that reflected not just population growth but economic increase, as slavery and cotton growing expanded apace. These early efforts created a black Methodist foundation in the state.[5] Nineteenth-century Methodist evangelists continued to affirm John Wesley's injunction against slaveholding, describing it as a moral issue, a message obviously attractive to blacks but eventually alienating to the emerging planter class.

Slaveholding, minus Methodism's moral antislavery sting in the South, established the basis for a society built on inequality. Because of slavery and cotton, Mississippi prospered to become the fifth-richest state in the nation in the two decades before the Civil War. The slave population grew by 100 percent in each decade of the 1830s and 1840s, most of it concentrated in the Delta area. Delta slaveholdings were large, with the median holding in the Delta County of Issaquena being 118; in a hilly place like Neshoba the comparable number was 11.[6]

Successful Delta planters set the social tone in the state, not by their numbers, but by their great displays of wealth, designed largely to impress other planters. Their conspicuous consumption made clear to poor whites and slaves just who was in charge. They indulged in imported goods: carriages, especially, which were often shipped from England and decorated with ornate woodcarvings. They sought consumer products too, such as French leggings, Italian medicated soap, French party dresses, and Swiss lace, which arrived in small Mississippi towns via transshipment from either New Orleans or Memphis.[7]

The emergence of this powerful planter class with its vast slave labor force, though located largely in the Delta, became the keystone of the remembered history of most whites in the South, many raised on the "Plantation Myth." This Plantation imagery grew during the two decades leading up to the Civil War, as planters evolved a system of white supremacy that would affect all slaves, many poor whites, and of course all planters themselves. With the Northern victory at Appomattox, white Southerners expanded their history by adding to their collective memory the "Lost Cause" interpretation of the war. According to this view, which had an enduring life in the Neshoba area, the South had been noble and honorable, defeated in war because crude and irreligious Northerners had invaded their land, ravaged the countryside, raped their women, and evidenced no experience living with blacks. The myth persisted, and served as a basis for suspicions about outsiders, "Yankees" in particular. It mattered little that Neshoba was physically spared much of the conflict of the Civil War. Memories thrive on imagination, and for many white Mississippians the Confederate defeat at Vicksburg and the struggle for control of the Mississippi River remained vivid overarching images. In Neshoba, shared stories and the local newspaper were reminders to residents of a battle that almost occurred in Philadelphia, Mississippi, in 1863—the same year as the battles at Vicksburg and Gettysburg—when Union officer William Grierson surrounded the town and made people promise to keep the presence of the soldiers a secret for twenty-four hours.[8]

When the war and slavery finally ended in 1865, abolitionists, "carpet-baggers," and "scalawags"—some black, mostly white—some from within the state but largely from outside, came to Mississippi hoping to develop a plan for Reconstruction that would provide ex-slaves with a form of freedom that would include justice and free land. The presence of outsiders exacerbated the fears of Southern whites worried about the loss of a black labor force and the possibility of black control.

The Longdale community was settled during this period, around the same time many other rural black settlements were springing up around the state. Philadelphia, eight miles west of Longdale, was a potential source of employment and supplies. Residents began to arrive between 1863 and 1877, and as with many institutions and policies that emerge in a period of social upheaval, the church the Longdale people built was stamped with the revolutionary ideals that gave it birth. Historians and others who have considered the consequences of the post–Civil War years, often reach widely divergent conclusions about just how revolutionary the moment was. The era still looms large in the memories of black and white Southerners.

Reconstruction provided the historical foundation for Mt. Zion, for the freed people who became Methodists. Later analysts of the era of Reconstruction, supportive of its aims, consider its policies part of an unfinished social revolution, with goals still to be realized. Critics at the time thought its policies were setting up conditions for "race war" and the continuing economic impoverishment of the South. Reconstruction's nineteenth-century advocates, similar to those of the activists of the "Second Reconstruction" of the 1960s, were most often enthusiasts and idealists with expansive plans for social change. Black and white spokespeople for Reconstruction called for a new beginning that started with rebuilding the South; they called for new schools for black and white children, and the black vote for their fathers. But beyond that they also called for other social measures, like charities, colleges, and hospitals that would come into being with aid from the federal government, meaning tax dollars. The Southern economy had been broken by the war and was obviously in need of help, but the industrial reformers who would initiate change did not come until later, and some were as corrupt as the politicians who wooed them. Proposed Reconstruction policies were expensive, expansive, and in their emphasis on black advance, controversial; the revolution ended almost before it had a chance to demonstrate its potential in the war-damaged South, though it left behind strong and enduring memories about social change in the minds of its partisans.

The freed people who settled Longdale and soon announced themselves as Methodists were among those who supported Reconstruction reforms, particularly the franchise—which some already possessed—and landownership. That was not an unlikely development, given that as early as 1867 the Mississippi Mission Conference had announced the "inalienable rights" of all, "at the ballot box" and in their "persons, property, business . . . liberty and religion," a position that aided the rapid growth of Methodists among blacks, whose numbers rose from 8,732 full members in 1869 to 26,100 in 1878.[9] But Mississippi was the Southern state most fiercely opposed to Reconstruction, and efforts to dismantle the new social programs began early, starting in 1874. Just a year later the Democratic "Redeemers," who would "redeem" the state from potential black control, put in place the Mississippi Plan of 1875 to manipulate the political process in order to end what was most worrisome to whites, namely black voting. In commenting on these efforts, one Mississippi historian observed, "Seldom have politicians been as irresponsible."[10] In its more benign form, the First Mississippi Plan, as it was called, required these new black voters to know the section, township, and range within which they lived, and to stay mindful of their polling places, which were changed regularly as white registrars relocated them without telling potential black voters. Then rumors and fears of "race war" whipped up a white frenzy, at one time forcing the New England-born governor of Mississippi, Adelbert Ames, to appeal to Republican president Ulysses Grant and the federal government for help with troops to suppress the "revolutionary measures" of the Democrats. His request was ultimately denied. Emboldened, these "Redeemers" resorted to outright violence against blacks and stuffed ballot boxes, so that in the ensuing election of 1876 Democrats swept into office and proceeded to organize impeachment proceedings against Republican officeholders.[11]

In Mississippi and elsewhere in the South, Reconstruction was the "Time of Jubilee" for the newly freed people, the long hoped-for time when they would experience the rights available to other Americans. When Reconstruction ended, freedom still meant for them the opportunity to choose their own life's path, a choice they exercised in different ways: some remained on the farms where they had worked for years and where they had kin; some went in search of family members taken from them; and still others moved to nearby towns and cities, where they established new communities, some like Longdale, which supported an inclusive society, and others like Mound Bayou, the entirely black town founded in 1887. They struggled to keep hope alive.

Longdale Creates Its History

The politics of this time of social disorder were the historical experience of the people who settled Longdale community. A few freed people had occupied and worked the land there as early as 1870, land largely untouched by the Indians who had once claimed it. A white clergyman, W. J. Seale, owned large tracts in the area surrounding Longdale, and timber companies, recognizing possibilities, laid claim to much of the rest. But the land had not been cleared or planted and it was only its timber stands that once attracted speculators and other white financial interests to it. These early black settlers employed a variety of strategies to gain land for their families; some, along with a few whites, homesteaded the land, then built on it and improved it for planting and cattle. Reconstruction reforms had aroused their hopes too, but when the brutal "Redemption" measures came and their revolutionary energies were challenged, they had only their church to maintain their aspirations.

People frequently made the long walk from Longdale to the developing white city of Philadelphia, and sometimes rode in wagons the forty-five miles in the opposite direction to the commercial center of Meridian, home to a growing black Methodist church. Five or six other small black settlements were nearby, creating a rural network of freed people with Longdale at the center. The people who came to Longdale were from places near and far; some from neighboring Lauderdale County, and others from more distant locations, like Alabama, Georgia, and South Carolina. They

were experienced farmers who hoped to become independent landowners, as virtually all freed people did. Their only capital was their labor,
which they believed that with help from family and neighbors could be
transformed into an independent livelihood, eked from the scrubby,
timbered land that whites did not covet. Longdale was far off the main
road, its nearest neighbors white Methodists who worshipped two miles
away at Pinehurst Methodist Church, founded in 1834. To get supplies, it
was best to make the trek to Philadelphia on Saturdays when there were
other people around, who could serve as protection from members of the
recently formed Ku Klux Klan, who might find sport in assaulting a lone
black pedestrian. Though Reconstruction was a brief moment in time,
Longdale's settlers held on to its goals.

Longdale's white neighbors in Neshoba remembered Reconstruction
differently, and they, too, passed that memory to their children. Seen not as
an era of progressive reforms beneficial to them as well as to blacks, white
Neshobans reframed Reconstruction as a scheme of the Republicans that
led to fraud, taxes, excesses, and the sight of black men in public offices.
They were confident, however, that the status quo antebellum would be
returned, if necessary by means foul as well as fair, which could involve
calling on violent Klan enforcers at the ready. The disenfranchisement of
blacks, they were convinced, would "redeem" them from the troublesome
outsiders who did not appreciate their culture.[12] Whites learned early to be
suspicious of anything that seemed to originate from "outside" the state.

Once Mississippi was successfully under Democratic control, its politicians rewrote the state constitution in 1890 to make segregation and
"legal" separation of the races mandated social policy. Evidence from state
voting registers indicate that Neshoba County was one of those places that,
for reasons unclear, did not fully comply with the disenfranchisement of
all its black voters until later in the decade. Some of the men of Longdale
who had secured the vote during Reconstruction proved unwilling to give
it up easily.[13] In other areas of life, the South's emergent "Social Code"
segregating the races could substitute for constitutional segregation until
an enforcement policy was firmly in place.

In the new "redeemed" order, churches, as well as any public place people gathered, were to be as segregated as all the others. Segregation was
an easy move for the Baptist churches that dominated the state because
they were locally governed and controlled, but separation was a more
complicated matter for those planters who perceived a status value in
being Methodists. Methodism was a connectional denomination subject

to control that could be local, as with quarterly and annual conferences, or more distant, as with bishops and the General Conference. Some of those planters, who had grown wealthy on cotton and slavery, had decided to leave Methodism well before the war began, hoping to find another denomination that would judge them less harshly for owning slaves, as the General Conference continued to do.

So for the Methodist denomination, with this hierarchical and connectional governance, the segregated church structure of the Old South that was being reimposed created new problems for its leaders. When the General Conference battled the race question in 1844 the result was a regional split. In the South, Methodists who called themselves Christian segregationists, joined the renamed Methodist Episcopal Church, South. Methodism nationally—which is to say largely Northeastern and Midwestern—had enjoyed a "meteoric" rise in membership during the first half of the nineteenth century, and during the White House years of President Ulysses Grant, between 1868 and 1876, it enjoyed yet more enthusiastic popular acceptance, with newspapers referring to the president's "Methodist court" and the "influence of Methodist priests."[14] Leaders of this branch of Methodism worried how the denomination could minister to all its flock as the new Southern racial code prohibited freed people—whom Methodists had once courted successfully for converts—from worshipping with their white co-religionists who were segregationists.

Despite the turmoil, Longdale farm families, though just recently settled into small shotgun cabins, laid plans for a church for their community to replace an outdoor hush arbor. The residents agreed that the settlement needed a church to anchor it. The prevailing political instability hardly made it a propitious time to contemplate institution building in Neshoba County, or actually anywhere in the South. Some Reconstruction measures, though reduced in scope, still remained in sufficient strength to persuade the people of Longdale their church plans could succeed. A number of male residents of the community still voted, and on the state level there remained the striking example of sitting black politicians, like Blanche K. Bruce, who remained in the Congress, and John R. Lynch and thirty-two others who served in the state legislature.[15] Longdale people may have felt empowered by these examples, for some men refused to be intimidated into conceding the vote until 1903.[16] Whites had regained control of all the bully pulpits throughout the state—politics, schools, churches, fraternal groups—and they could rely on local Klan hard-liners to coerce cooperation with the "Bourbon" white leadership to strip black voters of the franchise. Black residents, including Methodists, began to leave the state, while those who remained, including Longdale people, began to collect guns—for hunting they said.

There were other people recently freed by the Thirteenth Amendment who decided that safety and the comfort of community lay in another direction, in an all-black town where control and protection were entirely in their own hands, the best known of these towns being Mound Bayou, founded in 1887. So-called voluntary segregation had an appeal for some freed people, who assumed that segregation would be a way of life in their area, and they thought they might have an advantage in planning how it would be implemented. Mound Bayou announced "voluntary" black separatism rather than enforced segregation, and welcomed residents who accepted the "sacrifice" of their votes in exchange for what they were promised would be a fair and equitable application of the law in their community by the state's white officials. In a sense they designed a separate state. Isaiah T. Montgomery, Mound Bayou's founder, made what became a famous "sacrifice" speech in 1890 at the state disenfranchising convention, where he was the only black spokesperson present. In its early years Mound Bayou was an economic success, a model for black separatism.[17]

Longdale residents followed a different course from Mound Bayou, and most chose not to follow the migration patterns of other freed people and leave the area. They preferred to remain settled where they were. Perhaps unknowingly, they were heeding the urging of the pre-eminent black leader of the time, Frederick Douglass, who advised the freed people to remain at home and through their efforts and numbers effect change from within. From a different political perspective twenty years later, Booker T. Washington would ask Southern blacks to "cast down your buckets where you are."[18]

As much as the presence of Methodist missionaries—whose names are buried in history—the stormy political climate of the times may have influenced Longdale's decision to build a church in its community. They were political realists who surely perceived the value in being part of a denomination known for its historic antislavery stance. Being linked to a predominantly white "outside" religious body could be perceived as a subtle way to reject the totality of the Jim Crow agenda. Methodism's connectional structure would keep Longdale's residents in touch with developments outside Mississippi, while also making them members of a church that did not then sanction Jim Crow. And not incidentally, in its non-Southern incarnation, Methodism contained a significant vocal minority of supporters of the goals of Reconstruction. In the planning for their church, Longdale people also decided against another racially separate option, the appeal of three distinct groups of "African" Methodists who asked them to join their ranks. Mt. Zion Church chose to be part of the vast, nominally nonsegregated world of international connectional Methodism.

The memories of Longdale's early settlers and their descendants when combined with the limited available historical evidence help supply answers to the question of "why" Mt. Zion joined with the Methodists. The material to document "how" the church came into being remains in the realm of speculation, and is ultimately related to the dynamic, changing environment of the growth of black Methodism in the South. A likely explanation is that an itinerant Methodist missionary out of Meridian, someone black or white, visited among the settlers in Longdale.

Black Americans held a generally good opinion of Methodism, owing in part to the principles of its founder, John Wesley, which included labeling slaveholding a sin. Wesley had said slaveholders could not be members of the denomination. After American slaveholders became prosperous and more numerous, however, the church revisited this defining issue, and when no consensus could be reached, the denomination split regionally. The pro-slaveholding faction, essentially in the states that would form the Confederacy, became the Methodist Episcopal Church, South, with a mission that reflected the white supremacist ideology of its constituents. But music, liturgy, and evangelical preaching also brought black Methodists into the church. That part of the denomination that rejected slaveholding in 1844, sometimes called the "Old Church," was the branch to which Mt. Zion became attached. Essentially Northern and Western in membership, the "Old Church" contained enough supporters of early Reconstruction to send missionaries south.

When the (Non-Southern) General Conference met in 1864, the delegates anticipated the racial dilemma they would face with the successful (for them) ending of the Civil War. They posed to the Conference the now-famous question that resonates through Methodist history: "What shall we do with the blacks?" The answer, the Methodist accommodation to white Southern customs, was to create separate annual missionary conferences for black members, mostly in the conquered South. But the reform contingent within the church thought something else, more proactive, in keeping with the goals of Reconstruction, should be done, so General Conference agreed to send teachers and ministers south to help freed people obtain work and education, while also seeking converts.[19]

It was this small band of Methodist missionaries in Mississippi, initially no more than ten but numbering sixty by 1878, who helped inspire Mt. Zion in planting its church. John Wesley's message also counted for something among the freed people and Reconstruction missionaries, who had heard of his message to British abolitionist William Wilberforce: "Go on, in the name of God and in the power of His might, till even American slavery (the vilest that ever saw the sun) shall vanish away before it."[20] Wesley had opposed a settled ministry, and planned for elders, missionaries, and preachers to travel a circuit; typically three or four churches, sometimes more. There was no hiding place for these saddlebag ministers in Mississippi, who were readily identified by local whites as equality-minded carpetbaggers, who welcomed black members and accepted black elders as church leaders.

One of these early black leaders of Reconstruction Methodism in the state was James Lynch, previously an African Methodist Episcopal Church minister, who had left the North to go to South Carolina and then Mississippi to help create a "colorblind" church. Lynch was the most literal, the most extreme, of the Methodist leadership to argue for a church that denied racial distinctions. He died a very young man in 1870, after becoming a Methodist Church elder as well as virtual head of the Mississippi Republican Party. His close colleagues in building this new intentionally biracial Methodist Conference shared his views, the white A. C. McDonald making clear there was no place for racial division in the Mississippi Methodist Conference.[21] A few of these saddlebag Methodists journeyed to east central Mississippi, where they established a church and opened a school in the city of Meridian, to be attended and staffed by blacks, and sent out circuit riders—black and white—to assist freed people in creating congregations.

It was through some such serendipitous connection that the Methodist congregation in Longdale evolved, joined with the "Old Church," and also somehow connected to the color-blind missionary message of the Lynch-McDonald company. Some Longdale residents were possibly already Methodists through the efforts of early evangelists, or even through the work of the Methodist Episcopal Church, South—the pro-slavery element in the denomination—that had courted slaves prior to 1865, presumably to

keep control over black worshippers. The precise reason Longdale joined
with the "Old Church" is not known, but it was a decision that would put
them at odds with their local culture. The leadership of the denomination
was largely Northern, its mission worldwide. And during Reconstruction
in Mississippi it had welcomed blacks as leaders and members, and had
supported the goals of the reformers, especially the vote and justice for
black people.

Mt. Zion Church and Its Memories, 1878 on

Remember this.
PAUL RICOEUR, Memory, History, Forgetting

As long as the place of blacks in the nation's history went
unrecognized, blacks would remain relegated to the
margins of American life.
W. FITZHUGH BRUNDAGE, Southern Past

Mt. Zion's third generation of members, that is, those born in the twentieth century, cherish the memories of the founders, many of them relatives, and through their recollections help preserve the fabric of the community's history. Their collective memories locate Longdale in a specific place, east central Mississippi, within the context of Southern rural African American history. These grandsons and granddaughters of the pioneering settlers, many of them born in the first two decades of the twentieth century, remember the names of their ancestors, who were mostly newly freed people, and recall with pride their hopes and aspirations—for land, for the vote, and for a church where they could worship the personal Jesus they knew. Through the lives of their parents, as well as their own, they understood the painful experiences of segregation and Jim Crow policies, many of which visited indignities on people important in the community. These people included generations of Mt. Zion's Sunday school teachers, Methodist Conference delegates, caregivers, as well as farmers and parents. While historical data report the scandalous number of lynchings in the state, they don't define the full range of racial indignities regularly imposed on all black people who knew themselves worthy of respect. There were attentive white neighbors in Neshoba County who appreciated the great injustice of the situation; with few exceptions, however, they kept from speaking out because of fear of reprisal. In the opening decades of the twentieth century, it could be almost as hard to be labeled "nigger lover," as it was to be black.

Memories of the Founder of Mt. Zion: Ross Jones's Story

Thomas Jones, the first landholder of record in Longdale, holds a privileged place in the collective memory of the residents. The high regard for him is a tribute to the man, the family's long presence in the community, as well as to the recollections of his grandson, Ross Jones, one of Longdale's third generation. Thomas Jones's stature in local memory may be a consequence of not just his personal achievements, but also the example he left for younger generations who lived in hard times. Once a slave "tied up" by his master, he became a farmer of considerable means, a pillar of the church, the school, and the community. He was somebody.

Ross Jones first shared his recollections of his grandfather Thomas with me in 2001, when he was eighty-eight and his brother Wilbur, who also lived in the family home, was ninety-two. Tall, handsome, elegant men, they rocked on the front porch of their substantial two-storied house in Longdale, their home since childhood, and spoke feelingly of their grandfather, Ross occasionally taking leave to stir the cabbage on the kitchen stove. Over eight years of occasional conversations, Ross turned ninety-six, Wilbur died, and the details of Thomas Jones's life changed some in the telling. What remained consistent themes in Ross Jones's recollections of his grandfather was that Thomas had been born a slave in Alabama, had managed his way west to Neshoba County, and in addition to marrying his wife, Harriet, and having five sons and a daughter, had purchased sixty acres of land in Neshoba in 1879, a section of which he donated for worship purposes. The deed to those sixty acres of land had almost sacred implications.

In our earliest meeting, Ross Jones was most animated when he spoke of Grandfather Thomas Jones's daring escape from slavery in Alabama. There is no documentary evidence to verify Ross's account of Thomas's experience, but it was an important family memory for Ross, whose description of it was not challenged by his neighbors, and was supported by his daughter and son-in-law. Ross recalled a man who was wily and willful, and seemingly possessed of great physical strength. Brother Wilbur corroborated Ross's account, though otherwise spoke little, except to agree that their grandfather had been sold by his master to a planter in Mississippi. The man charged with escorting Thomas from Alabama to his new place let him ride in the wagon part of the way, an act of kindness Ross thought. But once in Mississippi, Thomas decided to run back to Alabama—for reasons Ross did not explain although it may have been to find Harriet, the woman who became his wife—and his return to the plantation made the old owner "crazy" because he had to give back the money he had received for his sale. The old master had Thomas "tied up." But he broke free and returned to Mississippi.[1]

All the early settlers of Longdale had once been slaves, except for the young children, and in their own way could have identified with the Thomas Jones experience. Thomas, perhaps like some of them, had escaped slavery by his wits, around 1862 or 1863, before official emancipation.[2] His wife Harriet is listed in the county records as age twenty-four, so born in 1846, although a tombstone indicates she was born in 1849. Ross Jones told the story of his grandfather's departure from Alabama slavery as the activity of a man alone, although his later escape may also have included Harriet. Records show that their son James was seven in 1870, suggesting that the parents did escape slavery about 1862 or 1863. That makes their successful venture even more notable, since Thomas ran west, rather than to a city or to the North, and then soon settled down in Mississippi.[3] Exactly when he put down his roots in Longdale is not clear, but by 1870, the time when he and Harriet show up in the county's register, there were at least three dozen other settlers in Longdale, the majority of them listed as "farm labor," young people who worked as hands on the farms of their families, or adults hired out for day labor.[4] Only Thomas Jones and a "D" Wilson are listed as farmers.[5]

Thomas Jones was obviously a man ambitious for himself, his family, and the small community they had joined. The County Deed Record Book notes that on March 21, 1879, Thomas and his wife Harriet Jones purchased their sixty acres for $124, making Thomas Jones the first official landowner in Longdale, and giving him a much desired status.[6] Like other slaves, Thomas Jones had left slavery behind with no capital: no formal education, no tools, no land, no social network, no inheritance.[7] He managed to eke out a surplus from the sale of produce—most likely cotton—he grew on the land. It was a momentous day when he arrived at court to sign the Deed Record Book as a landowner.

His life and Harriet's are the stuff of Longdale's collective memory. Just fifteen years out of slavery, Thomas Jones was able to donate land for a church. His story, and that of other Longdale residents, speaks of ambitious and religious ex-slaves who discovered a way to transform their lives and create community in very trying times. Their collective memory incorporates a past acknowledged as difficult, dominated, and impoverished, yet Mt. Zion's people have been inclined to focus on the future and the opportunities it holds.

Thomas Jones may have lacked material goods, but he was hard working and likely possessed a fair degree of self-confidence. But though eventually a landowner, he was not exempt from the challenges he and his community faced as Reconstruction reform ground to a halt. He was among the local blacks who still voted in Neshoba County in the 1880s, at a time when Jim Crow laws were trying to take away that right. There were others in Longdale still voting along with him, including Burrell Kirkland, Julius Anderson, Henry Wells, Jack Johnson, and about ten others, though the numbers declined every year.[8] In the estimation of their grandchildren, these were people of substance, slightly better off financially than most of their neighbors, possessed of a certain air of assurance. They knew that a few black men around the state continued to hold elected public office.

The Impact of Reconstruction's Demise

A notable black political figure during the Reconstruction years was Hiram Revels, who was not only a Methodist Episcopal Church minister, but in 1870 also became a United States senator, occupying the seat formerly held by the president of the Confederacy, Jefferson Davis. Like Blanche K. Bruce, James Lynch, and other black leaders of the times, Revels endorsed what Northern Methodists termed the "coincidence of principles," by which they meant the neat correlation of Methodism with Reconstruction Republicanism.[9] It was absorbed at Mt. Zion Church as one of its founding principles, a way of viewing the world members shared.

In a sign of the changing conditions being wrought by "Redemption," Hiram Revels was gone from the Senate by 1872, to become the new president of black Alcorn College, a land-grant school created to avoid any possible integration of the University of Mississippi. The restoration of white supremacy became inevitable after 1876 as the federal troops sent to protect black rights in the state were withdrawn.[10] Thomas Jones and his neighbors could see the impact of these changes on their community, but they continued to push the limits of Reconstruction reform as long as they could. Jones had first registered to vote on July 2, 1872, one of many freedmen who rushed to take advantage of what had been so long denied; his name last appears in the official election district register in 1892, followed by the notice that he is "dead."[11]

Despite the social turmoil accompanying the imminent return of white supremacy, Jones and his neighbors continued with plans for a community church. Longdale's first worship center was a fragile construction of pine poles covered with brush and pine branches built at a corner of the property Jones had contributed. An additional gift of land from another early landowner, Julius Anderson, with the help of the Burrell Kirkland family, allowed the men of Longdale to move the church to a different site and build a more substantial structure, remembered as "the log church." In 1899, this was replaced with yet another building, the one that served as Mt. Zion Church and community center until it was burned in the devastating fire of 1964.[12] Somehow it seemed a fitting end to the life of Thomas Jones that he died while helping with the building of the log church, the first real church in the community, which he would not live to see.[13]

Ross Jones at one point wondered aloud in his recollections if maybe his grandfather had been helped with a gift of forty acres and a mule from the federal government, a significant government promise in the minds of many other Southern black farmers.[14] Thomas Jones was an adept business negotiator, and he may have increased his land holdings through transactions with some federal agency. Ross Jones knew that freed people had hoped for, even expected, a program of land reform to help compensate for years of unpaid labor. Land ownership was the hallmark of the "coincidence of principles" between Republicanism and Methodism. A policy of land reform would give freed people the opportunity to participate in the free labor market and enjoy the fruits of their own labor. Many freedmen had pinned their hopes on the pledge of "forty acres and a mule," and Ross Jones knew the history of the promise and what had become of it.

What Jones recalled was known formally as Special Field Order No. 15, a command issued by Union General William T. Sherman setting aside land along the Atlantic coast from South Carolina to Florida for blacks to settle. The deed of 1879 shows that Thomas Jones purchased his first parcel of land himself without federal assistance of any kind, although during his lifetime his holdings increased, partly the result of familial inheritance and partly the result of additional but unknown business arrangements. Other Longdale residents eventually became landowners as well, but few through the assistance of any federal agency, other than limited provisions of the Homestead Act. Neither Sherman's plan, nor considerations by the federal Freedman's Bureau, nor potential options debated in the Lincoln and Johnson administrations produced the needed program of land distribution.[15] If Jones did manage to get some of his land through federal help, the lion's share of his holdings was achieved through his own hard work. The creation of a black yeomanry class, such as W. E. B. DuBois envisioned in his book *Black Reconstruction*, was never endorsed by white politicians. Though it would have been in keeping with the tradition of free land and free labor in America—"free men, free land, free labor"—it was a promise unfulfilled.[16]

Longdale was part of a network of six other black rural communities in the area, creating an informal association of farmers in the years after the war. In addition to Longdale, there were Poplar Springs, Northbend, Stallo, Muckalusha, and Hope, each with its own distinctive qualities and its own Methodist church. Early land records lack clarity when it comes to documenting the acquisitions of the pioneering black settlers in these communities, though the settlements shared ties of family and religion, and a common need for protection and shared resources.

Some of the earliest residents of Longdale, in addition to Thomas and Harriet Jones, were Burrell and Hannah Kirkland—to whom my guides Jennifer Hathorn and Freddie Grady were kin—Julius and Lou Anderson, George W. Johnson, J. C. Clemons, Harry Cattenhead, and Mary Snowden Calloway.[17] These path-breaking families hold a special place in community memory. The white clergyman W. J. Seale, who once owned much of the land in the area before selling parcels of it to timber interests, transferred—by sale or loan—other parcels to the black families as they arrived in Longdale, families like the Coles and the Steeles who later became notable leaders in the community. The new arrivals continued to be ingenious in acquiring property, negotiating arrangements with Choctaws, federal agencies, and people like Seale. Still others came by their property by purchasing it from Northern land speculators, investors who had gobbled up Mississippi land in the first years following the Choctaw Cession in 1830, hoping to get quick returns from timber sales. The new residents also recognized timber could be a money crop, but in these formative years cotton was a surer investment.

The Advent of Sharecropping

As another generation of settlers arrived in Longdale, they learned that instead of being welcomed by the Methodist concept of the "coincidence of principles" between Methodism and Reconstruction, they were greeted by Redemption-era discriminatory hiring policies and payment arrangements for black-grown produce. Rather than the "coincidence of principles," they were faced with "constricting possibilities." Unlike the opportunities that had opened up for Thomas Jones, newer arrivals had to forego land ownership, at least temporarily, and become sharecroppers.

Those who became croppers worked the farms of local whites and even some blacks, growing cotton and corn, and raising cattle and pigs. If they were lucky to hit good weather, they might accumulate enough money to buy their own land, but any misfortune would mean ongoing debt. While the hills of Neshoba County made cotton farming difficult, timber seemed there for the taking, but without a railroad there was no easy way to get it to market, so people continued to plant cotton.

Longdale's sharecroppers worked for the farmers who were willing to make them a decent offer: on occasion, despite the hard times, that farmer could be a black man. One was Will Jones, a son born to Harriet and Thomas Jones in 1868, and later the father to Ross Jones. Calloway Cole and Three Foot Cole, other prominent residents of Longdale with significant holdings, also required more farm help. Will Jones married Katie Cole, the daughter of a neighbor whose family was a Longdale landowner, and together Will and Katie had ten children: five girls and five boys and a growing farm. Ross was the youngest. Will Jones built what was then the largest house in the community, well off the main gravel road, back toward some piney woods. It remained as the Jones homestead. In a good season, he would hire black workers to help with the crops; he grew cotton and corn, raised cattle, and owned mules to pull the cotton wagon to the city of Meridian. There he sold the crop to cotton factors and used the money to buy supplies for the farm. The round trip journey could take a week over muddy and rutted roads.

Longdale Builds a School

By 1885, Longdale also had its own school, appropriately known as Mt. Zion School, and Will Jones was the first in his family to have the advantage of an education. The school had been created the same way the church had been, through the pooled resources and labor of the community. The church founders located Mt. Zion School just south of the church, readily accessible to all the children in the community. The farmers placed great store in the new school, tithing their cotton crop to support it as well as the church. In addition to maintaining their own school, they were subsequently required to pay county taxes that went toward the support of the whites-only schools, so in a sense they were double taxed.[18] The community's investment in its school, however, demonstrated the high value church members placed on the potential for schooling to offer a wholly new life, and provided capital that almost all of them lacked.[19]

Mt. Zion School offered eight grades, and Will Jones, an adolescent at the time the school opened, attended for several years. Community members all remembered the school fondly, even those teachers known as demanding and severe. Ross Jones, who was a trustee of the school for several decades, said there were usually two teachers in the school at a time for the thirty or more children in attendance, until a bulge in growth in the 1930s required an expansion in staff and space. The school was a modest building, heated by a wood stove, and equipped with an outside pump and the ubiquitous outhouse. The community also made housing available to its teachers so they would not be subject to the insults and discrimination of whites in town, many of whom mocked the idea of an educated Negro. It was helpful to the children, too, to have their teachers live and work in Longdale's protected environment. The seasonal needs of the cotton crop determined the length of the school term, which meant that the boys and girls who attended the school had farm chores to do before and after school, and had no school at all during the seasons for planting and chopping cotton. The school term ran four months, and parents were known to discipline their children by threatening to keep them out of school whenever it was in session.[20] There was a similar country school for black children in nearby Poplar Springs, and some of Longdale's children went there for their education.

Ross Jones was as proud of his father's accomplishments as he was of his grandfather's. A successful farmer, Will Jones, said Ross, reportedly sometimes got as much as $25 for a bale of cotton (he didn't mention the size of the bale) at the market in Meridian, less than white farmers received, but money that would go a long way in Longdale.[21] As the primary cash crop in Mississippi, cotton drove the price of everything else, and when the price dipped to heart-breaking lows, as it would do during the Depression, everyone suffered, black farmers most of all. Ross thought that in later years, during the depths of the Jim Crow period in the 1920s, by the time he had himself become a farmer with a cotton crop to sell in Meridian, he, too, was routinely cheated by the cotton factors, something that he didn't think had been as bad during his father's day. The economy was in decline during his own early trading days, but he thought that one advantage his father had had was that "Dad could figure," and "knew how to calculate his crops." His Dad was also "good at reading," as was his mother.[22]

One of Jones's contemporaries, the fiery Methodist minister Clinton Collier, part-time resident of Longdale, and full-time teacher and farmer, corroborated Jones's opinion that until the 1930s, black farmers were regularly short-changed on their cotton returns from the white agent in Meridian.[23] Both men believed that it was well known that open corruption took place at the cotton market, but the law at the time offered them no recourse. Each of them, Jones and Collier, had had some schooling; Jones a few years at Mt. Zion School, and Collier a few semesters at Howard University and then Jackson State. They both understood education as an important form of capital, for themselves and for their children, with their experience in the white marketplace an especially compelling argument in its favor. Jones would later send his own two children to college, including graduate school for his daughter, and also supported the higher education of a number of foster children he raised in his home.[24] Collier, an activist and a man who enjoyed his reputation for having a hot temper, lamented the fact that his "Daddy could not read or write" even though he paid taxes. That was reason enough, Collier thought, that blacks deserved reparations.[25]

For much of his life Ross Jones was a mainstay of Mt. Zion Church as well as Mt. Zion School. He served on the official board of the church for thirty years, many of them as financial officer, making sure the funds were raised and the bills were paid, a service he also performed for Mt. Zion School. Nevertheless, he recalled, although his father Will was smart enough to calculate the value of his cotton crop, and occasionally had years when he was able to hire black croppers, there were times when the money was too short to support a growing family of ten children. Some of the children left the area for a time, perhaps simply to stretch their wings elsewhere, or else, in company of other migrants, to escape Jim Crow. Two of Will and Katie Jones's daughters left home to go to high school—a luxury in the early twentieth century—boarding with friends in Meridian since Neshoba did not have a high school for black children. Three of the sons, as they grew older, at various times moved away from Longdale: Wilbur to the army; Ross to New York, from where he worked as a Pullman car porter; and another brother to Detroit. At one point all three brothers lived in Detroit. Ross returned to Longdale in 1942 when his father took sick and there was no one else to manage the farm; although he had enjoyed New York, Ross was happy to move home. When his father died, Ross became the new patriarch, contributing to the community while living in the family homestead, a place that was big enough to accommodate various family members when they returned to town, with some, like Wilbur, staying for over fifty years.[26]

Not all of Jones's neighbors shared in the community's high regard for the sons of Thomas Jones, the respected founder. Clarence Hill, once a sharecropper, then a trucker and a marketer of some of his own timber crop, thought Ross and Wilbur Jones were "secretive to protect what they had." The Joneses were considered better off than most of Longdale's residents. Ross Jones was a very light-skinned man, a quality people inevitably referred to when they described him. Clarence Hill also made and sold moonshine, something Ross Jones refused to do. Perhaps their distance could be explained as a class issue—Jones owned more land than Hill—or perhaps, as seemed likely, it belonged to some difference of opinion buried in the small community, best left unspoken. But one subject on which they did agree was the importance of education. Hill, too, sent his daughter to college, though he himself had had only two years of schooling.[27]

At Mt. Zion Church, the services that began in 1879 continued uninterrupted thereafter, maintained mostly by the energies and contributions of lay people, and the infrequent clerical services of an itinerant black minister with three or four other charges on his circuit. Mt. Zion was diligent about its finances, paying its assessment to the denomination, and compensating the minister and the Mt. Zion teachers on time. The original Northern white ministers who had arrived during the early days of Reconstruction were gone by 1892. Although the ardor for major social change had dissipated, the white activists had left Mississippi largely because of the 1890 state constitution that legalized Jim Crow segregation.

White Memory in Neshoba: Florence Mars of Philadelphia

Neighboring white Philadelphians and white Neshoba had memories that grew from different soil than Longdale's; they were formed in the heyday of the antebellum period—which Neshoba enjoyed only vicariously—and came to flower in recollections of the "War of Northern Aggression." An efflorescence of those memories came from one of its own matriarchs, Florence Mars, although not until 1977. Mars offered her version of white memory in an autobiographical account, *Witness in Philadelphia*, that purported to offer "facts" that conformed more closely to what really happened in the town's past. Not exactly a tell-all, Mars did have some scores to settle.

The daughter of an old and well-to-do family in Neshoba possessed of unusual interests for a Southern woman of the time—working as a photographer, traveling as a single woman, for example—Mars lifted the veil of social secrecy the white community maintained around its activities.[28] She was a leading figure in white Philadelphia, who in her book revealed the interests, habits, and social mores of her grandparents, her parents, her school chums, and of course, herself. Her memory reached back well into the nineteenth century. Mars presented an "inside" look at white Philadelphia generally ignored in the newspaper and other published documents; she presented a social context for understanding not only the area's white documentary history but its collective memory.

Unlike Longdale's past, white Neshoba's collective memory was considered the only history of record, and it therefore controlled the story of the past and its impact on the present. Mars' work relied only minimally on documentary material, like court registers, land documents, church histories, and the weekly *Neshoba Democrat*, whose editors she knew well. She provided documentary evidence when she felt it necessary, but for a book that was essentially a memoir, she relied heavily on memory, on conversations with neighbors, and what came to light through Philadelphia gossip. But her book, as well as the weekly paper, made clear that race was always the social signifier in the county as far back as memory and records go, separating everything along racial lines, or as the white Mississippi writer Willie Morris once bemoaned, "we are burdened by race."[29]

White racial "burdens," as Mars noted, were obviously of a different order from blacks. If whites felt guilty or shameful for their harsh treatment of their black neighbors, they did not let on. Only much later would some white residents realize that their complicity in violating the rights of others would come with a heavy personal price for them too.

In 1905, at the time the railroad finally came through to Philadelphia and telegraph contact was established, white residents of the small town remained as unfamiliar with their black neighbors in Longdale as from timber marketers up and down the Mississippi. Both Mars and the

documentary evidence note that whites knew local blacks as traders at
the various shops, and as occasional paid laborers, domestics, croppers,
and timber workers. In other interactions they might have with blacks,
white Neshobans believed their secrets and their conversations remained
among themselves, hidden from their black workers. They offered little
evidence of understanding the quality of life of their black neighbors.

Mars famously said that in Neshoba County—the one known by
whites—"the basement of the past is not very deep."[30] She believed that
"All the mysteries of the present seem to be entangled" with memories of
a past that stretched back to the county's founding in 1833.[31] She said everything was involved with race, with nothing changed about racial interaction over the past 150 years. She was convinced that despite grim evidence
to the contrary, her white neighbors still clung to a plantation image of the
South peopled by cultured whites and their loyal black servants. Though
as Mars said, it was a shallow image to be sure, it was likely deep enough
to hide feelings of guilt or remorse on the part of whites.

Ten years younger than Ross Jones, and living in town about nine
miles away, Florence Mars was one of only a handful of Philadelphia
whites who knew that Longdale people had lives more textured and complex than those of simple domestics or croppers. She had been born in
1923, and descended from a family that included landowners, shopkeep-
ers, physicians, and lawyers, so she knew well the priorities of those of her
class. She was also accustomed to making regular visits to Longdale, usually to transport a domestic, but she reported sometimes lingering on to
engage in conversation with residents, coming to regard some as friends.
An active member of First Methodist Church and also the owner of a cattle business, she was considered by her neighbors as a racial liberal—or
worse. She had, atypically, gone out of state to college and traveled on
her own as an amateur photographer. A proto-feminist, she experienced
the wrath of her neighbors in the 1960s when she dared question continuing community silence on topics dealing with race. In her opinion,
everyone in Philadelphia in those years supported the White Citizens
Council, which she derided as "the uptown Klan," and she assumed most
were pleased with the presence of a KKK chapter in the area, even after
everyone knew that Klan members had murdered the civil rights workers.[32] Why, she had asked publicly, had blacks been so continuously mis-
treated and discriminated against in the county? She got her answer when
Klan pressure caused her to lose her cattle business, then to be driven out
of Philadelphia's First Methodist Church, before suffering the ultimate

indignity for a white woman by being arrested by the sheriff for drunk driving, a police action unheard of for white ladies.

Although friends and older relatives repeatedly reminded her of the prevailing social mores of the town, especially those relating to blacks, Mars had been angered by the 1964 murders and the white silence that followed, as investigators tried to find the killers. She thought she had found the answer to her question about continued black discrimination: like everything else about Neshoba she had ever been taught, white racism was based on its unexamined past, one predicated on white supremacy. In the grammar school of her childhood she said she had been taught that "Southerners were white; Negroes were Negroes. The white civilization of the South was one of the greatest in the world."[33] She wrote her memoir after she had lost her cattle business to Klan threats, and after her humiliation by the sheriff, so there may have been an urge to overstate her case, but she was well attuned to the values of her peer group. She suspected they thought "I always wore the shoe on the wrong foot." Though she believed that on occasion she heard a dissenting liberal opinion on racial matters in the white First Methodist Church—which had no contact with Longdale Methodist Church—she was convinced that the accepted view among almost all whites grew out of reference to the Plantation Myth. And since all whites in the county were kin, related to each other in the temporal and geographic ways a tribe might be, she assumed that their views on cultural norms were widely shared.

Freely paraphrasing William Faulkner, Mars said that in order to understand Neshoba County one needed to live there a hundred years, her reinterpretation of the Faulknerian statement that "To understand the world, you have to understand a place like Mississippi."[34] Perhaps the meaning of both is best comprehended in the context of the mysterious and complex imagery projected by the place. As Diane McWhorter said, it is home to brambles as well as magnolias, where things are not what they seem, and where traditions run deep and violators of them are not readily tolerated. The effort to understand Mississippi culture has tempted many, including its own Willie Morris, the writer who temporarily relocated to New York City, to conclude that the place can be known only in terms of a kind of double-sidedness: an open, almost giddy, hospitality, that is combined with a hiddenness, a suspicion of outsiders trying to pry into its past.[35] Mars shared Morris's view, convinced that Mississippi itself was ironic. It cultivated mystery and inwardness as well as openness and generous hospitality; it nurtured a covert and suspicious side while projecting an air of ease and comfort. Mars recalled a beloved black family servant, "who had cooked my dinner that day," but nevertheless was allowed to die in a cabin behind her family's home for want of simple medical care.[36] Everything, she was convinced, was involved with race, but shame, guilt, and hypocrisy were heavily papered over by a cover of secrecy and denial.

Sex and alcohol, she believed, were important components of Neshoba's hidden history. White men tried for years to keep quiet their liaisons with black women without success. The appearances of Ross Jones, Clint Collier, and mulatto mothers with white-appearing babies, gave the lie to the limit of segregation; Mars called it "nighttime integration." And everyone seemed to know that it was a black woman who had been violated. Mars told of hearing from her grandfather, Oscar Johnson, that his own grandfather had "retained a woman," a not-uncommon practice after the Civil War, he said, when white slaveholders built houses in their backyards for preferred former female slaves. When she asked her "Pappy" how white women felt about this relationship, she replied, "Pappy chuckled and said, 'Well, it was just sort of convenient.'"[37]

Hidden behind the same veil of secrecy was the use of alcohol, which Mars remembered being the most discussed topic in her church when she was growing up. [38] It was not just that her Methodist Church advised abstinence, but that Neshoba County was an officially "dry" county. By the end of the nineteenth century, abstinence had become part of evangelical religion and conservative politics, not just in Mississippi but in many areas of the South and West. Preachers called on Scriptural texts to remind congregations of the evils of drinking whiskey. In the antebellum period, abstinence had been more important to some reformers than abolition. Yet the Reverend Clay Lee, who in 1964 became the minister of the First Methodist Church in Philadelphia, thought "there were more alcoholics in Philadelphia than in other towns of comparable size."[39] While he served the church in Philadelphia he counseled numerous alcoholics in the congregation, and was aware that "white lightning" and whiskey were consumed in many homes and at social events. The sheriff, mandated to confiscate beverage alcohol and destroy the illicit stills people kept out in the countryside, would occasionally comply, collecting the extra tax fees that followed a raid. More frequently he was a consumer.

Out in Longdale few residents—except perhaps some church ladies—ever expressed any moral qualms about the making and selling of whiskey. It had a very practical function; it was a way to make extra money and to buy protection. The sheriff was a steady customer of

Longdale producers—the same person officially charged with destroying stills—along with his deputies, who visited the community to secure their own supply.[40] Mars believed strongly that the hypocrisy about alcohol laid the basis for the moral compromise with racism: "illegal" alcohol consumption had opened a moral breach for her white neighbors, a sin they seemed to believe was more personal, more egregious, to them than the evil of racism and injustice. Having once sinned greatly, it was easier to sin on something they defined as less personally damning.

Racism and the Railroad

The most important event in the remembered lives of white Neshobans after the 1890 racial coup bore little relationship to the characteristics Florence Mars later pointed to as defining qualities of the community. For white Philadelphians, the most significant development at the beginning of the new century was not black disenfranchisement, legalized Jim Crow, or the surreptitious use of alcohol, but rather the appearance of the railroad in 1905. A symbol of modernization, the rail line meant that large and small timber interests could more easily get their product to market and enjoy higher profits shipping their goods around the state and the nation. They might stand a good chance of making more money dealing with an outside world, while still keeping intimate community secrets, their collective memory of the past, under wraps at home.[41]

3

"I Was Never Scared"

MT. ZION IN THE JIM CROW YEARS, 1890–1954

By the close of the nineteenth century, the future of the Negro in American life had been settled for the next fifty years. It was clear that the black ballot would be virtually silent; that the two races would continue distinct castes.

BULLOCK, History of Negro Education in the South

There is great unrest and growing discontent among the Negroes. They are beginning to feel friendless and hopeless.

CHARLES B. GALLOWAY, Bishop, Methodist Episcopal Church, South (Mississippi) 1904

This is home.

ROSS JONES, Longdale, 2005

Longdale's Methodists

Although Mt. Zion Church was born during the experiment with inter-racialism that was basic to Reconstruction, its congregation and leaders had no experience with inclusive fellowship with white Methodists until long years after the murders of the civil rights workers. The rigid lines of segregation that became more entrenched during the pre–First World War years meant that Mt. Zion had little contact with its parent denomination, the Methodist Episcopal Church. State laws now separated Mt. Zion from all white institutional life, including the annual white Methodist denominational conferences, of which there were two in Mississippi.

Mt. Zion Church grew to maturity simultaneously with the expansion of Jim Crow segregation in law and custom. The reality of white supremacy penetrated all aspects of black life, from religion to the economy and into the black community itself, persuading some Longdale residents to abandon Mississippi for places advertised as more hospitable to black migrants. During these early decades of the new century it was not only in Mississippi that crude racism raised its ugly head; the entire country—indeed most of the Western world, intoxicated with ideas of global expansion—seemed besotted with varieties of white supremacist ideas. These were hard times for a little country Methodist church working to hold up its people and their sense of dignity. Some of their black friends in town and in the state wondered why more of Mt. Zion's members didn't protest segregation by leaving Mississippi. Growing numbers of migrants were already heading north, hoping to leave behind the most degrading aspects of Jim Crow, and setting in motion a massive tide of migration.

Longdale residents could have listed a number of reasons why it was not a good idea for them to join the departing throngs. Some simply couldn't afford to leave Longdale for lack of necessary resources: they were too encumbered with family or with debts, so leaving was not an option. But others stayed in Longdale because of the positive reasons that had attracted them to settle there in the first place: because it was a community that felt welcoming and because Mt. Zion Church provided a comforting sense of family. Mt. Zion's experience during the most oppressive Jim Crow years of 1890 to 1940, is an example of how one community of faith, and likely many others like it, offered its people qualities not available to them in the larger society, such as joy, dignity, and hope for better times. Those who lived through these years and their descendants were proud to describe how they had managed back then. Many of Longdale's residents, when they reflected on the old days of dread and abuse from the distance of sixty years, said "I was never scared," an affirmation that floated from their lips like an echo over the country roads. They credited their confidence to the support of the community and the ministry of the church. In the final analysis they knew they held the moral high ground on both fronts—the church and the state—in the struggles over inclusion, and that counted for a lot.

Why Not Just Leave Jim Crow?

Life for Southern black people in the years between 1890 and 1920 has been described as "the nadir of the Negro," a period said by some writers to be "worse than slavery."[1] Violence and intimidation kept black voters disenfranchised and politically powerless—the state constitution of 1890 had added a poll tax and an "understanding clause" for just that purpose—and lynching became the ultimate means of enforcing the invisible strictures of the southern social code that maintained white supremacy. The Magnolia State led the nation in lynchings. Surely, whether or not to join the Great Migration headed north and west had to be a subject most black Mississippians considered during these years; in Mississippi the heaviest outmigration to another state occurred in the years between 1910 and 1920, sooner than other Southern states.

Because of the new white segregationist measures, Mt. Zion's members could be expected to look to their local church, whose affairs they controlled themselves, for support and emotional uplift, and that was surely a factor contributing to the growth in church membership at the time. It is telling that in 1890, right after Mississippi mandated segregation, Mt. Zion Church enjoyed its largest membership to date. The southern social code controlling custom and segregation had ways, both civil and crude, to remind black worshippers that they were not welcome at white churches. To borrow a phrase from historian Christopher Lasch, a church of their own could prove to be a "haven in a heartless world."[2]

But for Mt. Zion's people it was more than a search for a haven that determined their choice to remain in Longdale. The inclusive Methodism that had attracted their ancestors had become an integral part of their own identity by the end of the century, and they remained attached to the northern Methodist Episcopal Church and all that its heritage represented in a time not long gone. In the South, the values of Reconstruction Methodism remained dear to freed people; not just interracialism, but its companion ideology of free labor, free land, free men. Methodism at the time of Reconstruction included country black people within a worldwide network of churches, and introduced them to the Republican version of free-labor ideology. Then, too, the Methodist emphasis on education and social policy complemented their own position on these issues.[3] Worldwide Methodism aspired to be an exception to Jim Crow, even though segregation was part of the local Mississippi conference beginning in 1890. So Mt. Zion's members did not seem to feel that they were bringing competing values—to accommodate or protest, to stay or to go—to their choice of remaining in Longdale during the toughest years of Jim Crow. In the context of the Jim Crow South, Mt. Zion's people defined themselves as social reformers—a few, like Clint Collier, even revolutionaries—who, despite having lost the reform war, could, through their lives and institutions, continue to witness for equality and social justice right where they were; in east central Mississippi and in the Methodist Episcopal Church. The church could, if necessary, serve as a retreat and a sanctuary where members were renewed for the struggles ahead.[4]

The harshness of the Jim Crow laws, however, rendered it all but impossible for Mt. Zion to have anything but the most indirect contact with its parent denomination. Instead, their denominational involvement was with the black Mississippi Methodist Conference, which until 1920 was presided over by a visiting white bishop. Both their religious and secular concerns were addressed there by delegates, usually elected, to the annual conference meetings, who considered the interests of the denomination at large, as well as the hopes and fears of local Mississippi congregations like Mt. Zion. The visiting bishop typically conducted the business of the conference, asking delegates to promote denominational literature, to pay their assessments, to endorse temperance, and to stay current with the goals of various denominational boards. But the delegates themselves found ways to use these meetings as an opportunity to address their own issues; at one session they commended one of their own who had "manfully condemned the 'mob law' of this country," and at another they praised the politicians who "stand against lynching."[5] On a more personal level, they appropriated money for "a new suit of clothes" for a recently ordained elder in the conference. The records of these conference sessions make it possible to learn many of the problems of local congregations, and it was this conference that provided the ecclesiastical support for Mt. Zion Church.

One consistent urgent concern in Mississippi conference sessions was the need for education. "Next to personal salvation," delegates were advised, "preach personal education."[6] The Methodist denomination had built schools, colleges, universities, and academies in the state, and it was incumbent on the black delegates assembled to accept the responsibility to persuade their congregations back home to take advantage of the opportunities. Education, delegates were reminded, was vital to the church, to the community, and to the race.

The Great Migration

An attachment to Methodism therefore factored into an individual's decision whether to join the Great Migration headed north as worsening Jim

Crow conditions convinced thousands to leave. It was never a collective congregational choice at Mt. Zion to stay or go, although there were other churches where people decided to leave en masse. Those who decided that they would leave Southern settlements like Longdale for the seeming safety of the North may have had trouble understanding why their neighbors stayed behind. The migrants and Northern black newspapers did their best to encourage people to leave; they told of jobs, opportunities, and a sense of freedom to be found in new urban centers in Chicago, Detroit, and New York. Some Longdale people did leave, for a year, several years, or a lifetime. But a surprising number, like the Jones brothers and many Second World War veterans in the 1940s, came back. The world was a tough place, perhaps irredeemably corrupt, and yet the God who was worshipped at Mt. Zion Church had promised to help this community of believers achieve progress toward the goals of fairness, freedom, justice, and salvation. They encouraged each other in their beliefs, and in their desire for land, education, and personal dignity.[7]

Out in the countryside, Mt. Zion could seem the very model of a protected haven, a place that afforded shelter from the worst of the racist storm. According to Henry Bullock, a student of black education in the South, settlements like Longdale helped form Southern black residents into a unique people; their strong kinship ties and shared "positive" outlook helped them get through the hard times, and shaped "Southern Negroes into a particular kind of folk."[8] But Bullock also argued that there was a downside to this rural isolation in that it kept black residents from interacting with the white local culture and the wider world around them. This criticism had no supporters at Mt. Zion, largely because members found rewards in continuing contacts with the local conference and, though indirectly, with the denomination. In addition, Longdale was home to ambitious, entrepreneurial people who had established a variety of trading arrangements with whites, so their isolation was not complete.

But even places that can seem like havens are not fully autonomous units, and Longdale residents were not misled into thinking that God and their rural location protected their church from physical danger. Stories from slavery and the current oppression of an evolving Jim Crow system were alive in their lives and collective memory. For people under siege, the concept of haven is an illusory thing. Residents were nothing if not vigilant: they kept guns in their houses and on their person, yet even that was not enough to prevent the white sheriff and his rogue colleagues from patrolling their roads at will and creating havoc.[9] It remained the case, however, that Longdale's rural isolation did afford a degree of protection not found in the city of Philadelphia, where blacks were constantly on the defensive against the assaults and insults of whites. In a way unknown to most moderns, the Longdale church grounded its people spiritually and temporally, just as churches had served similarly for other immigrant groups in the past.

The depredations of the looming Great Depression also added to the harshness of life for blacks in the rural South. For some Mt. Zion people and their friends, the collapse of the economy provided the final motivation to leave, however great their distress at arriving at such a decision. If the choice seemed clear to those who made it, it was never easy to implement. By going north the migrants put Southern segregation behind them, but they also left behind many of the appealing things associated with home: not just furniture and goods, but family, friends, church, food, hunting, slow Southern accents, the comfort of warm sunny days. There was pain that came from pulling up roots, despite the constant danger of life in Mississippi and Neshoba County. But some people did leave Mt. Zion and Neshoba County.

The writer Isabel Wilkerson has gracefully recaptured the story of the Great Migration in the years between 1915 and 1970. During that period over five million people left the South, and Wilkerson has noted the suffering on both sides of the emotional equation of those involved in the choice; the promise of new beginnings, but also the uncertainty, the fear of never seeing loved ones again, the dangers faced by those who remained.[10] The majority of those who left tended to be healthy, relatively young, unencumbered, possessed of a measure of education, and as befits most of those who choose to become migrants, determination and spiritedness.[11] Wilkerson thought no one single factor led people to leave, but rather an accumulation of issues over time persuaded them when the time was right, though a search for better wages, schools, and an alternative to Jim Crow would have been prominent considerations. Common to all leavers, she believed, was the desire to be free.

Black Methodists were as desirous of freedom as other black Southerners, and conference records reveal a loss in membership between 1916 and 1940. In the black Methodist Conference of Upper Mississippi the greatest loss of members to the Great Migration came after the First World War, or about the same time the largest number of black residents left the state. Between 1916 and 1919, the conference lost approximately a quarter of its members, going from 25,079 to 19,100.[12] A Methodist observer explained the drop as a result of "the Old Plantation system," low wages, and the devastations of the boll weevil.[13] The Mississippi Conference to which Mt. Zion belonged (as distinct from the Conference of Upper Mississippi) also lost membership though more gradually, attributed by conference delegates to an insufficient number of clergy. A similar, gradual pattern of outmigration was in evidence at Mt. Zion Church, where individuals like Ross and Wilbur Jones left in the 1930s in search of better jobs, only to return after the Second World War. In their case and that of other leavers from Longdale, they were no poorer or more burdened than others who made the choice to go. Wilkerson has indicated that another consideration may have been involved for those who, unlike the Jones brothers and others, decided not to go but remain behind; Wilkerson suggests they may have been "more conciliatory than many of the people in the Great Migration," presumably more willing to show whites the deference demanded by the invisible southern social code.[14]

The circumstances of Mt. Zion's members were sufficiently complicated to disallow such an easy explanation. As heirs of Reconstruction, they had adopted integrationist ideology and continued to witness for an inclusive society. Longdale was not Mound Bayou. They interacted regularly with whites over economic matters like cotton sales, timber sales, loans, and jobs, while the men of the community continued to press for the right to vote. Years later, members remembered a persistent urge to resist Jim Crow, even through small acts of protest. Their white neighbors were sufficiently uneasy over the behavior of blacks in the area that they stayed alert, but only the most daring of black residents challenged social expectations overtly. For black Neshobans, interactions with whites in Jim Crow Mississippi almost mandated deference to the southern social code during these years. The Reverend Clint Collier, occasional Longdale resident and the most outspoken leader of black opposition in the area, was once jailed on trumped-up charges to keep him out of sight during a Martin Luther King visit; when he reflected on his life during the Jim Crow years, however, he joined the chorus of others who said, "I was not scared." He had lived in Washington, DC, in the 1950s and said he found that a scarier place because of "the threat of nuclear war in Washington." Collier claimed he found it "scarier" because of the "potential for an invasion by outside terrorists," his definition of terrorism having a different meaning for him in those pre-9/11 years.[15] For Collier, for Ross Jones and his brothers, for the dozen or so others who left and returned, the North was not the Promised Land. If

Longdale people looked more "conciliatory" to those who left, they would most likely have debated the charge.

The Great Migration, with millions involved, came to have a profound impact on American life, both in the lives of the migrants, and on the nature of Northern culture itself. It affected the communities they left behind as well. Historian Neil McMillen referred to the migration as a "folk movement of incalculable moment."[16] The influence of Southern black music, religion, dance, dress, food, speech, sense of community, proved lasting in the places where migrants settled, while at the same time helping to loosen the hold of Jim Crow on the South. But one overlooked consequence of the movement was its indirect effect on Southern black history, and how the culture of those who remained influenced Southern white culture. Because of those who stayed—in Longdale and similar rural hamlets—there were people to be integrated into a multicultural environment; into schools, and shops, and buses; to continue the agitation for justice, opportunity, and a place of recognition in Southern history: to be the witnesses for an inclusive society.

The Witness of a Longdale Family

Jeff Steele of Longdale was one of those black Mississippians who chose to remain in the South. In 1925, while in his early thirties, he moved with his young family from nearby Kemper County to settle in Longdale. He and his wife had two young sons, Cornelius, five, and Jeff, two; a third son, William H., would arrive in 1927. They moved into a sharecropper cabin at the Cox Place in the Sandtown area of the county, near the white Pine Grove Methodist Church. Their new home was a few miles from the Longdale settlement yet close enough for them to be part of the neighborhood community. Perhaps Steele had thought of leaving segregation behind and joining the other migrants headed north. For the Steele family, however, Longdale offered compensations of its own; there was already a community in place, they could work with other croppers toward personal land ownership, join the church, and send the children to school. Had they left, they would have constituted a poor and vulnerable traveling group. Longdale was a welcoming community with an institutional life.

It was also true that they were vulnerable in Longdale as well, and to the most violent of crimes. Although no lynchings occurred near the Longdale area until the 1964 Klan murders, there had been seven lynchings in the county between 1875 and 1902.[17] Vigilante groups were known

to roam the area, their actions unpredictable, and the town had a reputation for being a tough place. Lynch mobs typically sought out victims
among those who "did not know their place," that is, individuals who
demonstrated in various ways signs of aspiration or personal pride, qualities thought to undermine white control but actually encouraged by the
preaching at Mt. Zion Church. The reality, however, was that victims were
sometimes chosen because they happened to be in the wrong place at the
wrong time.[18] The daunting data about lynching shows that Mississippi
lynched 539 blacks between "the end of Reconstruction and the modern
civil rights era," according to historian Charles Payne, the most of any
state.[19]

The tradition of white Southern violence against blacks was as old as
the nation itself, though black people were the most likely to remember it.
To the crowds of white observers who showed up when a black killing was
announced, it was pornographic violence. For the Steeles, and for virtually
all Southern blacks, stories of white assaults against black people formed
part of the storehouse of memories they always possessed. What Jeff
Steele's personal religious beliefs were at the time he settled in Longdale
are not obvious, although he soon joined Mt. Zion Methodist Church, a
congregation committed to what historian Eric Foner has called the common faith outlook of Southern black church people, namely a "messianic
vision of history."[20] Themselves under great duress, they found confidence
in God's promise to the Jews in the book of Exodus that they would be
delivered from bondage, a belief strong enough to provide intermittent
comfort and to shape collective memory. A harsh past would inevitably
give way to a liberating future. Their attachment to this Old Testament
Exodus covenant combined easily with their view of Jesus as "a personal
redeemer offering solace in the face of misfortune." Through a lifetime
lived in Longdale, Jeff Steele showed a courage and confidence compatible
with spiritual ideas of this sort; his confidence was likely bolstered as well
by his impressive physical strength and the gun he always carried. His
Longdale neighbor, Mabel Wells, a Sunday school teacher at Mt. Zion for
most of her life, and a teacher at the school, expressed her religious views
more explicitly. Frail and elderly at the time she witnessed to her faith in
her small shotgun cabin in 2002, she spoke of the Exodus account, as
well as the comforting presence of Jesus she found in the gospel of John.[21]
Her convictions—and presumably those of Jeff Steele as well—were not
pie-in-the-sky religious affirmations, but were offered with an absolute
certainty that God acted in their world, and would protect them in the end.

They knew, of course, that lynching killed people and they meant to take precautions, but their faith was born out of tragedy, bestowing a spiritual awareness that sustained their daily life experiences.

The majority of Longdale residents who decided to remain in the area were not without resources, although sizable land holdings were not one of them. Most had some material resources, and while not a part of the "Negro vanguard," they had had some education at Mt. Zion School. Immaterial forces, including collective memories, played a part in their choice to remain; Mississippians in general and Neshobans in particular took delight in their natural surroundings, possessing a keen sense of place, of family, and rootedness in the community. A sense of rootedness may have been even more true for women raising large families, and for those too elderly to undertake the journey.

Part of an in-migration, new families continued to arrive in Longdale in the opening decades of the twentieth century. They were voting with their feet against the harshness of Jim Crow in other parts of the South, hoping to find, if not the Promised Land, then a land with some promise. The possibility of acquiring their own land was an important incentive to settle there, as new residents focused on economic considerations. When Jeff Steele—later known as "Old Man Jeff"—had arrived in 1925, he and his family were part of a third generation of settlers, some already interrelated by marriage at the time the Steeles got there.[22] It was from this third generation that the Great Migration claimed most of its Longdale participants.

The Steele family established connections in Longdale, and before long its members became among the more prominent in the area. They had a visible presence in the community and were pillars of Mt. Zion Church. They also realized their hope of becoming landowners. Their son Cornelius eventually became known as a man of influence and authority, not just in Longdale but in Neshoba County as well. At one time he had the reputation of being "the most powerful African American in the community."[23] Cornelius's son, John, said his father always carried a weapon, and was "not a nonviolent man, someone more like Billy the Kid or Wyatt Earp," who would not let others push him around.[24] Because of his reputation, Cornelius would be one of the first persons the civil rights workers contacted in the 1960s, under the protective cover of darkness, to lay out plans for a Freedom School at the church that would help people register to vote. Cornelius was one of a group of men in Longdale who tried to register to vote in 1945, and continued the challenge in the years following. A story circulated in the community that a voting registrar once asked

Steele "how many bubbles are in a bar of soap" as a means of keeping him from the vote.[25]

Mt. Zion Church carried on with its usual activities during these very difficult decades, holding Sunday worship services—or sometimes just Sunday School—summer revivals, sumptuous "dinners on the grounds," and gathering with other black Methodist churches for local conference meetings. They sang hymns from the Methodist hymnal, listened to passionate but dignified sermons, and generally conducted their worship like most other churches in the denomination. They sent delegates to the annual conference, and were saddened to hear back that in 1929 a popular Methodist preparatory school for black children in nearby Meridian would close, a victim of the Depression era and its disproportionate effect on black people.

"The Nadir of the Negro": Jim Crow Settles In

Whites also suffered economically in the years surrounding the Great Depression, yet for most there was always the belief, rooted in memory, that their power—if not their vast estates—was secure as long as they held hegemonic control of the culture. The Jim Crow laws also made it possible to engage in a steady redefinition of what "whiteness" meant, a concept further refined in the 1960s through the efforts of the Mississippi State Sovereignty Commission. Whiteness was understood as not just racial identity and skin color, but as a sign of privilege that was startlingly flexible "in redefining itself and group boundaries."[26] The race-based humiliating social code proved remarkably adaptable at finding new ways to assert white supremacy, affirm black inferiority, and wound black pride. At the time, during the early decades of the twentieth century, it seemed that Mississippi was in company with much of the Western world in capitulating to extreme positions on white supremacy. During this so-called "nadir of the Negro," it was a constant struggle for black people to be prepared for the next demeaning white social invention.

Social Darwinism, another definition for white supremacy, had currency throughout the Western world during these years, as pseudoscientific theories of racism replaced progressive hope. Some white Baptists in 1903 complained that people who don't have time to read the Bible were reading a book called " 'The Negro a Beast' and talk[ed] about the poor negro as being some kind of a brute without a name."[27] Literature and scholarship combined to devalue the black person. A measure of how ubiquitous was the idea of white supremacy is an entry in the prestigious

Encyclopedia Britannica of 1910 that stated, "[T]he negro would appear to stand on a lower evolutionary plane than the white man."[28] The hegemonic control of whites in the modern world spurred the "reconstitution of whiteness" that benefitted a ruling class convinced that its mission was to colonize "less civilized" societies.[29] How that global redefinition got manifested among whites living in Neshoba County—ancestors of Florence Mars—was through increased violence toward blacks and freshly invented extensions of the social code intended to protect white control.

Whites who shaped the southern social code understood that domination over small things assured authority over larger ones, namely control of the culture. In the city of Philadelphia, for example, that was interpreted to mean that blacks from Longdale had to give way to whites on the sidewalk. They were reminded to avoid direct eye contact with whites, an action whites considered impudent. Black men were expected to remove their hats in a room where white men kept theirs on. Ross Jones remembered one such experience when he was at the tax office paying his assessment. Told to remove his hat, he doffed it briefly and then immediately replaced it on his head.[30] A small gesture, but in the context of Jim Crow Mississippi a sign of black resistance to white supremacy.

Jones recalled an even more potentially violent episode from which members of Mt. Zion's congregation rescued him. Some six decades after the event occurred, Jones told of a startling demonstration of how whites understood the power implicit in their whiteness. A young man at the time, he was in a car on the way to Sunday worship at Mt. Zion Church when he and his friends passed a white man at the side of the road changing a flat tire on his car. Later, settled in his pew at Mt. Zion, Jones was confronted by the angry white man, who had followed him into church, planning to accost him. The white man's anger had been fueled by what he alleged were the "smiles" on the faces of the black men as they observed his predicament in their drive by. He was intent on fighting Jones in the church if people in the congregation had not stopped him.[31] Demonstrations of actions of white supremacy could appear in the least expected places, and it required black vigilance and group cooperation to resist it.[32]

White Memory and the Politics of Mississippi Segregation

The aggressive racist politics of Mississippi in the first half of the twentieth century tore at the people of Longdale and their Methodist church, as they did blacks throughout the state. Whites were conscious of the fact that Mississippi was a black-majority state where black voters, if they were ever enfranchised, could gain political control. Cornelius Steele knew that too, and that knowledge probably kept him among those who regularly advanced on the doors of the voting registrar's office. But the harsh reality was that between 1904 and 1947, that is, between the administrations of Governor James Vardaman and Governor, then Senator, Theodore Bilbo, white political leaders were determined to maintain hegemonic control in the state through policies that were unabashedly racist. They were not embarrassed to gain white votes by playing the race card.

Longdale residents, not just the Steeles, also knew that they were the state's majority. The population of Mississippi in 1930 stood at a little over two million, more than a million of them black. The figure represented a 12 percent gain over the previous decade despite little change in the ratio; in 1920 the population totaled 1,790,618, with 953,184 who were black.[33] These figures were alarming to white politicians, who remembered Reconstruction and the consequences for white control from an enfranchised black population. All forms of authority in the state were thus rigged to prevent a black electorate; the politics, the economy, the social climate, were all designed to keep the state's black residents marginalized and nonvoters.

The state's politicians and candidates for office in the first half of the twentieth century tended to focus on two of the hottest of the race issues, namely the continued disenfranchisement of blacks, and the foolishness of educating black children. When Vardaman was campaigning for the governorship in 1904 there was no mistaking his message: "When I speak of educating the people, I mean the white people." He agreed "The Negro is necessary in the economy of the world," but only as a "burden bearer."[34] In office, he called for a state Textbook Commission that would oversee rewriting the current "Confederate standpoint" of the history of the Civil War to make it "fair and impartial," but the proposal never went very far largely due to the lack of political support.[35] Thus, students continued to be taught the "Confederate standpoint" of the war, ensuring that white memory for the next generation would remain built around the Old South image.

During his terms as governor and senator, Bilbo remembered Vardaman's advice that to ensure blacks never got to the polls, it was important to visit them "the night before the elections." Since only 6 percent of blacks were registered as late as 1964, it was hardly a major political problem for the white leadership, though it did reveal the depth of white fear of a black voting bloc. Unless any of his listeners were unclear about the intention of his message, Bilbo spelled it out directly: "I call on every red-blooded white man to use ANY MEANS to keep the nigger away from the polls."[36]

As Vardaman had made plain earlier, limited black education was an integral part of the administration's racist political agenda. Political office-holders statewide spoke candidly about eliminating most, if not all, forms of education for black children. The state needed laborers who worked cheap, not laborers who could read. Why, the politicians often asked, should white taxpayers pay for education for black students when what the economy required was cheap manual labor? This view of education left blacks doubly disadvantaged during the Depression because, in addition to the problem of the shrinking job market, they had little to no education or skills to offer. Mt. Zion and other black Methodists struggled to keep education a priority.

Black men in particular knew they were vulnerable to more than joblessness, but to the ultimate weapon of white control, lynching. The evidence on the practice is stark, showing that there were almost 2,500 black victims in ten Southern states between 1882 and 1930, or "on the average, a black man, or child was murdered nearly once a week, every week" in these years.[37] Terrorism, such as lynching, succeeds when it manages to intimidate potential victims and forces them to live in fear; Mt. Zion's mission to its members, to quiet fears and provide reassurance, succeeded among those many people who affirmed "I was not afraid," and "I was not scared." After 1935 the number of lynchings throughout the South began to decline, although the threat continued, along with assaults that inevitably went unpunished.[38]

*Longdale Combats Jim Crow through the Post-*Brown* Years*

Although Longdale residents collectively recalled in the twenty-first century that they had not been "scared" during the terrible years of Jim Crow, they agreed that having weapons always available to them helped keep fears at bay. In 1930, a lynching occurred in nearby Kemper County, a place close enough to Longdale to keep people on edge. As a protective measure against gang violence they adopted a system of residential patrols: people from the community, usually armed, who monitored community roads when an alert was called or in particularly tense times. According to Arecia Steele, who had married into the large Steele clan descended from Jeff Steele, white folks knew "that any shot fired into a cabin would be returned by the mens inside."[39] The conviction that they held the moral high ground was probably the most powerful weapon they possessed, but they also kept their guns loaded.

Their conviction of the moral power of their position was put to the test following the passage of the 1954 *Brown* decision by the Supreme Court. At the time, black protest against the growing white onslaught was most commonly revealed through nonviolent, nonconfrontational means. The tiny octogenarian Mabel Wells, who gave most to the community in her capacity as a teacher, thought she was one of those who contributed to local security at a time when she worked as a domestic. During the course of cleaning the closet of the owner of the house, she discovered Ku Klux Klan robes, a product of the revitalized Klan of the 1960's. Her employer was not publicly identified as a Klan member, and while she continued to work for him because she needed the money, she alerted all her friends to the fact that he was a Klansman and they needed to be on their guard.[40] Women like Mabel Wells who worked as maids had regular access to the white community and its affairs, and could provide a steady stream of useful information.[41]

Mabel Wells and others like her were forced to be more vigilant as the racial environment grew more heated following the Supreme Court's decision. For a long time, before a lack of customers forced its closure, there had been a grocery store at the end of Longdale's Church Road, owned by a Klan member who was known to the community. The Klansman often sat in the front of the store playing checkers with his friends, likely Klan members as well. His store carried many of the household goods Longdale people needed, and from time to time he would hire someone from the community to work for him. For Longdale residents it was a calculated choice almost every day: to patronize the nearby Klan-run store with its crude racist and sexist owner, or travel the distance to Philadelphia. Aware of what they faced, women customers in particular, residents shopped for supplies at the store only as need dictated, always on guard and apprehensive.[42]

When the civil rights movement entered the area in the sixties, white aggression and black protest kept pace in the region. Longdale men like the Steeles—father Jeff and son Cornelius—kept up their pressure on whites through their attempts to vote. Ross Jones had earlier angered whites with his 1932 bold, in-your-face gesture of driving through town in a brand new car, a show of his financial status and the respect he enjoyed in his community.[43] Clint Collier, regarded by blacks and whites as the most aggressive and persistent protester in the area, was most active during the 1960s and 1970s, but even earlier he showed a willingness to spend a few days in jail in order to make a point. For many years he attempted to organize people for political action, and at various times conducted boycotts of stores in Philadelphia. In 1962, he, Burline Kirkland, and a couple of black residents of Independence Quarters in Philadelphia traveled to Washington, DC, to attend Martin Luther King's March on Washington. Community observers said they took heart when they saw community members take public stands such as these.

A less political challenge to white control had been the continuing attempts to expand black landowning. Black landowning in Longdale had been a restraint on white hegemony from the beginning. Possessing land contributed to a sense of pride, and although virtually all residents considered themselves landowners, in fact probably half were sharecroppers who didn't own their land. But a sharecropper today was preparing to be a landowner tomorrow. Landowners belonged to a small elite category in black Mississippi; in the earliest years of freedom, 1865 to 1890, they constituted only about 5 percent of black farmers.[44] By 1900, ten years later, the number had increased to more than 15 percent, a record high for the pre–Second World War years. From that point, the percentage declined in every decade of the Jim Crow period until 1940.[45] Black land ownership was not inconsiderable, but that still meant, according to historian Neil McMillen, "approximately 85 percent of all black [farm] operators in any given decade did not own the land they farmed."[46] Longdale farmers grew crops on hardscrabble land that whites did not want, and in the Depression decades leading up to the Second World War, the holdings shrank and more farmers had to supplement their earnings with sharecropping. In those pre-war years, the number of Neshoba's black farmers dropped to less than 300.[47] Those who did hold on to their land had to conduct business transactions with white tradespeople in addition to working especially hard to make marginal land productive. Most of these activities required them to operate within the prevailing social code.[48] But landownership, of even small and marginally productive holdings, conveyed a sense of status, a symbol of proprietorship and personal ambition, qualities that did not go unremarked by Longdale's white neighbors. Florence Mars confirmed that white Philadelphians generally regarded the Longdale residents as reliable and industrious, in a category apart from other black Neshobans they met.[49] Even some black residents of the Neshoba County area, who moved into houses in Independence Quarters built for them in the post–Second World War years, thought Mt. Zion people considered themselves "special." And most did regard their rural lifestyle as a better one.[50]

Longdale residents also appeared to be apolitical, though not nonpartisan, their progressive views kept under wraps during the Jim Crow years. Most black Methodists of the time, including those at Mt. Zion, because of outward appearances—a measured approach to worship, conservative dress, and eagerness for education—were assumed to be supporters of the Booker T. Washington gradualist approach to social change. No evidence would suggest that Mt. Zion people ever joined the ongoing Washington-DuBois debate, although sympathy for Washington's views surfaced among the black Methodist denominational leadership. At Mt. Zion, people's beliefs were influenced by the immediate political and physical conditions of their environment, sustained by faith and hope for the future; the only label that defined them was Methodist.

Getting by in Hard Times

Their environment temporarily changed for the better in 1905 when the railroad came to Philadelphia and a trunk line was added to Longdale. Just before the railroad, Neshoba County in 1900 had 12,726 people; 9,874 white and 2,852 black, virtually all described as "rural," including whites in town who ran shops, worked at trades and professions, owned timber mills, and ran banks.[51] Longdale people were farmers and household laborers, although the occasional Methodist elder lived there, and a teacher or two. The arrival of the railroad promised whites easier access to markets, but it would prove beneficial to black residents as well. Timber was the dominant product in the county, with cotton the king in most other areas of the state. The railroad was a boon to large timbering interests but also an advantage for small landowners. Many Longdale families became involved with the timber industry as timber workers but also as limited business partners, benefitting as small shareholders of timber land. The timber companies possessed much of the county land in the early years of the twentieth century, with the DeWeese Rodgers Lumber Company (now Weyerhaeuser) leading the way after 1915.[52] Longdale was a hub of a small trunk line that a timber company ran into the community to get timber to the mills. A cooperative relationship gradually developed between the lumber interests and the residents of Longdale. Numbers of black men went to work at the mills in town where the work looked steady and more predictable than farming.

As the industry grew, a small contractual trade in timber emerged, one not available to those black Mississippians who lived in areas with little marketable timber.[53] For Longdale farmers, the timber leasing agreements they worked out with the owners provided an additional source of income. Companies typically leased as much as 90 percent of a farmer's land in a heavily treed area, leaving the owner with 10 percent for personal use.[54] This became a regular supplement to the farmer's income, and was surely an advantage for the timber men. Most landowning residents of Mt. Zion participated in these leasing arrangements with mill owners. When Longdale resident Clarence Hill spoke of his early days in the community, he said he leased his treed land first to the Molpus Lumber Company, and then to Georgia Pacific. Leasing agreements remained in place into the twenty-first century.[55]

As long as the timber supply held up, this was a good financial arrangement for both parties to the contract. But eventually it proved to be not an especially wise investment for either, since the race for profits led to overcutting of virgin timber with minimal regard for replacement. By the 1930s, although Mississippi was third in the nation in timber production, the industry suffered from the financial crush of the Depression. Timber men, taxed on the same basis as producers of agriculture, though their product took years, often decades, to come to market, were unable to keep up with their taxes. Workers were let go from their jobs, and that included mill hands from Longdale who worked in town, their terminations recalled as a personal loss by those owners who had come to know some of their employees directly. Unique among industries in the state, timber and its owners maintained a congenial rapport with black workers and farmers. Nevertheless, with few people able to pay their taxes, the state treasury in 1932 held a balance of $1326.17, while the state debt amounted to over $50 million.[56]

Mt. Zion's residents also grew some cotton, like virtually everyone else in the state, the land for growing limited by their leasing contracts. Cotton was usually a dependable cash crop, although Longdale growers believed they did not fare as well in their transactions with cotton agents as they did with timber owners. In the Depression years they were exposed to the drop in cotton prices, as everyone else was. In Longdale, sharecropping residents relied on cotton profits to help them buy land, and they also tithed 10 percent of their profits to support Mt. Zion Church and Mt. Zion School. The few black landowners with sizable farms hired black croppers to work their land, attempting to help them out in hard times. Ross Jones described himself as a generous landlord who returned half the profit from sales to the croppers who worked on his farm, an arrangement he pointed out was unusual in the cotton economy, where croppers typically ended the year with only debts.[57] There is no indication of what his workers thought about the arrangement, although Jones said many came back to work in subsequent years.

The best year for cotton sales statewide was 1919, just after the First World War, when the price per pound reached an all time high of 35.34 cents. Because cotton was king, its value determined the condition of the whole economy. After 1919, the price began a precipitous decline due to the presence of the boll weevil, bad weather, and then the gathering clouds of the Depression. By 1931, the price for cotton per pound had dropped to 5.66 cents, a measure of the hard times that settled over the state in those years.[58] Everyone connected to the cotton industry—which is to say almost everyone in the state—suffered terribly. A gloomy Governor Bilbo said in 1930 that he feared that as supplies ran out Mississippians could face "sickness, sorrow, distress, death, and starvation . . . everywhere," though he could have been talking about the daily circumstances of life for most black tenants.[59] By 1930, deprivation was general as well as disproportionate. Now large planters needed even fewer croppers and black workers feared being replaced by machines. The New Deal helped with limited financial aid to encourage farmers to plant less cotton and give welfare to destitute blacks—although since funds were filtered through the hands of white power brokers, blacks saw little of it. Areas like the Delta and other areas planted heavily in cotton suffered terribly, while a place like Neshoba, with its more limited cotton growing, suffered less. Mt. Zion School actually witnessed a growth in the number of pupils in the 1930s and had to arrange for larger facilities and another teacher.[60]

The Economy of Longdale

The Depression visited hard times on Longdale, although residents remember the era differently depending on their age. People in their eighties and nineties in the early twenty-first century, who lived through the experience, remembered the abject poverty of the times and the creative ways people responded to it. Those from a younger age cohort, born after 1935 or 1936, expressed greater concern with discrimination and ill treatment than with the dismal state of the economy, though they still worried about limited job opportunities and low wages. The Depression years were not the same defining moment for the younger people that they were for their older neighbors.

For Wilbur Jones, the older brother of Ross and a member of the older generation, the late 1920s provided his breaking point, his story another reminder of how the Depression brought greater misfortunes sooner to blacks than to whites. By then, he said, he was tired of being a day laborer, working sunup to sundown to "chop, hoe, and weed" cotton for a dollar a day, and that was when he left for Detroit, as eventually did his other two brothers.[61] Women left the area too, knowing they could find work as underpaid domestics. Some of them also returned to Longdale after years away. For Clinton Collier, who was born in 1909, the Depression coincided with his coming of age, robbing him of youthful opportunity. In his case, he left the area temporarily to join the growing war industry, and then to join the army itself. But he was convinced the people of his father's generation, those who had experienced the period known as the "nadir of the Negro," had known an even harder time. His father had been born to a sharecropping family in 1878, and then became a cropper himself at age eleven. Through hard work and help from his large family of eleven children he acquired 80 acres, and leased even more. Collier said he loved his Daddy, but as he himself grew up, "I know the condition we were living in. My Daddy had been pushed around. His cabin had a dirt floor. My uncle had been a medical doctor, but he was waylaid and shot by the Ku Klux Klan." Since there was no organized Klan in Neshoba in the 1920s and 1930s, the event probably occurred some other place.[62] With 80 acres and more, his father still lived with a dirt floor. Collier himself became a Methodist minister in 1954 because he saw it as a vehicle for protesting racial injustice but also because it offered financial benefits.[63]

Longdale got through the difficult years of the Depression because of its small, diversified, if marginal, economy and the help neighbors gave each other. Some men continued to work in timber even as layoffs occurred and other jobs were lost, and timber contracts were renegotiated. Residents continued raising cotton and suffered along with everyone else as the price dropped. Besides timber and cotton, Longdale's farmers found resources in corn, oats, kitchen produce, and in raising chicken, hogs, and cattle.

The trade in cattle, a small but notable dimension of Longdale's mixed economy, was a demanding business governed by a rigid racial code. The cattle were taken to the stockyards on the outskirts of Philadelphia for sale, and for those who came from Longdale that was an unpleasant, sometimes dangerous, occasion. Whatever civility prevailed in transactions between lumbermen and growers, or between cotton drivers and their companions on the road, was lost at the stockyards. The prevailing social code required that blacks stand while whites sat to evaluate their sales and purchases—an indignity not to be forgotten—and the interactions at the yard could be rough. In later years Collier and Ross Jones recalled that they were allowed to participate in the bidding to buy, but were forced to accept whatever the auctioneer decided they would be paid for the animals they sold.[64] The white cattlemen were a tough and rugged bunch, prepared for anything. Collier said that as late as 1966 he nearly lost his life in a stockyard fight. A white man who wore brass knuckles threatened him, and were it not for Cornelius Steele—about whom Collier (as well as Jones) later had second thoughts—and help from Cecil George, a white neighbor, he might have been killed. As at the cotton market, the black men thought they were cheated out of their full payment at the stockyard. Whether trading or farming, the men of Longdale were almost never unarmed.

While the primary business of Longdale, even during the Depression, remained timber sales and cotton growing, there were other entrepreneurial enterprises that helped sustain the residents. Women continued to be domestics while also working as cotton choppers, all the while holding the church together. Some people continued to sell illegal whiskey because, even though Prohibition had ended, Neshoba County was still theoretically a "dry" county. A few creative folk read Tarot cards, and others performed healing and midwifery. Mt. Zion's school teachers, resident in the community, were paid their salaries right through the Depression years.

The school actually did very well during the 1930s. In 1935, the parents of children in Mt. Zion School erected a new building, the third school since Longdale was settled. The school being used at the time was the former commissary of the A. DeWeese Lumber Company, and according to the parents, "because the families of the community were growing," it was time to construct a bigger facility. The resources to build a school, at a time when other communities were closing schools and letting teachers go, seem to have come from a variety of donors: the Methodist denomination, a local philanthropist, and several of the larger landowners in Mt. Zion itself.[65]

The memories of Mt. Zion's members do not fill in all the spaces of ordinary life during the Great Depression. It is recalled as a hard time, but most past time was hard time. Young people left, but a surprising number returned, some after an absence of thirty or more years. Industrial jobs in the North imposed their own cyclical lean times. And for those who returned, it was the memories which drew them; of school and church and community and family. When Ross Jones was asked why he returned to Longdale from New York City, he said simply "This is home."

The stories from their past that Mt. Zion's people remembered were the basis of the collective memory of the community, unknown and likely unimaginable to white residents of the area. But while they told of hard times in the past, their focus was on an improved future, an equally difficult concept for their white neighbors to grasp. For blacks and whites, memories followed the color line.

The Great Anomaly

The Methodist Episcopal Church and Its Black Members

PART TWO

The Great Anomaly:

The Methodist Episcopal Church and
Its Black Membership

4

Sanctified Segregation

BLACK METHODISTS AND THE CENTRAL JURISDICTION, 1920–1940

The rumor got abroad that the Methodist Episcopal Church was "Massa Linkum's" church.
MORROW, Northern Methodism and Reconstruction

It is inconceivable that I should believe that my people are being bartered from Church to Church "as if they were mere chattels and pawns in a game," even the great game of unification of American Methodism.
SPEECH OF IRVINE G. PENN, 1919, MEC

So we do not lose heart. . . . For this slight momentary affliction is preparing us for an eternal weight of glory beyond all comparison.
2 CORINTHIANS 4:16, 17

A Conversation about Religious Racism

"How much do you know about the Central Jurisdiction," the Reverend Harry Bowie asked me at the outset of this study in July 2001.[1] Bowie's question referred to the administrative unit within Methodism that was the price the denomination paid in racial politics to reunite its northern and southern branches in 1939. He knew I was at work on the history of Mt. Zion Church, and the point he was making was that any study of the church had to be viewed within the context of Methodism's bruising struggle over racial inclusion. Both an insider and an outsider to Methodism and Mississippi, Bowie was particularly well suited to comment on the tumultuous religious life in the state in the recent past. He had been a civil rights activist who had moved there in the 1960s and then stayed on. His practical work in the movement was combined with a broad liberal education, first at Hobart College and then at General Seminary in New York. Most of his civil rights activism had been with the Delta Ministry, a mission to Mississippi's needy, supported by funds from mainline Protestant churches channeled through the National Council of Churches (NCC).[2]

Bowie's argument was straightforward. Mt. Zion had battled the state of Mississippi over racial equality, essentially a political fight, whose broad contours were familiar to most students of American history. But it had also endured another bitter confrontation, this one with its own Methodist denomination, which within the larger construct of morality and human values was, Bowie suggested, more consequential. Because the struggle within Methodism was implicitly involved with moral values, namely how the church could simultaneously support an inclusive denomination while also serving Southern "Christian segregationists," it had a profound effect on how the culture viewed segregation. When the denomination pronounced a blessing on segregation, it made it easier for secular leaders in the state to justify their white supremacist policies.

In 1939, at the time the black Central Jurisdiction became a segregated reality within Methodism, white supremacy had already established a firm grip over matters dealing with race in Mississippi, and most other parts of the South. As Jim Crow matured into its second generation, Mississippi black people found themselves denied basic human rights as well as legal rights. In a sign of the absence of fundamental courtesy, black people were never addressed by titles. In interactions with whites, black people knew that regardless of age or status, they would be referred to by first names, or by a variety of diminutive terms like "auntie," or "uncle," or "boy," with only those who believed themselves more gracious calling them "niggrahs." In the 1939 South, blacks lived in dilapidated cabins on dirt roads, their children sent to poorly served black schools, while the parents worked on the land or at underpaid jobs. Law enforcement agencies were a foe and not a friend. When such dire living conditions prevailed among its members, did it make any difference that the second-largest denomination in the state—and a power in the nation—the Methodist Episcopal Church, was willing to accept a constitution that mandated internal segregation in the church? That was the issue implicit in Reverend Bowie's question to me: there was a correlation between the abject living conditions of Southern blacks and the moral implications of the new Methodist policy. Roman Catholics and Jews in the state did not follow suit, but their numbers were

small, and members tended to follow the custom of the South and volun-
tarily worship apart. With the creation of the Central Jurisdiction, separate
congregations were required, with nothing voluntary about them.

The decision by the Methodists, long in coming, affirmed the blessing of this mainline church on the practice of segregation. In the name
of a unified church, it accepted the demands of its Southern constituency
to separate out some of its most loyal members, the mostly Southern
black Methodists. Might the outcome—years of racial struggle and violence—have been different if the Methodist Church had maintained its
commitment to an inclusive church? Bowie's point was that the Methodist
compromise lent moral authority to the continued denial of the rights of
black Methodists, a policy that continued for another thirty years. It became
a challenge Mt. Zion had to confront: whether to remain in a segregated
Methodist Church, or leave and join a black-only Methodist denomination.
They stayed within the denomination, becoming part of "the faithful Black
Remnant" within Methodism, regarded by many both within and outside
as the conscience of the denomination.[3] Bowie was right: to understand
how Mt. Zion endured and what it believed, it was necessary to understand
what informed the creation of the Central Jurisdiction.

The Central Jurisdiction (CJ) was the denomination's answer to the
famous question raised in the name of reunification of the church, north
and south, which was, "what shall we do about our Negro members?"
The answer that the leadership arrived at was this artificial, unwieldy con-
glomeration, meant to be the jurisdictional center for all black churches,
including rural Mt. Zion in Longdale. In Mississippi the CJ remained in
existence until 1972, although the denomination officially voted its demise
in 1968, at which point black conferences were to be aligned with neighboring white conferences. Mississippi remained a holdout until 1972,
thanks to the efforts of outspoken segregationist laymen in the state, and
a lack of clerical leadership at the highest levels. Bowie noted the irony of
the Methodist solution for healing a regionally divided church: although
it was a self-consciously connectional church, supposedly seamlessly
attached to its local congregations, it was willing to revise its constitution
to segregate some of its most devoted members.

Harry Bowie's assessment of the Central Jurisdiction had been shaped
in important ways by his time with the Delta Ministry, which was a
hands-on mission focused on the poorest of the poor in the Delta and
other selected parts of the state.[4] He saw that as a far cry from the racially
driven politics that had created the Central Jurisdiction. Largely young

clergy and some lay people, black and white, worked in The Ministry and cooperated often with black activists in protesting the conditions of the local poor. White Mississippians viewed the Delta Ministry from a very different perspective: they saw it as an offensive outsider, an intruder on local customs, whose workers held questionable values that included interracialism, socialism—sometimes described as communism—and an alternative lifestyle that might be fashionable someplace else. As a progressive and a movement activist, Bowie was at odds with this white Mississippi consensus: for him the Delta Ministry was the last "hoorah" of Rooseveltian liberalism, which breathed its last in 1968 when he wound up his work with it.

According to Bowie, the Delta Ministry blended politics and religion so completely that it had no identifiable theology, but instead had a "social gospel" outlook that encouraged fellowship with the Mississippi Freedom Democratic Party.[5] In many ways The Ministry had much in common with the Methodism of Mt. Zion's founders, a compatibility that continued to foster cooperation between Delta Ministry and other black Methodists in the state. Bowie's fond recollection of The Ministry as color-blind, generous and idealistic contrasted sharply with his view of Methodism's Central Jurisdiction, which he viewed as a compromise with segregation.[6] The Central Jurisdiction, he believed, was the denomination's capitulation to "Christian segregationists," and a moral blot on its history.[7]

The white Methodist Church, he said, was a powerful institution in Mississippi, an appendage of the sociopolitical structure of the state.[8] The church maintained contact with its white members not only through the clergy and the bishop, but through local denominational publications and prosegregation organizations that sought validation through church alliances. Black Methodists came to realize that they, too, had power within their own conference, the Mississippi Conference of the Methodist Church, CJ, and they used it to advance their own issues with national denominational boards and commissions. Mt. Zion was a small voice in this much larger denomination, the largest Protestant body in the country, its future and political fortunes determined by a remote national institution.

The Creation of a "Church within a Church"

The interwar years, 1920–1940, had been especially hard on Mt. Zion's members, due in large measure to the extension of white supremacy into virtually all aspects of black life, but also from the burdens of the Great

Depression. There was no relief to be found outside their own community, yet most residents remained where they had planted their roots.

Their local black Methodist conference had been meeting apart from white Methodists since the early 1890s, an arrangement required by state segregation laws, and for all that time leadership of the conference had been managed by white bishops. In 1920, the national denomination responded to the repeated requests made by several black conferences for a bishop of their own. Church commissions had been debating similar requests for at least twenty years, before they finally agreed that black conferences could be served by black bishops. But before that change could take place, the denominational constitution had to be altered to allow for racially limiting the services of black bishops. Methodism's founder, John Wesley, had originally planned for an itinerant superintendency, which meant that potentially a black bishop could preside over a white conference, and a white bishop over a black one, a development white Methodists in the state could not accept. Mississippi's black Methodist conferences were pleased to learn that they would finally be getting a black bishop in 1920, but displeased that his authority in the denomination would be limited in ways that did not apply to his white colleagues.[9]

The overriding goal of the denomination at the time was healing the regional breach, opened in 1844 over the question of slaveholding. The issue of reunification in 1939 still carried racial implications, and since 1915 had taken precedence over all other matters. The black Methodist agitation for black bishops, an issue as early as 1900, was an aspect of the regional split. Since the idea of a black bishop was totally unacceptable to white Methodists in the South, the denominational leadership eventually hammered out a compromise, following long debates and commission sessions, which limited the duties of a black bishop to just black conferences. Mt. Zion and other Southern black Methodist congregations were pleased when it was announced they could have a bishop of their own, but most also understood it was an accommodation to Jim Crow.

Segregation divided many institutions in the nation at the time. The postwar years had been trying, not just for Methodists, but for virtually every other institution, all of them at sometime caught up in the tumult over racial matters. The election of black bishops was a commentary on the times, consistent with the color line drawn in all areas of collective life. Race riots and killings shadowed the entire country. Black Southerners who had moved north expecting to find safety and opportunity found their hopes chilled. In 1917, a year before the First World War ended, a white mob in East

St. Louis, Illinois, a white mob murdered thirty-nine blacks who had moved to the area seeking defense-industry work.[10] Postwar readjustment failed to include significant numbers of new black residents in matters of housing and job opportunities, and shortages led to more racial conflict. In 1919 alone, race riots occurred in over twenty-six towns and cities, including Chicago.[11] In the face of these outrages, W. E. B. Dubois and the NAACP made it clear they were not going to continue a policy of nonresistance and cooperation—as they had during the First World War—but would be more militant and fight back. Racial violence in the North was matched by news of lynchings in the South. It was in this tense environment that the Reverend Robert E. Jones was elected the first black bishop to serve in a nonmission capacity in the Methodist Church.

In the black Mississippi Methodist Annual Conference in 1920, the primary concern of the delegates, apart from celebrating the announcement of the new bishop, was understandably the safety of their people amid the violence continually directed at them. Delegates voiced a sense of despair about worsening conditions facing their members and the hostility that confronted them in their daily lives. The possibility of better educational opportunities seemed to hold out one glimmer of hope, and with that in mind the conference drew up two resolutions to the Mississippi legislature, both of them related to education. The first one focused on public education and its basic unfairness to black children, and the other said that taxes paid by whites should not be used exclusively for white schools. The measures were essentially the social gospel message of progressive Methodism, one that called for harmonizing political matters with religious beliefs.[12] Mt. Zion's delegates endorsed the resolutions, which had direct relevance for their school problems at home. Although Mt. Zion School, small and sparsely supplied, was adequate for young children, the community had no high school for its older children. In the matter related to tax revenue, segregated schools—especially segregated schools—needed more financial help from state tax resources. Education remained a priority for the conference as it was for Mt. Zion.

The announcement of the new bishop was the other major item on the conference agenda. Aware that it was a recognition of segregation, the delegates knew they needed to have leadership of their own if they wanted their concerns represented on church boards and in debate. They accepted the constitutional adjustments the denomination made so that Bishop Robert Jones, the newly elected bishop for the Mississippi Methodist

Conference, could replace the white bishops who had previously served in the post.

Jones's election acknowledged the racial separation of the conferences. The bishop was already a prominent figure in the denomination, having served in a number of official capacities, including as editor of the conference journal, the *Southwestern Christian Advocate*, the voice of black Methodism. His election announced the end of the long struggle for a black bishop. It had taken a rejection of Wesley's concept of itinerancy and a revision of the constitution to achieve it, no small changes.

The new bishop was charged with ministering to all black Methodists in the state, in its two conferences and even beyond. Mt. Zion Church was a member of the Mississippi Methodist Conference; the second black conference in the state was known as Upper Mississippi Methodist Conference. Black Methodists now had their own bishop, just as those in independent Methodist denominations had had for years, beginning with the African Methodist Episcopal Church in 1815. By the time of Jones's election, black membership in the Methodist Episcopal Church was approximately 300,000, and most of them endorsed the prospect of a black bishop, although many were disappointed by the limits placed on his leadership.[13] For Southern black Methodists—and they were the majority in the denomination—having a black bishop, even with restricted responsibilities, seemed at first to be desirable.

Bishop Jones brought his broad experience to the post, along with unusual credentials to manage a delicate job in stressful times. Better educated than most of his peers, he had studied at Bennett College and Gammon Theological Seminary. It probably did not hurt that his complexion was reportedly so light that he could have "passed"; he said himself that he was "black by choice." A social conservative friendly with Booker T. Washington, he was quiet on the subject of social equality, as were others in the leadership of black Methodism.[14] Along with his professional preparation for the office, his appearance and nonstrident approach to the vexing social issues of the day probably facilitated his election. In the recent past, he had been a member of the Commission on Unification that had studied the reunion of the two regional branches of Methodism. The day following his election, Matthew W. Clair and Alexander P. Shaw, two other black Methodist ministers, were also elected bishops.

Once in office, it was Jones who presided at the Mississippi Methodist Annual Conference sessions to which Mt. Zion sent delegates. The clergy and lay representatives at the conference spoke of their pleasure at his presence, "taking advantage of the disadvantage" of Jim Crow. That reality, the disadvantage of Jim Crow, would become more vexing to black delegates over the next two decades. The delegates from Mt. Zion joined with the others to welcome Jones as one of them, someone who had shared life in the black South. Bishop Jones could promote issues on their behalf and see that colleagues were appointed to denominational posts. His election, determined by the Joint Commission on Unification, was a step in the direction of the reconciliation and reunification of the two branches of Methodism. Southern black churches remained supportive of their bishops over the years, although they were increasingly vocal about how the limited black episcopacy contributed to religious segregation.[15] Bishop Jones became another member of a growing class of black leaders, who were, however, excluded from the coterie of white officials who made and shaped policy in the church and in American culture. With black bishops limited to black conferences, and white bishops assigned to white ones, the black episcopacy helped create a church within a church for black Methodists.

Since its inception, the Methodist Church had prided itself on how well it meshed with popular culture. In its struggle over a racially divided episcopacy, it once again announced its place within the cultural milieu. The racial distress in the country raised a problem familiar to Methodists: namely, how to minister to black Methodists in an inclusive church and at the same time serve the needs of self-styled Christian segregationists. To a northern bishop like John W. Hamilton, at one time a member of the Joint Commission on Unification, the issue was precisely its moral and human consequences, ones that called the church to set an example. Hamilton once said to his fellow delegates, "They [black Methodists] have come into our fellowship through our tuition. Now, are we going to stand up and take each one of these members individually and say to him: 'You go off'? . . . I have no more right to tell him to go out of our Church than he has to tell me to do the same."[16] But Hamilton's insinuation of the need for social equality was not in sync with the majority in the church, and Jones was assigned to a black conference.

At the time of Jones's election in 1920, the denomination seemed far different from the one that Mt. Zion's founders joined in 1879. That nineteenth-century church identified with antislavery and Republican Reconstruction. Even as the twentieth century unfolded, there were Methodists who continued to support a new social gospel, one that gave aid to the poor, the immigrant, the needy, and the marginalized. The Methodist Church of James Lynch, Hiram Revels, and A. C. McDonald during Reconstruction had welcomed black Methodists and whites alike, and supporters of that sort of approach remained in the denomination, if more quietly. In 1920, instead of the inclusive, connectional denomination known to Mt. Zion, the denomination seemed on a slide toward the segregation policies adopted by Mississippi in 1890. Reunion, not social issues, was the major denominational preoccupation. And the whole discussion of reunion, church leaders knew, had to be handled gingerly. At one Joint Commission meeting on the question, however, an invited Southern delegate, A. J. Lamar, chose to state the problem bluntly: "We all know and we have known from the beginning that the crux of the situation is that [*sic*] Status of the Colored Membership in the Methodist Episcopal Church."[17] As commission discussions unfolded, representatives from both sides saw obvious advantages accruing to their churches from reunification: the South would gain access to the multitude of resources possessed by the Northern branch, and the North would lay claim to the membership-rich South. But compromise was elusive on any proposal in which black members were treated as equals.

Implications of the Central Jurisdiction in the Black South

Historians within Methodism, from an historically distanced position, were sympathetic to Harry Bowie's assessment of the Central Jurisdiction, that it had cast a dark cloud over the church's ministry to its black members.[18] The move to create a racially separate entity within the church was also a response to vast cultural dislocations such as the Great Migration and the Depression, changes that were not well handled by either the state or the church.

In 1939, not only the church failed its Southern black members, so did the federal government. As late as the 1960s, Attorney General Robert Kennedy could say of Mississippi that it resembled a Third World country. What historian James C. Cobb observed about the Delta's glaring inequities during the Depression years could well be applied to the rest of the state, namely that "global and national economic influences" confirmed the Delta's inequality and "reinforced its anachronistic social and political order as well."[19] During the thirties, it was not just the Delta but all of Mississippi that was an anachronism. The state's utter neediness had been compounded by the Depression. The federal government went on with its quid pro quo arrangement with the state, allowing it to maintain its "way of life" in exchange for support for measures the Roosevelt administration desired. Washington for the most part kept its distance on matters internal to the Magnolia State, although it funded programs for agriculture and social welfare in the Delta that, unfortunately, held the potential to make things worse by filtering money and power through the hands of the planter elite and enhancing their control.[20] The unique hardships of all Southern blacks during the interwar years went largely unrecognized, not only by the federal government, but by other agencies of church and society as well. The Methodists were not alone in abandoning hope—for a time—for an inclusive society. None wanted to be drawn into the seemingly insoluble affairs of Mississippi.

Occasionally social reformers, alone or in groups, attempted to address the problems of Southern black people. Northern progressives, largely from mainline churches, tried to intervene on behalf of Mississippi's rural black poor. One group of highly visible public figures, including Reinhold Niebuhr, Norman Thomas, Sam Franklin, Sherwood Eddy, Howard Kester, and others, attempted to investigate the plight of black tenant farmers and sharecroppers through the work of the Delta Cooperative Farm and the Southern Tenant Farmers Union. Despite their commitment and prominence, however, these notables were eventually forced to abandon hands-on activity, and by 1954 were essentially forced out of the state by the attacks of the recently formed White Citizen's Council. Niebuhr concluded sadly that the "organized church does not adequately serve [the black sharecroppers]."[21] Public activists such as these were few, and even they were discouraged by conditions in the state and the inadequacy of the church. Before the Methodist Church adopted reunification in the 1930s, it might have listened to the advice of people like Niebuhr, who called for a way forward by incorporating black members equally. There was also the nagging appeal of the Southern segregationist constituency. Instead of listening to voices like Niebuhr's and other progressives, the church settled on the "Great Compromise," what black Bishop James Thomas referred to as the "Great Anomaly." Thomas thought the latter description was especially apt, since Methodist polity was said to derive from the "radical inclusiveness" demanded in the New Testament while the creation of the Central Jurisdiction contradicted that view.[22]

Reunification, however described, was achieved when both regional branches of Methodism, along with the Methodist Protestant Church—a relatively new addition to the projected union—agreed they could become one denomination with a new name, The Methodist Church. Reunion would involve major structural changes in church government and policy, all of it hinged on the segregation of black members. The reorganization plan created not just the Central Jurisdiction but five other geographically defined regional policymaking bodies, also called jurisdictions. It was an organizational model entirely new to the denomination: the five jurisdictions were the Northeastern, the Southeastern, the North Central, the South Central, and the Western. The sixth, however, was the Central Jurisdiction, which had no geographical identity, but was a sprawling entity stretching virtually coast to coast, binding black congregations to black conferences across the continent.[23] Each of the six bodies would elect its own bishops, promote denominational interests in its region, and determine the boundaries of its own conferences. The newly-official policy of segregation also replaced central control of the denomination with regional control, a highly desirable outcome for the South. Additionally, it created a Judicial Council to arbitrate church disputes. "Jurisdictions divided Methodist fraternity by race," decentralizing the organization of the denomination, or as one church historian described it, it "ensmalled" the church.[24]

The reunited denomination celebrated the work of reunion at a grand "Uniting Conference" of Methodism in Kansas City in the spring of 1939. Three Methodist bodies merged to become The Methodist Church: the Methodist Episcopal Church; the Methodist Episcopal Church, South; and the Methodist Protestant Church. This was a time when denominationalism mattered; as a consequence of merger The Methodist Church was now the largest Protestant body in the country, with over eight million white members and more than 300,000 black members. The records of the Kansas City event note that after the vote was announced, the assembled white delegates to the conference stood and sang lustily "We're Marching to Zion"; the black delegates meanwhile sat and wept.[25] Mt. Zion was a constituent member of this new administrative creation, and like most black Methodists did not favor it, but cultural conditions had rendered it virtually inevitable.

The Central Jurisdiction and Its Opposition

It did not take long for black Methodist critics to line up against the Central
Jurisdiction, recognizing it as the imposed segregated arrangement that
it was. It was unclear just what Bishop Jones thought of this new construction of the denomination. "Bishop Jones did not want the Central
Jurisdiction," claimed his biographer. Among many Northern liberals the
arrangement was regarded as temporary, but white Southerners believed
it was a sacred contract. Bishop Jones once rationalized that the new order
at least did not make things worse for blacks, it did not "segregate them
any more than was already the case in the Northern church." His biographer said Jones accepted it as an "expedient accommodation."[26]

The segregated arrangement afforded some privileges for a few black
Methodists. It allowed for the appointment of more black clergy and lay
people to denominational boards as representatives from the Central
Jurisdiction. Ministers in leadership positions had access to better salaries and pensions, and clerical salaries in general were meant to increase,
although they remained lower than those of white colleagues, sometimes
by half.

Many, seemingly most, black Methodist ministers did not share the
view of Bishop Jones that the Central Jurisdiction did not make things
worse than the way they were before. The Reverend Lorenzo H. King, a
prominent black New York clergyman who would later become a bishop
himself, went as far as to ask the NAACP to intervene with legal action to
stop the implementation of the unification plan. He could not get enough
support in the church to go ahead with the idea.[27] The *Christian Century*
magazine published an editorial about King's proposal, saying that "it
becomes increasingly evident that the white majority in that denomination [the Methodist Church] has assumed a rather terrifying responsibility.
It is one thing for a majority to overrule the mere wishes of a minority; it
is quite another for that majority to force the minority, however small it
may be, into what that minority considers a morally untenable position."[28]
The *Southwestern Christian Advocate* ran articles and letters in the months
surrounding unification sent by readers who described their displeasure
with the new order, an arrangement most agreed was imposed on them,
and was another example of institutionalized segregation.

The votes from the uniting conference told the story. Of the forty-eight
black delegates at the 1939 conference, thirty-six opposed unification and
the Central Jurisdiction, and only eleven supported the measure. In the

General Conference as a whole, where whites were the clear majority, the vote was 470 in favor and 83 opposed.[29] No one knew how Bishop Jones of the Mississippi Conference voted on the matter, but the word leaked through the black press intimated that he had abstained because he opposed the Central Jurisdiction.[30]

By the following year black Methodists could claim four bishops, including Jones, whose episcopal residence was transferred from New Orleans to Columbus, Ohio. Lorenzo King was made a bishop and moved to Atlanta, and Bishop A. P. Shaw was the resident in Baltimore. Another bishop, W. A. C. Hughes, was elected to replace Jones in New Orleans, but, tragically, he died soon after and had to be replaced.[31] These men held leadership roles in their conferences and on denominational boards. When Robert N. Brooks, the black editor of the *Christian Advocate*, learned that Bishop Jones was the presider at the 1940 reunited and interracial General Conference, he likened the inspirational importance of the event as akin for black Methodists to a Joe Louis fight.[32] Brooks and others like him were among those who thought their members and colleagues were the refining fire of Methodism.

Sociologist Dwight M. Culver in 1953 did the first careful study of segregation within the Methodist denomination. In his book, Culver concluded that "Negro segregation in America is the expression of the 'white man's' theory of color caste . . . a theoretically fixed caste line [that] cannot be crossed successfully," whether by education, social integration, or individual advancement.[33] Although the Central Jurisdiction was marketed to black constituents as an expanded opportunity for leadership, a majority of black clerical leaders now recognized it for what it was, said Culver, a powerful symbol of prejudice and discrimination.[34]

The Central Jurisdiction evolved into an essentially Southern institution, since the vast majority of the denomination's black churches were located in the South, many the products of energetic missionary work during Reconstruction. The church was strongest in just those areas where segregation was well defended: Mississippi, which in 1939 claimed to have the most Methodist churches; South Carolina, Louisiana, Tennessee, as well as Maryland and Washington, DC. Texas soon outpaced Mississippi in having the most churches.[35] In addition to being Southern, most Central Jurisdiction churches were rural, with the majority of their congregations made up of women—farm workers, domestics, or teachers—and their children. The men in the churches were farmers and teachers, too, with some business people and professionals included. These churches paid

their denominational assessments, contributed to missions, and supported a minister or supply pastor with the rest, perhaps like Mt. Zion
using a percentage of farm receipts to meet their budget.[36] Black ministers remained underpaid compared with their white counterparts, and
once the denomination added educational requirements for clergy, including seminary training, the supply of preachers began a gradual decline,
followed by the membership.[37] When ministers assigned to the Central
Jurisdiction were asked about the greatest obstacle to their development
as leaders, they responded variously "no comment," "segregation," "racial
barriers," and notably "The Central Jurisdiction."[38]

By 1952, Mississippi CJ churches boasted the largest church memberships, with 28 percent of them reporting between 251 and 500 members,
making it the leader among black conferences in the denomination. In
the whole of the Central Jurisdiction only 16 percent counted more than
250 members.[39] The members of these churches were people who had
remained at home and had not joined the Great Migration north and west.
The Methodist churches in Mississippi tended not to attract the very poorest of residents; it cost money, after all, to maintain a building and pay a
minister, something the most impoverished could not do. The sociological
structure at Mt. Zion Church probably resembled other black Methodist
churches in the state, being working class and lower middle class with a
few teachers and business people. The membership at Mt. Zion fluctu-
ated between a high of 467 in 1910, to 300 in 1931, and then later as the
Depression and migration took their toll, to 174 in 1940.[40] Membership figures are traditionally unreliable, depending on who is doing the counting,
yet if the prewar number is accurate, the congregation was sufficiently
steady for it to meet its expenses, a point of considerable local pride.
Several decades later, in the 1960s, membership began another growth
spurt, as some former residents returned and the civil rights movement
energized communities like Longdale to be engaged with their churches.

Harry Bowie thought that Mt. Zion had always supported the idea
of an inclusive society despite being placed in the segregated Central
Jurisdiction. Some of its members may have held on to the colorblind
beliefs that were expressed in 1867 by James Lynch, although Dwight
Culver said such ideas were obsolete by 1953. In Mississippi through most
of the twentieth century, religion was tied to race, which meant it was also
about politics. For black Methodists, like those at Mt. Zion, the objective
was always an inclusive church, a view which clearly set it apart from the
mainstream of Southern white Methodism.

A Coda

The time Bishop Robert Jones presided over the General Conference in 1940 was a shining moment for black Methodists and undoubtedly for some whites as well. It was a public symbol of the church's ability to be inclusive, at least at the upper echelon. But as significant as the image it presented, the reunited church was a new creation, with no history or depth to it; it was not the image of the church—interracial and inclusive—most Methodists remembered and carried in their heads.

Jones himself considered the capstone of his career to be something else entirely, namely the creation of Gulfside, a Chattauqua-like retreat in Mississippi on the Gulf of Mexico. Gulfside had been built according to the principles of Booker T. Washington, favoring separate development, not inclusiveness, and the facility provided an educational and recreational retreat for black people not duplicated elsewhere. When he retired from the church in 1944, the bishop was celebrated mostly for Gulfside. A Southerner and a realist, Jones himself may therefore have realized that his presiding over the General Conference had been a fleeting honor.

A more poignant, perhaps lasting, memory for him might have been the marginalized treatment accorded him by his white colleagues. One such event occurred at a meeting of bishops in 1926, not long after Jones was elected to the episcopacy. He and his wife had been included in a meeting of bishops in Washington, DC, along with two other black bishops and their wives. When they arrived at the banquet hotel, the black attendees were all refused admission to the formal dinner being held inside; no place cards had been set for them, and they were not even allowed to enter. The white bishops explained they had not been party to the planning for the event, and after the insult to Jones and the others, they vowed not to meet in segregated facilities in the future. Yet when the General Conference met in Atlantic City in 1932, black delegates, including bishops, had to find segregated facilities in restaurants and hotels that would accept them.[41]

The Segregationist Insurgency and the Politicization of Mississippi Methodism, 1940–1954

To question the [Democratic] party which prevented Negro equality was to question the "Southern Way of Life."
NASH AND TAGGART, Mississippi Politics

[T]he Central Jurisdiction is unethical, immoral, unsound, and basically unchristian.
CHRISTIAN ADVOCATE (CJ), April 1948

Remnant or Residue?

In basic human terms, the changes wrought by reunification and the Central Jurisdiction made visible what had previously been invisible, that the "church within a church" that was black Methodism had an identity as the Central Jurisdiction. Black Methodist scholar William B. McClain has said that the creation of the Central Jurisdiction removed "the illusion that The Methodist Church was somehow an inclusive fellowship of Jesus Christ that worshipped a God who is 'no respecter of persons.' "[1] Since 1890, Mt. Zion had been sending its delegates to a black conference, and now with the arrival of the Central Jurisdiction in 1940 it sent its delegates to a similar conference, the difference being that within the CJ conference segregation was now de jure when previously it had been de facto. Black Methodists were involuntarily segregated by the church, and while that led to numerous administrative changes—notably the reality of a racial jurisdiction—it produced little difference in the operation of a local congregation like Mt. Zion. It did, however, make a difference in their lives as residents of east central Mississippi. It gave added strength to the state white conferences whose members could now unapologetically identify themselves as "Christian segregationists," and merge their interests with those of the many segregationist organizations taking root in the state. Just as there were two legally defined race-based school systems, there were now legally defined race-based Methodist conferences in the state and also the nation. The appearance of the CJ publically defined the Methodist denomination as pro-segregation, although operationally black Methodists worshipped as before at black Methodist churches and white Methodists at white ones. In the earliest years of the life of the CJ, black Methodists in the state were inclined to give it grudging acceptance—it meant new opportunities, greater conference power, a chance to be the "refining fire" of Methodism, as the "faithful remnant"—but within a decade that changed to virtually total opposition. They realized they were in a Jim Crow position in the church, the residue that remained when answered the question, "What shall we do about our black members"? by creating the CJ.

The Mississippi Conference CJ in that first year had a membership of slightly over 20,000, about what it had been throughout the decade, despite outmigration and the effects of the Depression. Surprisingly, membership in the Philadelphia Circuit to which Mt. Zion belonged dropped dramatically in 1942 for no clear reason.[2] The delegates seemed to enjoy a sense of enhanced power from being part of the largely autonomous Central Jurisdiction; they were better positioned to nominate members to official boards and commissions, to elect their own bishop, to set their own financial priorities. But, as noted, within a decade it was clear that white Methodists were engaged in a marriage of convenience with the political segregationist groups in the state, including some of the most rabid. Black Methodists who were part of one of the three African Methodist denominations called out to their co-religionists to join them, wondering why they would remain within a church that consigned them to Jim Crow status: considered not a "faithful remnant," but the residue left when white Methodists reunited.

Why Would You Want to Be a Methodist?

The question of why black Methodists remained within the denomination would be asked of them—and they would ask it of themselves—repeatedly in the future, though perhaps less frequently at Mt. Zion Church than elsewhere. Formally segregated by their own denomination, black Methodists could wonder what value there was in remaining within the church rather than just leaving. Grant S. Shockley, a black Methodist theologian, said it was a perennial question members asked of themselves: "The enticements and the provocations for blacks in The Methodist Church to seek spiritual peace and personal dignity elsewhere," he said, "are an indelible part of Methodist history."[3] Brutalized by the state in its desire to enforce segregation, Mississippi's black Methodists could feel deserted by its denominational mainstream. But there was no large-scale defection by black members from Methodism in Mississippi in the years after the appearance of the CJ.

The most common answer black Methodists gave as to why they remained was similar to the response Ross Jones made when he returned to Longdale from New York: "because it is home." The Methodist Church was their church as much as it was the church of whites. The members of Mt. Zion, like black Methodists elsewhere, had chosen Methodism as their spiritual home, with some people in places like Maryland and New York becoming adherents as early as the eighteenth century, when the Wesleyans first appeared in America. They did not intend to leave; those who did not want them there should leave instead. The struggle over race was the single most definable issue for the denomination through much of the twentieth century, more so than either alcohol or tobacco, though ministers were required to forswear both, but not segregation. The struggle to remind Methodism of its pledge of inclusiveness became an important part of the faith of many black Methodists like those at Mt. Zion, whom Shockley would describe as the "primordial conscience of [a] United Methodism."[4]

But there were other reasons people remained Methodists. Students of religion have explained that there were spiritual, theological, and cultural factors that made Methodism appealing, and one was its compatibility with the historic African American experience. William McClain has suggested that early in their association with the denomination, black people discovered the adaptability of Methodism to a "bicultural synthesis" that allowed them to fashion a "Christian tradition to fit their own situation."[5] This explanation of the adaptability of evangelical religion to the black experience has been noted by others.

Historian Donald G. Mathews, for example, in examining black Methodism, concluded that belief in Methodism "removed blacks from their slavery and the subordination of race" through what Mathews described as the experience of the "liminal self."[6] Becoming Methodist required the initiate to encounter the salvific effect of the New Birth, a time when they were suspended in life between one form of existence and another, which served as a kind of rite of passage where none of the old rules applied. Methodists named this transformative process "holiness," which led one to discard the values of the old order and embrace a new transcendent one of holiness "liberty." Most Methodists, black or white, also grasped this idea experientially, but for black Methodists it held the potential for being emotionally very freeing. The experience of being a Methodist was the experience of conviction, a rebirth.

Arguing from a different but related historical and theological perspective, historian of religion Charles H. Long has said African Americans have traditionally been drawn to the progressive witness of societies like The Methodist Church, particularly when its prophetic witness is most in evidence. In his important "systematic study of black religion" in 1971, Long noted that three themes, or "symbolic images," defined African American spirituality, and all of them related to the connection between religious belief and a lived experience.[7]

Images of Africa and the memory of slavery figure importantly in Long's systematics, which come from beliefs derived from folklore, social protest, black fraternalism, life experience, and biblical imagery. The three themes most evident in this belief structure, he says, are recurrent images of Africa, the experience of slavery, and a particular understanding of God. For Long, to be an African American meant to understand God only within this threefold context, and it was that totality which represented one's religious consciousness. A person, he said, had to feel loved and cherished as a child of God, which for black Americans required transforming the negative and limiting experience of their lives as lived in America into something new. God was that transformative force, the shaper of their consciousness, and the resource that allowed them to "maintain their human image without completely acquiescing to the norms of the majority population." Long, too, believed in a new birth experience, which could be for some people a voice from heaven, or perhaps a light in the sky. Religion was ultimately about God, politics, and lived experience; as at Mt. Zion, it was about community.[8]

The Significance of the Social Gospel and Black Methodists

As Harry Bowie noted in his assessment of the social gospel appeal of the Delta Ministry, Mississippi's poor black people, including Methodists, responded positively to The Ministry's message of liberal biblical theology and a social-conscious witness. From their earliest association with Methodism in the eighteenth century, black people had been attracted by the denomination's blend of evangelical religion with social witnessing, a prophetic message that was, however, muted as the denomination flourished in the culture. The gap between cultural acceptance and prophetic witness narrowed as the church identified more fully with its secular environment. A notable iteration of its old antislavery message occurred during Radical Reconstruction, when social witnessing again became a major emphasis of the church. But as a growing denomination, popular in the culture, it was difficult for Methodist leaders to resist the claims of those who called for a close compatibility with secular priorities.

That changed at the beginning of the twentieth century, when the social gospel movement found small pockets of adherents within most mainstream denominations, including Methodism. This new/old strain of Methodism was prevalent almost exclusively within Northern circles, where it was led by the Reverend Harry F. Ward and Bishop Francis McConnell, clergy leaders considered too extreme in their views by many white Methodists, even in their home territory. The positions of these spokesmen for the liberal social gospel were foundational to the Methodist Federation for Social Action, a new denominational body highly critical of church policies that condoned Jim Crow and segregation. In rural Longdale, Mississippi, small congregations like Mt. Zion could be introduced to this message in denominational tracts and through Sunday school literature that showed a tan-skinned Jesus surrounded by children of color.[9]

Through the agency of the Federation for Social Action, social gospel representatives like Ward and McConnell attempted to revitalize the church's appeal to its black members, whose earlier expectations had been dashed by the collapse of Reconstruction and the emergence of Jim Crow. They conceived a denominational statement known as "the Social Creed" of the church that marked Methodism's entry into the social gospel arena.[10] At the time of its adoption, the creed called for "equal rights and complete justice for all men [sic] in all stations of life," and offered a list of principles, largely economic in nature, that its authors believed the church should address: the rights of labor, arbitration, a living wage, safe working conditions for women, and an end to child labor. Controversial in many areas of the church, particularly the white South, the creed spoke to the concerns of all black conferences, including Mississippi. Conservative laymen found the creed's positions untenable, and criticized authors Ward and McConnell, as well as their associates, Frank Mason North, Edward

Devine, and Worth Tippy, referring to them as socialists, extremists, and even fellow travelers. The federation had a political agenda as well as a spiritual one, but that had always been true of Methodism; this agenda endorsed clear political choices while also condemning racism, issues then at the margin of the mainstream church.

By the time of the creation of the Central Jurisdiction, Methodist leadership had decided it was advisable to rework the Social Creed by selecting pieces from edited versions from the past.[11] As support for reunification grew within the white Southern Methodist Church, enthusiasm for the Federation for Social Action decreased. Its decline stilled criticism of Jim Crow within the church just at the time that segregation measures were growing more harsh and pervasive. The change yielded a toned-down Social Creed, applauded by white Southern Methodists, including the Mississippi Conference. Following reunification, with segregation an increasingly hot issue in the culture, the General Conference in 1952 agreed to break formal ties with the federation, and the Social Creed was redefined as a living document, meant to be responsive to the needs of the times, though still a statement of principles appropriate for use in public worship.[12]

White Methodists in the South were pleased by the decision to disconnect from the federation, an agency perceived by them as an intrusion by outsiders who were water carriers for far-left politics.

White Southerners had Mississippi resident John Satterfield, the delegate who best represented their interests, to thank for the critical report that led the General Conference to distance itself from the Federation for Social Action. Satterfield had become the best-known spokesman for the large white Southeastern Jurisdiction, while he also served other conservative organizations supportive of segregation, like the Mississippi Association of Methodist Ministers and Laymen (MAMML), the right-wing Circuit Riders, and a Washington lobby group promoting segregation. Satterfield's damning report on the work of the federation pushed the General Conference decision. As an experienced corporate lawyer and active Mississippi Methodist layman, Satterfield enjoyed a large reputation within the denomination, the Southeastern Jurisdiction, and in the nation as a whole.[13]

The Politics of White Methodism in the State

In writing about Mississippi, historian Joseph Crespino documented just how entangled the Methodist Church became in the prolonged state struggle over racial issues.[14] As sides were drawn within the denomination over the future of the Central Jurisdiction, it was the white Southeastern Jurisdiction, formidable, conservative, membership-rich, that appeared to have the advantage. One distinct advantage it enjoyed was having John Satterfield as a member and as an advocate. Satterfield was repeatedly returned as a delegate to General Conference because members of the Southeastern Jurisdiction knew he was a powerful defender of their values. The advocates of an inclusive, nonsegregated church in the state could count on the support of faculty and administration of prestigious Millsaps College, the editor of the Methodist regional journal, Sam Ashmore, all black Methodists, and some leading clergy scattered about the state's few cities, but they were no match for Satterfield and the influential Southeastern Jurisdiction.[15]

Satterfield was respected throughout the rest of the denomination. A commanding presence at General Conference, he was a devoted layman, a lawyer whose national reputation would get him elected president of the American Bar Association in 1960. *Time* magazine once called him "segregation's best defender." For a while he taught the popular Men's Bible Class at Jackson's Galloway Church—known as the "cathedral church of Mississippi Methodism"—where he was able to recruit socially prominent laymen to support his interest in the White Citizen's Council. He served along with another prominent attorney, Charles Parlin of Englewood, New Jersey, on denominational commissions elected to consider the future of the Central Jurisdiction.[16]

In the white Mississippi Methodist Conference the fight over segregation increased in intensity after the Second World War, as black veterans came home, and white laymen maneuvered to gain control of the conference machinery. Black Methodists continued to report abuses against their members, their clergy, and their facilities. Many whites seemed to believe, as Satterfield did, that by preserving the church as they remembered it, they were saving the soul of the "Southern way of life." Neither side viewed these as incidental issues. Within Mississippi's white conferences, segregation's supporters were mostly laymen, who got themselves elected to conference meetings and boards where they gained a stranglehold on conference policies. Their tactics could resemble those of their secular colleagues who manipulated the machinery of state. The roots of the conflict were deep and extended over the reach of the entire state. It led to a temporary realignment of local Methodists, one that saw black Methodists working with the small band of white Methodist integrationists, and white Methodists considering secession from the denomination. Leaders of the segregationist Mississippi Association of Methodist Ministers and Laymen (MAMML) proposed leaving Methodism for their own small, ultraconservative, independent congregations.

The Postwar Black Awakening

Only an estimated 2,000 blacks were registered to vote in the state at the time the Central Jurisdiction appeared on the scene. After the war, numbers of returning veterans attempted to register, only to be turned back by various tactics employed by the Democratic political machinery; still, by 1947, the number of registrants had risen to 5,000.[17] The change was attributable to a new activism among black residents and the recruiting efforts of national organizations like the NAACP. Whites looked on the NAACP as dangerous and subversive and Alabama declared membership in the organization illegal. Small, local groups continued to operate clandestinely, and there were rumors abroad in Neshoba that there was a chapter that met at Mt. Zion Church, though the rumors were never confirmed. White poll officials discovered the surest way to keep blacks from voting was by invoking the "understanding" clause of the state constitution, requiring those hoping to register to interpret an obscure section of the document to the registrar's satisfaction. Mississippi officials were inclined to resort to actual violence, bringing in police dogs and crowds with clubs to intimidate blacks trying to register. Lynching, though in decline, was still a threat after the war, employed against those who refused to "keep their place."

Six black men were lynched in the state between 1943 and the end of the decade; three in 1943, and one each in 1944, 1946, and 1949.[18] By this accounting, Neshoba County had ten lynchings between 1875 and 1964, while neighboring Kemper County, known as "Bloody Kemper," had thirty-four during the same period. The death of the Reverend Isaac Simmons, a farmer, in 1944, was a murderous reminder that no class of blacks was immune. Many believed that in "timber counties" like Neshoba, blacks were statistically at greater risk of being lynched, although the threat was constant everywhere.[19] These abuses against blacks—the attacks on ministers, the lynchings of the six men in six years—were never investigated by police or law enforcement. A kind of symbiotic relationship grew up between white hooligans, some actually criminals, and law enforcement, which allowed them to turn a blind eye to violence against blacks.

It required people with an immunity to fear to challenge these white assaults, and there were people of extraordinary courage in the postwar years willing to do it. Veterans returning home anticipated a change in the old ways, and when there was no evidence of progress they tried to make it happen. Veteran Amzie Moore of Greenwood was considered the most fearless of this younger group of black resisters, who intended to capitalize on the Supreme Court decision in 1944 outlawing the whites-only primary. In Neshoba, Cornelius Steele kept up his efforts to register, although he was repeatedly turned away. This new group of activists was encouraged by the civil rights initiatives of President Truman, ending discrimination in the military and banning segregation on interstate transportation. Their goal was to transform Mississippi into a more modern, urban, and diverse place.[20] The segregationist opposition, initially surprised by the intensity of younger blacks who showed an unwillingness to play the role of accommodating Negro, dug in its heels more firmly, bent on maintaining the customs that made up the "Southern way of life."

Social critics from outside the state raised their voices above the din to criticize white churches and white clergy for their silence regarding racial assaults, especially lynching. One of these was Dr. Arthur Raper, who had headed the Commission on Interracial Cooperation in North Carolina in the 1930s, and who noted that while "Methodists and Baptists" often sparred with each other, they found common ground in a shared prejudice against blacks. Raper thought the two denominations had a shared attitude toward lynching, which served in a bizarre way as a class and social unifier. In his view, some church leaders advanced their personal interests by appeal to racial fears in the same way that politicians did, which seemed to be the case in "the arguments presented in the Methodist controversy over unification in both secular and religious press."[21] Walter White, the NAACP leader and social observer, made the chilling observation that there appeared to be a high correlation between lynchings and the presence of Methodists and Baptists in the area, the two groups that had represented 87 percent of church membership in the state in the thirties.[22] Mississippi historian Neil McMillen, referring to yet another critic, concluded that "Perhaps lynchings would not have been so common in Mississippi during this period if more clergymen and congregations had taken strong stands against it."[23]

Mississippians described lynching as a necessary means of social control, even in the postwar years, and they could count on the tacit approval of many members of the United States Senate. That federal body had repeatedly refused to pass an antilynch law in the years between 1921 and the Second World War, due largely to filibustering by Southern senators. In the meanwhile, the Mississippi Methodist Conference CJ delegates continued to condemn mob violence in all its forms.

Segregation and the Mississippi Methodist Conference CJ

Methodism in Mississippi had clearly become a politicized institution, its ministers and members constantly bombarded by segregationist tactics and appeals. In the postwar years and even earlier, the records of the black annual conferences are filled with references to the violence and abuse arbitrarily imposed on their clergy and laity. At the conference in 1942, for example, delegates noted that the minister who served on the rural Philadelphia Circuit, which included Mt. Zion Church, the Reverend L. W. Smith, was regularly subjected to harassment, perhaps a contributing factor in the temporary decline in membership. Particularly in rural areas, white thugs, alone or in groups, would set upon the clergy, conspicuous by their Bibles and their preaching suits, as they went from one assignment to another. Mr. Smith was assigned to four churches, all of them on the rim of the city of Philadelphia, which meant he had to use a bus or walk to get to his church appointments.[24] Since he had not yet met his educational requirements for ordination—a limiting condition for many black clergy—Mr. Smith served his charges as a supply minister, a fact that reduced his already low salary even more and kept him carless. When Mt. Zion gave him the use of a parsonage with a kitchen garden, it was a welcome perquisite that limited his exposure to white toughs. But it was not in Longdale that he needed protection.[25] The conference acknowledged that his commitment to Methodism came at a high personal cost, but that did not relieve his financial situation. As a supply rather than a settled minister, his salary would have been less than the $1,000 a regularly appointed CJ pastor received.[26]

Traveling had always been part of the risk for Methodist circuit riders who, in a previous age, had told of the dangers encountered in wild, unsettled territories, contributing to the mystique of frontier Methodism. But traveling in twentieth-century Mississippi, particularly rural Mississippi, posed frequent, not just occasional, threats for black Methodist clergy. Delegates reported that the Reverend Smith was subjected to constant verbal attacks as he made his rural church rounds. In addition to serving

Mt. Zion, he ministered at Hopewell, Prairie Chapel, and sometimes Dixon, all many miles distant from Mt. Zion, so he was constantly exposed to hidden dangers on the roads.[27]

Even after the 1939 reunification, belonging to a white-majority denomination was no advantage to Mississippi black Methodists. The dangers kept pace with the threats they faced; one CJ delegate submitted a report to conference on the hazards faced by itinerant ministers. According to this report, preachers wearing their Sunday clothes became targets for racist rowdies while simply waiting at bus or train stops, or just walking on the road. They were, it said, subjected to "mistreatment humiliation [sic], and violence."[28] The report described one assault on a minister who had tried without success to attend a district conference in Canton, and of another who was attacked on the way to a missionary meeting at Gulfside. This awful record of violence prompted delegates to ask: "These conditions are causing our people to wonder, and ask the question, Why? Why? What next? What have we done?" The answer, they all knew, was that they lived in a dangerous apartheid state.

Sometimes ministers were able to buy or borrow cars, but because the war effort limited supplies of rubber, and thus tires, automobile transportation was not something they could rely on. In any case, cars were no sure protection against white violence, it seemed. Delegates at the 1946 conference learned of "Bro. Daniels, who had been beaten and dragged from his car without reason."[29] Conference delegates also addressed the difficulties faced by their lay people who were "embarrassed and humiliated" in their workaday lives. Still, they agreed not to be discouraged by the problems of the present hour: although the road ahead was "dark and fraught with trouble," said one delegate, these Methodist folk would continue to rely on "all peaceful means of democracy," chiefly the struggle to gain the ballot. Life was about getting on, staying safe, supporting each other, and working for change through the vote.[30]

Black Methodists Oppose the Central Jurisdiction

By the end of the decade of the 1940s and throughout the 1950s, Mississippi's black Methodists made clear in a variety of ways their conviction that the Central Jurisdiction was an immoral witness to segregation. In its denominational journal, the *Christian Advocate*, writers frequently referred to the "immoral" nature of the decision to create the CJ. Said one contributor in 1948, "At present The Methodist

Church stands in grave danger of being unethical, and immoral and unchristian, as it faces the proposition of retaining or dissolving the Central Jurisdiction," which the writer clearly believed needed to be dissolved.[31] Another contributor objected to the patronizing quality of racial remarks in General Conference, such as "We love our colored brethren."[32] One subscriber said, "As long as it maintains the Central Jurisdiction, there will be a spot on [The Methodist Church's] government."[33] Virtually no support for the CJ could be found in the pages of the *Christian Advocate*, yet for white Methodists its creation had been a condition of their rejoining the denomination, and that remained for them a permanent contract.

Contributors to the *Christian Advocate* didn't limit themselves to observations about the CJ. They were Methodists after all—embattled Methodists to be sure—and like most Methodists their interests were expansive. Many writers worried about the threats to the daily lives of church members, wondering how these might be avoided or prevented. Some contributors made obvious political remarks, calling for an end to the white primary before that was abolished, and an end to other discriminatory measures like the poll tax. Many wrote about lynching. And several writers referred to surveillance of their church services and conferences by the police. One writer spoke of a CJ conference interrupted by a policeman who walked in, only to retreat when he noticed the town mayor and the white Methodist pastor in attendance. Others similarly referred to annual conference meetings disrupted by police looking for sympathizers of the Methodist Federation for Social Action, suspecting "subversive activities." In a sign of black support for the Federation, CJ bishop Robert Brooks was elected as the president of the federation in 1948, and served as well on one of its advisory committees.[34]

Southeastern Jurisdiction leaders also harbored some criticism of reunification, although their concerns were quite different in kind from those of the black Methodists in the CJ. The white Southerners worried that in this new reunified church, national values and policies might eventually overwhelm and replace their Southern regional priorities. They resented the occasional appearance of an "outside" visitor from an agency like the Federation for Social Action, but found no problem at all with the presence of far-right Circuit Riders agents, whose speakers were funded by conservative Methodist laymen and their fraternal groups. The white Southerners felt singled out by some in the church as sinners because of their stance on segregation; they did, however, speak a truth when they said, "We refuse however to accept the charge that segregation is a child of Methodist Union, or that it is a product of any one section of our nation."[35] Segregation was a national reality.

Black Methodists kept up their efforts to chip away support for the Central Jurisdiction by encouraging the criticisms of their members and by sending protests to the national denomination. Letters and articles in the *Christian Advocate* continued. But so did attention to larger needs, such as supporting the NAACP, aiding missionaries in Africa, and maintaining mission stations in Liberia and other places around the world. By 1960, black Methodists were ready to create their own Committee of Five to plan for the dissolution of the Central Jurisdiction.

A *Church Taken Hostage*

Black Methodists in Mississippi and elsewhere believed that the way the Methodist Church dealt with its black constituency was a revealing study in American morality, and developments in the state during the 1950s confirmed that view.[36] Religion and politics by then were inextricably bound together: white Methodists were almost invariably segregationists and were either a part of, or supportive of, an array of segregationist organizations. They acknowledged the gain John Satterfield had achieved for them when the 1952 General Conference decided to neutralize the Federation for Social Action, but they remained troubled by other manifestations in the church that appeared liberal. The most ardent among them became members of one of the segregationist groups, which usually numbered as many Cold Warriors as segregationists.[37] These critics of the mainstream church complained that it was losing its way in a grand crusade for "one world, one race, one church."

United in support of the Central Jurisdiction, these Methodist anti-integrationists found new cause for alarm when the Supreme Court decision in *Brown v. Board of Education* came down in 1954. The court's announcement encouraged segregationists to fervent new actions, aided by the newly created White Citizen's Council. Chapters of the White Citizen's Council frequently met at churches, as they did at Galloway Methodist Church in Jackson, creating opportunities for new alliances among segregation's various factions. Black Methodists were convinced that their white Methodist brethren would sometimes send spies or informers into their churches to learn their views regarding integration, the *Brown* decision, and civil rights.

These white activists tried, with considerable success, to tame the few moderates in the Mississippi Conference. Many, but not all of them, had ties to Millsaps College in Jackson. The segregationist constituency in the Methodist church was largely lay-led, increasingly vocal, and after the *Brown* decision, growing in membership. Its harshest criticism was reserved for the national church, which was perceived by them as having leaders who tilted toward modernism and socialism. They were fearful of latent sympathy for the Federation for Social Action, suspicions they believed were confirmed when the denomination announced its participation in the socially engaged liberal Delta Ministry (in which Harry Bowie had so passionately served) that would be working in their state in 1964. A story illustrative of their views went the rounds in white churches. It told of a visiting Northern Methodist integrationist minister who was asked to read from Ephesians at a local church. After thumbing through his Bible for a bit, he was forced to ask the resident preacher where Ephesians could be found. For those who relished the story, the moral was clear: not only did these politically oriented ministers not understand the "Southern way of life," including living among black people, they did not even know their Bible. In the integration fight, the issues in church and state were so commingled, that the language of the struggle sometimes employed the same words, as in "all deliberate speed."

In the years following *Brown*, young Methodist seminary graduates failed to return to serve in Mississippi, unwilling to cope with the "white supremacist oligarchic regime that had run the state since the 1890s," by which they also meant the church.[38] A stalwart group of moderates struggled to get their message out, and their names also belong to the history of the Mississippi struggle: there was Sam Ashmore, editor of the white conference journal; the Reverend W. B. Selah, well-known Jackson clergyman who resigned in protest over segregation policies in the church; the Reverend Ed King, chaplain at Tougaloo College and social provocateur; the Reverend Clay Lee, who held to his views while serving a segregationist congregation; and the courageous efforts of conference laymen John Garner and J. P. Stafford, who were exposed to abuse even more than the clergy. In 1963, twenty-eight young pastors aligned themselves with this body of moderates by signing the locally controversial "Born of Conviction" statement—interpreted by critics as supportive of integration, though its most "political" comments dealt with support for the public schools and an open pulpit in the churches—as well as most of those associated with Millsaps College and Tougaloo College.[39] The efforts of these Mississippi moderates, who tried to be reasonable and diplomatic in their encounters with the segregationists—excepting the more assertive Ed King—were no contest for the full-throated harangues of their opposition. Nor were the efforts of such early black activists as C. C. Bryant, E. W. Steptoe, Emmett J. Stringer, or T. R. M Howard a match.

The fight within white Methodism had started as a backroom quarrel, or a church basement argument, until it became increasingly public following the 1954 *Brown* decision, when the conference journal became involved. Sam Ashmore tried to hew to a moderate course. But even Ashmore finally had to concede to the ingenuity of the lay opposition. He had heard that a warning had gone out to Methodist churches in the state—presumably the work of the Citizens' Council or MAMML—that churches had to abandon not only the theme of "Christian brotherhood," but the actual words.[40]

The *Brown* decision brought together the issues of race, religion, and politics in a perfect storm of passion and persecution that had been lying offshore. Mississippians determined to defy the court's decision found support from their senator, James Eastland, who said "The South will not abide by nor obey this legislative decision . . . of a political court."[41] Because Eastland was chairman of the Senate Internal Security Subcommittee, he contrived to hold showcase hearings meant to reveal the sinister, anti-American intent of liberals and radicals in the church, state, and civil rights groups. The entire Methodist denomination was decried as subversive, integrationist, and overtly secular by this band of Eastland segregationists. For those in the Eastland camp, despite the fact that the Methodist Church approved the segregated Central Jurisdiction, it was still viewed as a church where "the community of faith and the community of race [are] essentially one and the same."[42] White Methodist segregationists prepared themselves for a new round in the struggle, energized by the *Brown* decision, to prove that their community of faith would not be joined to a community of mixed races. They were simultaneously Christians and segregationists and admitted to no contradiction in that identity.

6

In the Aftermath of Brown

THE RACIAL STRUGGLE INSIDE THE MISSISSIPPI
METHODIST CHURCH, 1954–1964

> *[T]he court has found in our favor and recognized our
> human psychological complexity and citizenship and
> another battle of the Civil War has been won.*
>
> RALPH ELLISON, 1954

> *[W]e must proceed gradually, not upsetting habits or
> traditions that are older than the Republic.*
>
> DEMOCRATIC PRESIDENTIAL CANDIDATE ADLAI
> STEVENSON, 1956, COMMENTING ON *BROWN* AND
> MURDER OF EMMETT TILL

> *[T]he murder of Emmett Till and the subsequent trial of the
> two men accused of the crime . . . aroused greater emotion
> in Mississippi than the 1954 school desegregation decision.*
>
> MARS, WITNESS IN PHILADELPHIA

Rendering to Caesar?

With the 1954 Supreme Court decision of *Brown v. Board of Education* that
required desegregated schools, the gulf between The Methodist Church
at the national level and its local black Methodist congregations and conferences grew more obvious. The Court in the *Brown* case ruled that black
children deserved equal access to schooling, raising anxieties within the
Mississippi Methodist Church conferences and in the state of Mississippi
about how to respond to this federal assault on segregation. Initially, most
white Mississippians indicated that no response was necessary since the
decision would simply never be implemented in their state. Nor did most

white Methodists in the Mississippi Conference give evidence of any support for the decision—in fact, just the opposite. As everyone in the state
knew, the Court could make legal decisions, set precedents, influence
national conversation, but it could not enforce change on the ground.
Compliance, the Court implied in a follow-up decision on the case, would
come at the local level at a time when the environment would accept
it. The Methodist denomination, internally conflicted over the continued
existence of the Central Jurisdiction, took no action to support the implications of *Brown*, nor did it resolve the CJ debate. But even at rural Mt.
Zion Church, teenager Jewel Rush—later Jewel McDonald—was aware
that the *Brown* decision had provoked new conversation in her community.[1] Like black Methodists everywhere, Mt. Zion supported the *Brown*
decision to the limit possible in Jim Crow Mississippi. Some leaders in
The Methodist Church nationally also spoke in favor of compliance. But
within the decade it became clear that among the possible responses to
Brown, including full compliance or total resistance, both the state and
the white Methodist church opted for gradualism, postponing compliance until external forces threatened to take action to impose desegregation. Data about the rates of violence and the continued denial of voting
rights during the period revealed the cost of delay.

During this so-called "classic period" in the civil rights movement, Mt.
Zion's members were the local people whose work created the conditions
hospitable to change, once a critical protest mass formed. They were not
the movers on the national stage of politics or the church, but the agitators
who laid the foundation. They were marchers on the long road to an inclusive church and inclusive schools. When Jewel Rush McDonald thought
back on the impact of the *Brown* decision on her young life decades before,
she decided that the most significant change was the ability to ride the bus
to school. Her elders knew of the decision, likely through overheard conversations on the sidewalks in Philadelphia since newspapers were few
in their rural community.[2] The Court's opinion did not mean she could
attend an integrated school, or that her parents could vote, changes that
would come much later. She and other members of Mt. Zion Church, 210
of them in 1954, learned the full substance of the measure in the same way
they learned of the Methodist creation of the Central Jurisdiction in 1939,
through experience and through word of mouth. The church continued as
home to a small group of activists, led by Cornelius Steele, Clint Collier,
Burline Kirkland, and some others willing to take large risks to protest
discrimination.

Though not obvious at the time, the preferred strategy of both state and church in the decade between 1954 and 1964 was revealed to be delaying tactics and go-slow policies. White institutional leaders in the South denied their fears of school integration, which seemed too remote to be a concern, while they showed great concern over matters related to the Cold War—the potential threat of communism, the need to be vigilant to ensure "containment"—which they saw as an immediate threat. The reality, however, was that segregation and Cold War anxieties were conjoined in the South, and politicians—as well as many church leaders—worried that seeming soft on one would be interpreted as being soft on the other, and it often was. Integrationists, or "race mixers," were suspected of plotting to advance a communist agenda. Cold War hawks said the standoff with the Soviet Union called for a tough stance, firm language, and military preparedness. Why not, some of the more militant cold warriors asked, take a similarly hard line against implementing *Brown*? Eventually, the considered response of both church and state to desegregation was to make small changes that gave the appearance of accommodating to the Court and conference decisions. Events in the decade following *Brown* revealed an increase in violence, including the murder of black teenager Emmett Till, and the mob riot at Ole Miss following James Meredith's enrollment at the school that left two dead.

The Court's follow-up ruling to *Brown* in 1955, sometimes called *Brown II*, was a welcome adaptation of the original decision for those who endorsed gradualism. It said that compliance with the 1954 decision must be made "with all deliberate speed," language Mississippi decision makers interpreted as a justification for delay. The Court had not said "immediately," nor did it set a date certain for desegregation. Neither did Methodist General Conference delegates hear in the *Brown* opinion a goad to action on the question of the Central Jurisdiction. Gradualism was the strategy of both institutional bodies, although it was soon clear that in Mississippi any level of compliance would be accompanied by struggle, violent and sometimes brutal, at the local level, as moderates were increasingly intimidated into silence.

The *Brown* decision had an opposite effect on a new and younger group of civil rights activists, for whom the decision was a catalyst to greater activism in the black freedom struggle, the more youthful group included people like Martin Luther King, Jr., Fred Shuttlesworth, Joseph Lowery, their student allies, and women from the many black churches. These new volunteers eventually replaced the pioneering workers who had made *Brown* possible, and they were characterized by an impatience with gradualism, wanting to replace it with the kind of nonviolent activism that would become the hall-mark of the Freedom Rides and sit-ins.

Along with an increase in black protest, the white response to the *Brown* decision was similarly marked by new activism in Mississippi. It was initiated with threats and fury, intended to silence moderates in the state who might harbor sympathy for the Court's decision. For white Methodists in the state, the target became the local conference, defined as too moderate for Mississippi, which had the effect of turning Methodist laypeople into combatants against their own church. The white Methodist opposition to *Brown* was, insofar as it was a battle between segregation-ists and moderates, an internal church conflict, but it quickly bounded over conference borders into the political and institutional offices held by prominent Methodist laypeople. Unfortunate consequences followed, as careers were destroyed—particularly for teachers and clergy—and as lead-ers, like the Reverend Ed King, were jailed and assaulted, and mixed-race groups of worshippers were turned away from Methodist churches.

While the Court decision brought the heated situation in Mississippi to a boil, it did not by itself cause a conflict that was actually generations old. Activists on both sides of the racial divide knew the issues had taken root far back in time, and the new struggle was not, as some recent legal historians have alleged, "a fight created by *Brown*," critics whom James C. Cobb refers to as being "Down on Brown." *Brown* was a wake-up call to white Southerners about just how urgent was the sense of black protest, which they experienced as a strike at their history, their memories, and their segregated society.[3] Within Methodism, racial conflict dated from at least 1939, over issues unresolved since 1844.

Incremental changes within Methodism began to take place slowly in the years after *Brown*, the product of the synergistic efforts of local peo-ple and the national church. Local people and local churches—mostly outside the South but black Methodists from within—sought out those in the Methodist denomination who supported integration. Tomiko Brown-Nagin has written about this need for cooperation between local groups and their national sponsors, saying that "National organiza-tions must seek to collaborate with local organizations in ways . . . that maximize the scale, expertise, and agenda-setting capacities of the national-level organizations . . . and promote local knowledge and lead-ership."[4] Black Methodist activists understood the need, and kept up a lively conversation between local churches like Mt. Zion, and reached

out to the conferences and the national church. White liberal congregations did similar things.

The Meaning of "All Deliberate Speed" in Mississippi

The Court order for compliance with "all deliberate speed," minus an
accompanying timetable, allowed white Southerners to breathe more easily. White Mississippians were especially deliberate about their opposition
to *Brown*, though the general assumption in the state seemed to be that
the vagueness of the "deliberate speed" clause meant that any decision
about how and when to respond was in their hands. White Southerners
had known for years that the NAACP legal team as well as other civil
rights organizations had been battling in the courts to overturn segregation. In a "very long civil rights movement," the end was far from
sight. Anticipating that one day the courts might rule for the plaintiffs,
Mississippi and other Southern states tried to bargain with black leaders
to get them to accept segregation by proposing newer, though still separate, facilities. The Methodist Church tried a similar strategy. In an effort
to demonstrate that separate could be equal, the denomination directed
new funds be sent to black institutions, a move critics called an attempt to
dampen sentiment for integration. In the early 1940s the denomination
appropriated new monies to Mississippi's black institutions, most of it to
the college and school, but also to the hospital and other social agencies.
The white Mississippi Annual Conference supported the action, and in
addition announced a fund-raising program to assist Rust College, the
black Methodist school in Holly Springs; only 86 of the 308 churches in
the state sent any money for the school. The conference proposed another
initiative that called for the creation of committees on race relations in
local churches, and that produced even more disappointing results. Only
thirteen churches participated.[5]

The most conspicuous model of a separate institution in the state,
visible in every community, was the grossly unequal public school, the
intended target of the *Brown* decision. Black schools were historically
underfunded; figures from the 1930s show that white legislators at the
time appropriated 80 percent more resources for the education of a white
child than for a black child, and the great disparity continued.[6] Politicians
who read the handwriting on the wall made another attempt at offering
improved facilities in exchange for "separate but equal" schools. Robert
Margo, an economist who studied the process, noted that as part of a

white effort to get support from black teachers, their poverty-level salaries were increased so that, "In real terms, the average annual salaries of black teachers increased 82 percent between 1940 and 1950." Even then, their salaries remained well below those of white teachers.[7] It was a measure of what whites were willing to pay to keep their institutions racially separate.

In Neshoba County, school officials knew well the harsh reality of these unequal conditions in their schools. A state school report on facilities in the county explained that while white schools were "well adapted to the needs of the school and the community," black school "buildings are generally small, the furniture and other equipment obsolete and the surroundings unattractive."[8] The superintendent of education in Neshoba County told an agent from the Sovereignty Commission that he had to get "some new schools and new school busses for the negroes . . . [because] they are badly in need of these facilities."[9] But shortly after the *Brown* decision was made public, the newly elected, presumably moderate, governor of Mississippi, J. P. Coleman, revealed the intentions of the state when he said in August 1955 that there would be no fundamental change in educational policy, offering as his "solemn pledge" that the public schools would not close "nor will there be any mixing of the races in these schools."[10]

Noncompliance in Church and State

Active, organized opposition to the Court decree surfaced in the state as early as two months after the announcement of the *Brown* decision. The White Citizens' Council became the heart of noncompliance. Protest to recent developments had been building, and opposition to *Brown* set it off.

Reaction within the Methodist Church at the level of the General Conference was one of concern, with many delegates from the Northeast supportive of the Court's ruling. The General Conference meeting in 1956 came just two years after *Brown*, and delegates to the conference learned just how much heat had been generated internally by the Court decision, most of it focused on the status of the Central Jurisdiction. The conference appointed an unwieldy Committee of Seventy to study the CJ, and a compromise measure, which came to be known as "Amendment IX," recommended the "voluntary" merging of black and white conferences. CJ leaders responded critically to this strategy of "permissiveness," which was seen as simply a proposal for a long and lingering death for the segregated jurisdiction.[11] Southeastern Jurisdiction representatives urged delegates to reaffirm their commitment to keep the jurisdictions separate.

At the time the *Brown* decision became public, the editor of the *Central Christian Advocate*, black Methodist Prince A. Taylor, perceived the responsibility of the church in a way very different from the Southeastern Jurisdiction. Taylor wrote in the *Advocate* that the Court decision had not ended segregation, but simply "destroyed the barriers and the real task has just begun," which was for the church to take on the "inescapable responsibility" to work for a just and equal society. Readers familiar with the position of the *Central Christian Advocate* knew that he meant abolishing the Central Jurisdiction.[12] Unlike the Southeastern Jurisdiction delegates, Taylor thought it the duty of the church to lead the campaign for the full implementation of *Brown*. Black Methodists were quick to understand the implications of *Brown*.

Following the 1956 General Conference session, the Council of Bishops found it incumbent on them to listen to the concerns of their Southern colleagues. At a meeting in November that year, the Southern bishops told their Northern colleagues that while they might have some personal sympathy with *Brown*, they "minister[ed] in a region where acute tensions are developing." When they finished explaining their views, the vote of the Council showed that regional differences had once again resurfaced, with bishops from the Southeastern Jurisdiction opposed to the implementation of *Brown*, and the rest of the bishops supportive. The outcome disturbed Bishop Marvin Franklin of Mississippi—a major figure in the developing Mississippi struggle—who agreed with those who said the matter would have been better left alone.[13] Gradualism, if not denial, was the favored approach of the Southern bishops. Ironically, both the bishops who were supportive of *Brown* and those who were opposed agreed that the controversy would finally be "determined in the hearts of the people," but it was the segregationists that had the better organized "hearts and minds" campaign in Mississippi. Still, it appeared that bishops North and South were prepared to wait for the people to have a change of heart, for the church to reflect the culture rather than lead it.

The MAMML Campaign

Within the local Mississippi white conference, the Methodist segregationist insurgency and the White Citizens' Council program rolled out with breakneck speed. The Mississippi Association of Methodist Ministers and

Laymen (MAMML), the most aggressive of the Methodist protest agencies, emerged as the most vocal segregationist group in the conference. It called its first meeting in 1955 out of state, in Alabama, and according to its leaders attracted an audience of between 200 and 300 people. It quickly mounted an active and contentious attack on the denomination and the local white Methodist conference from a base created in Mississippi.

Tightly organized, MAMML exerted influence all out of proportion to its limited size. One unnamed religious leader described it as "the best organized opposition to integration in the church."[14] It relied on a lay constituency energized by the *Brown* decision, a core group of people whose criticism of the church went back to 1939 and beyond. Many felt unequally yoked to a liberal faction within the denomination found mainly in the North. MAMML's ominous reference in its literature to a "Russian Black Republic" in the making showed how it connected segregation and the Cold War. It warred against liberal pronouncements by the denomination, including the stripped-down version of the Social Creed, and the continuing attempts to get rid of the segregated Central Jurisdiction. Curiously, for a religious group, MAMML had no distinctive theological center, but shared with most Methodist segregationists the general assumption that God had ordained the separation of the races. When partisans attempted to explain their message, they built on a straightforward, unsophisticated rationale: a literalistic biblical interpretation about "preferring to be with one's own," and the "curse" of Ham related in the Genesis 9 account. Its publications, however, were strewn with references to God's blessing on their work.

Some clergy members of the conference were on MAMML's list of supporters, but it was predominantly an organization of conservative laymen, dependent for resources and mailing lists on other right-wing groups, particularly the Cincinnati-based Circuit Riders, Inc., an older organization. Layman John Satterfield was responsible for the contact between MAMML and Circuit Riders: what he seemed to have learned from his success in crippling the left-leaning Methodist Federation for Social Action was that a well-organized conservative lay movement could exercise considerable power over a range of issues. Satterfield sat on the executive board of Circuit Riders, which was a collective voice of conservative lay opposition to all liberal, or "pink," denominational policy, especially in the South. Myers G. Lowman, a disaffected Methodist layman, was its executive secretary. Its *raison d'être* was ending all traces of the liberal Methodist Federation for Social Action and the influence of the Social

Creed; MAMML labeled Harry Ward, the designer of these two efforts, "the Red Dean of the Communist Party in the religious field."[15] By deliberately widening its focus from the Cold War to segregation, Circuit Riders could tap into the monies raised by laymen's groups like MAMML, and enlarge its resources for white Mississippi Methodists. MAMML especially targeted white moderate and liberal support for integration, but it also kept close watch on the activities of black Methodists with the help of spies from the Mississippi State Sovereignty Commission—the secret civil rights surveillance group—in the two CJ conferences, who reported on the comments of ministers and lay people.

After MAMML had been created in the spring of 1955, it worked closely with the White Citizens' Council, the two groups having an overlapping membership. Satterfield was the man out front, the featured speaker at MAMML's organizational meeting and an active participant and advocate. MAMML's criticism of the national church increased, until by 1960 it had begun to insist that secession from the denomination was the only option, a move Satterfield ultimately rejected, noting his family's long history with Methodism. By that time he was a nationally recognized figure in the denomination and could hardly consider leaving. MAMML was the loudest opposition voice within white Mississippi Methodism, and it was the most threatening. Yet despite the ferocity of MAMML, small pockets of organized moderation in the Mississippi conferences remained, notably in the Mississippi Methodist Student Movement, and for a while longer in the Woman's Society of Christian Service (WSCS).[16]

MAMML and the White Citizens' Council had a talent for seeking out supporters among leading citizens in the community. The two groups shared mailing lists, meeting rooms, and skill at circulating notices around the churches. MAMML published its own newsletter along with pamphlets and news announcements. Both were grassroots organizations nominally committed to nonviolent noncompliance; for MAMML, noncompliance meant criticism of conference leadership locally and nationally as well as any church commissions dealing with race, while for the Citizens' Council, noncompliance was grounded in resistance to the Court's decision in the *Brown* case. For Mississippi blacks, the strategies of the two groups presented a distinction without a difference, as white retaliation to growing black protest claimed more black victims. By the late 1950s communities of whites warred against the NAACP and threatened its leaders. In 1955, cases that attracted national media attention—a relatively new development—were the murder in Belzoni of the Reverend George Lee, a staunch advocate for the black vote, and the brutal shooting of his friend Gus Courts, a former NAACP local president. A Delta town, Belzoni was a hotbed of Citizens' Council activities as well as home to black residents increasingly angry with the white resistance movement.[17]

For *Brown* supporters around the country who wanted to have immediate desegregation, the Court's imprecise call for "all deliberate speed" was a disappointment. White Southerners opposed to desegregation gave the phrase their own meaning, which Satterfield and others suggested meant "when you get around to it." Despite the fearless efforts of activists like Courts and Lee, both backers of *Brown* and vocal proponents of the black vote, by 1954 in a place like Neshoba County only eight black people were registered to vote.[18] During the 1950s, black assertiveness was met by the white resisters in church and state. A telling commentary on white aggressiveness was the assertion of famed Mississippi writer William Faulkner, who reportedly said that if forced to choose, he would "fight for Mississippi against the United States even if it meant going out into the street and shooting Negroes."[19] The strategy of delay in accepting a racially inclusive society would result in more black deaths.

The Killing of Emmett Till

In the same year that George Lee and Gus Courts were attacked, white racists murdered Emmett Till, a black teenager from Chicago. When Florence Mars assessed the white reaction to the *Brown* decision in Neshoba County, she decided that her white neighbors paid little attention to it because no one believed it would ever be implemented. What did grab their attention, she believed, was something more immediate, and that was the murder of the fourteen-year-old Till, killed by two white men whose widely publicized trial was a blatant celebration of whiteness. The murder, the trial, and the national attention they received were a demonstration of the consequences of delay in implementing *Brown* in the state.

The young Till had been on a visit to Money, Mississippi, from his home in Chicago when he allegedly whistled at a white woman working in a grocery store, a violation of the "Southern way of life." His adolescent behavior was seen as the sort of threat to whiteness that had to be squelched immediately, without any delay, legal or otherwise. The *Brown* decision, as Mars observed, was comparatively far less threatening, since it was the action of a court remote from life in Neshoba County. Till's body was dragged from the Tallahatchie River a few days after he disappeared, and the two accused of killing him, Roy Bryant—the woman's husband—and J. W. Milam, were brought to trial in Tallahatchie County. After a show trial for the two men, attended by Florence Mars, the jury deliberated briefly—only long enough to "smoke a cigarette," she recalled—and returned the unsurprising verdict of "not guilty." Two months after their acquittal, and in exchange for $3,500, the men confessed to the Southern writer William Bradford Huie, in an article published in *Look* magazine that they had indeed murdered Till.[20] The defense attorney for Bryant and Milam, J. J. Breland, said of Till's death that it was an "approved killing," necessary to "keep our niggahs in line."[21] Breland was likely correct, that some Mississippians were willing to take action into their own hands to defend whiteness and ensure white supremacy.

If the intention of Till's murder was to strike terror in the hearts of black men and suppress rising black anger, it came short of its goal. Most NAACP activities were driven underground—like the alleged NAACP-like gatherings at Mt. Zion Church confirmed by Mars—but activists frustrated by white delaying tactics recommitted to efforts to bring inclusion to the state.[22] They would become known as the "Till generation," with the Till case named as a turning point in the attitudes of Mississippi's blacks. The most fearless leader to emerge was Medgar Evers, a returning war veteran who became NAACP field secretary in Mississippi in 1954, a job that called for him to travel the state to see to the organization's business.[23] His brother Charles, perceived as a more controversial civil rights activist, lived at the time in Neshoba, and he frequently hosted his brother, the presence of the two men stoking white fears. But neither the efforts of the Evers brothers in the county, nor the advice from the black Methodist conference to keep on the pressure to vote, resulted in new names on the voting rolls. The Mississippi Methodist Annual Conference (CJ), which could hardly disengage from the implications of the *Brown* decision or the continuing fight in its own denomination about its very existence, continued to urge members to attempt to register, and to remain alert to changing conditions. Increased black resistance and the presence of the Evers brothers convinced Neshoba County to add a local branch of the White Citizens' Council. Black Methodists affirmed the moral high ground as their incentive, and the white Methodist Annual Conference developed yet more heated political rhetoric.

7

"Segregation Is Not Unchristian"

METHODISTS DEBATE DESEGREGATION, 1956–1964

> *In 1960, the Central Jurisdiction Organization still had value for some special interest groups within The Methodist Church.*
>
> W. ASTOR KIRK, Committee of Five, Central Jurisdiction

> *Identity was the defining element of this long-term denominational power-struggle [in The Methodist Church].*
>
> MORRIS L. DAVIS, *METHODIST UNIFICATION*

> *Racial divisions survived the elimination of the Central Jurisdiction on a congregational level and in appointment patterns.*
>
> RUSSELL RICHEY, *METHODIST CONFERENCE IN AMERICA*

Methodists Revisit the Central Jurisdiction

In the years between the *Brown* decision and the events of Freedom Summer, there was no better example of what Gunnar Myrdal in 1944 called the "American dilemma" over race than the Methodist Church. What Myrdal had noted in his two-volume study was the nation's moral and political dilemma over how to reconcile its self-image as democratic, humane, even Christian with its actual racist behavior toward nonwhites. Good intentions did not match political reality.[1] Something similar occurred within Methodism. What had been for many an attractive feature of Methodism—its attention to issues in contemporary culture—had become for many of those same people (outside the Southeastern Jurisdiction) the church's great liability; in creating the Central Jurisdiction, Methodism presented a moral defense of segregation, while also holding out an inclusive church as the ideal.

The Methodist Church left no space, offered no reasonable argument, about the conflict between the values it claimed to honor and the segregationist requirements of its white Southern constituency. In its General Conference and commissions, as the denomination continued to debate the future of the Central Jurisdiction, it balanced the value of voluntary desegregation against mandated desegregation in a way that resembled the government's indecisiveness in implementing school desegregation.

During these years, as civil rights activists made notable gains, if at great cost, Mississippi emerged as the white-hot center of the struggle. But as the Methodist denomination fiddled, Mississippi burned. Its powerful white churches in the state and its numerous black ones were fully politicized, embroiled in the segregation fight, though in different ways. White denominational leaders at every level in the state counseled delay, and then stood powerless as laymen closed the church doors to black Methodists, and black churches were torched. For their part, black Methodists relied on their annual conference sessions to support each other, exchange information about local dangers, and importantly, in their Minutes, to have a record of what damage had occurred to their churches and their people. With neither the media nor law enforcement recording offenses against black residents, the Minutes became a reliable source of information about church burnings, attacks on parsonages, disruptions of meetings, and the lengthening list of racial disorders. People at Mt. Zion Church had their guns for protection against nighttime cruising by local toughs or one of the sheriff's deputies. Whites could imagine danger arising from even a small church like Mt. Zion, which was assumed to have members involved in the protest movement, and which was known to have contact with a national denomination beyond the control of Mississippi's segregationist network. It was, however, the Mississippi Annual Conference CJ that was the best source of support and information for a local church like Mt. Zion.

The evident denominational ambivalence about segregation in the national church was not matched in the local white Mississippi Conference. Church leaders and laity there were candid about their support for segregation, and forceful in their opposition to any signs of an emergent moderation within the conference and among the clergy. They had been reared in a culture that understood segregation as the basic foundation for the "Southern way of life." The arrival of the first Freedom Riders in 1961 produced the anticipated escalation in racial tension, and the inclination of the white Methodist Church in the state was to avoid direct confrontation with protest activities and let law enforcement and the groups allied with it manage the dangerous situations. A strategy of delay was still the most popular approach on the local level, but with the appearance of newer forms of nonviolent direct action by movement participants, segregationists turned to more vigorous and hostile tactics in response. Yet while the conflict escalated in the years after *Brown*, the Methodist denomination continued its cautious, indecisive, approach when dealing with the future of the Central Jurisdiction. The General Conference elected commissions and created study groups to debate the issue, even as Southern segregationists and movement activists grew more assertive. Meanwhile people died in Mississippi's racial strife.

The quadrennial records of the Methodist General Conference shed light on how Methodists regarded their moral dilemma. The quandary appeared as a relatively simple bureaucratic decision, though actually it posed a great ethical problem: how to accommodate the demands of the Southeastern Jurisdiction with the denominational objective of inclusivity. Conference records show that there was sustained majority support for the Central Jurisdiction from 1939 until its disbanding in 1968.[2] The agonized arguments during these years occurred within a static moral environment, one seemingly dismissive of the condition of Methodism's black members. The church was immobilized by its history, until finally it was ready to discard its old wineskins and be replenished by the fresh ideas of the Second Reconstruction.

At the first quadrennial conference in 1956 following the *Brown* decision, some delegates believed they sensed a new willingness to resolve the problems posed by the Central Jurisdiction. Representatives at the General Conference tested the political waters and decided there was sufficient support for a constitutional amendment that could put the Central Jurisdiction on the road to dissolution. The amendment, remembered as "historic" Amendment IX, proposed the merger of black conferences with white neighboring ones, but based solely on the principle of voluntarism. It was a compromise measure that had no future at all in a state like Mississippi. According to the proposal, merger could take place when all parties to it, the churches as well as the sending conference (a black conference) and the receiving conference (a white conference), agreed to it.[3]

As with the Supreme Court's *Brown* decision, the measure offered no time frame for these proposed transfers. Yet even without dates, Amendment IX became contentious. It proved to be unacceptable to the Southeastern Jurisdiction because it raised the specter of the end of the

Central Jurisdiction, and it was unpopular among black and white liberals who thought it did not go far enough. What the amendment meant, essentially, was that in Border States, where the races were not as polarized as they were in the Deep South, black annual conferences might gain acceptance into nearby predominantly white conferences with relatively little fuss. Overall, however, the amendment was proposing an extremely slow process to dissolve the Central Jurisdiction by attrition, sparing General Conference the need to trudge across the minefield of an acceptable moral solution. Delegates optimistically created the Committee of Seventy to study the amendment.[4]

General Conference was locating its hope, as well as its credibility, in some distant future, when the time would come when there was "no place in The Methodist Church for racial discrimination," or "enforced segregation." To achieve that end, delegates recommended "that discrimination or segregation, by any method or practice, whether in conference structure or otherwise, be abolished with reasonable speed."[5] Again the term "reasonable speed" was the caveat; it was an unwillingness openly to challenge voluntarism, uncannily similar to the Court's call for "all deliberate speed."

Siege in Mississippi

While both the federal government and the Methodist Church weighed their options, Mississippi became a battleground. The first group of Freedom Riders from the Congress of Racial Equality (CORE), who arrived in Jackson in the summer of 1961, was followed closely by another busload of Student Nonviolent Coordinating Committee (SNCC) students who had been recruited by the indomitable Diane Nash. Along the way, riders encountered fights and firebombs, and went to jail rather than post bail. Claiming to be exhilarated rather than frightened at the time, CORE leader James Farmer said that their crusade against illegal segregation on interstate vehicles had become "a different and far grander thing than we had intended."[6] Years later when Farmer reflected on that bus trip into Jackson he had a different memory: "I was frankly terrified with the knowledge that the trip to Jackson might be the last any of us would ever take. Who, indeed, ever is . . . [ready for such threats?]"[7] The federal government, especially President Kennedy and his brother Robert, the attorney general, worried over a real potential for civil war in Mississippi.[8]

More volunteers, mostly students, arrived in Southern states to challenge segregation, with Mississippi, because of its violence, attracting disproportionate numbers along with media attention. When outsiders spoke of events in Mississippi after 1960, they used language that sounded like synonyms for war: it was "a state under siege," and a place where James Farmer feared dying on a bus ride. Mississippi was the epicenter of noncompliance, of massive resistance, and for the unarmed protesters, it was a place where "redemptive suffering" held promise of brighter days.

In such an environment, white Methodists who had any sympathy for the *Brown* decision knew there was considerable danger attached to speaking out. It was known that the mobs had been especially hard on the few white participants in the Freedom Rides. The historical record would indict white Mississippi Methodists for their "sinning by silence," and for having "laryngitis." By coming forward, white racial moderates would place themselves in the middle of the fight between conservative segregationists on the one hand and denominational integrationist liberals on the other. Racial political identities ran deep.[9]

Nevertheless the white Mississippi Conference still counted its moderate exceptions—Sam Ashmore, Ed King, Clay Lee—as well as the twenty-eight ministers who signed the "Born of Conviction" statement. Forever remembered for their action, the young ministers endorsed the need for public schools, for freedom of the pulpit, and for resistance to discrimination and communism. It was hardly a radical document, yet it generated immediate controversy and disrupted the lives of the signers. The men were catapulted into the limelight, harassed at home and at church by segregationists, and quietly applauded by supporters who viewed them as advocates of an authentic Methodism. By the end of the year nineteen of them were gone from their original pulpits.[10]

The General Conference of 1960: Failure to Cross the Rubicon

By the time the Methodist General Conference met again, in Denver in 1960, the white Mississippi Conference was deep in a conflict frightening and fierce. Since the last conference, the Mississippi State Sovereignty Commission (MSSC) had begun working hand in glove with the White Citizens' Council and also with MAMML, effectively closing off all opportunities for dissent. The Sovereignty Commission functioned as a watchdog for what had become a police state, its investigators, often retired FBI agents, constantly snooping for hints of support for integration.[11] The commission offered cash payments to informers, black and white, for anything that could be turned into incriminating evidence against supporters of integration. Agents seized on information about rumored heavy drinking, infidelity, indebtedness, assertiveness, socializing with the other race, anything that could be turned into damning evidence. The Sovereignty Commission did the bidding of the White Citizens' Council, and helped underwrite its work. It put everyone on alert by tracking car license plates, enlisting informers, and intruding unannounced on gatherings suspected of having a civil rights agenda, even the most innocent.

Citizens' Council member John Satterfield employed his legal skills to exacerbate still further the difficulties confronting the white Mississippi Methodist Conference. He drew up a Church Property Bill that he then introduced to the state legislature. The bill, intended to give local congregations legal title to their real property was, in fact, a thinly veiled attempt to give property control to any dissident segregationist congregation that wanted to bolt the denomination. Though opposed by the Methodist Bishop and other mainline church leaders, the bill passed.[12] During debate on the measure, one legislator suggested that the entire Methodist Church in the state be abolished.[13] MAMML supported both measures, and proposed that the best solution to the denomination's problems was a mass withdrawal from the church.

Satterfield was again a delegate to the General Conference in 1960, more popular with segregationists because of his success with the Mississippi legislature.[14] At the conference, his failure to endorse MAMML's schismatic suggestion to take the Mississippi Methodist Conference out of the denomination came as a surprise to delegates who knew of his many pronouncements against the national church. Satterfield was relying on the ability of Mississippians to get their support from the Southeastern Jurisdiction, and together win the fight for Southern values. The actions at Denver gave him hope.

Conference delegates proved unready to move decisively on matters of race. Instead of enacting dissolution measures for the Central Jurisdiction, delegates once again approved continued study of the subject. Leading black Methodist activist W. Astor Kirk, frustrated by the delegates' failure to act, described the Denver meeting as "the year the Methodist Church failed to cross the Rubicon."[15] The former "Committee of Seventy," created to study the Central Jurisdiction, was replaced by the "Committee on Interjurisdictional Relations," with attorney Charles Parlin as its chair, and John Satterfield, soon to be elected president of the American Bar Association, as another of its powerful members.[16] The Denver conference

kept the principle of voluntarism intact, affirming that churches and conferences could continue to act on the basis of the wishes of their members.
Denominational indecision allowed Southern delegates to believe they had
won another round. Delegate Harold Case of Boston offered an amendment to conference proceedings to set 1968 as a date certain for ending the
Central Jurisdiction, though that amendment, too, failed to win approval.

So despite daily front-page evidence of a national urgency to deal with
racial conflict, the General Conference of 1960 persisted with the same
tired efforts of judgment by committee, voluntarism, and delay. Satterfield,
and likely most others from the Southeastern Jurisdiction, were satis-
fied with the results of the Denver meetings, while black Methodists like
Astor Kirk felt betrayed. Consequently at their own Central Jurisdictional
Conference meeting later that same year, black delegates appointed their
own Committee of Five—resolution by committee seemed common to
all Methodists—to develop concrete plans for eliminating the Central
Jurisdiction.[17]

The proposal the black Methodists designed tapped into the concerns
of all black Americans. Their plan was far more comprehensive and specific than any General Conference measure. It laid out the mechanism
for church transfers—the most frequently debated topic regarding the
Central Jurisdiction—but that was just part of a grander scheme to integrate all Methodist facilities: schools and colleges, hospitals, and nursing
homes as well as church boards.[18] The black Methodist proposal called for
an end to the Central Jurisdiction and the beginning of inclusiveness in
all aspects of denominational life, indeed, an end to all racial discrimination.[19] The black Methodists planned to teach their white co-religionists
something about moral values, although the timing that year was not in
their favor.

A Mississippi Methodist historian said of the actions taken at Denver
that "at the time the General Conference of The Methodist Church was
going Mississippi's way," a fact not lost on worried white Mississippi
Methodists.[20]

The Effects on Longdale Methodists

In the meantime, Longdale Methodists, who would later say they "were
not scared" during these frightening times, wisely created increased precautions. Law enforcement agents from the county continued to patrol
their roads, not to offer protection but to buy liquor and intimidate the

residents. The Klan members who worked or shopped at the store at the end of Church Road practiced the same kind of surveillance of the neighborhood. In addition, MSSC agents roamed the area, working with informers to learn of any civil rights activity happening locally.

Longdale residents armored up. A woman from Mt. Zion Church remembered that "The mens defended our road."[21] Ross Jones kept two guns, one always hanging over the front door.[22] Others willing to accept the hazards of being clandestine activists were some of the usual leaders, Clinton Collier, Burleen Riley, Cornelius Steele, subsequently joined by Luther Riley, Ernest Kirkland—all Methodists—and Fred Black from town, occasionally cooperating with other close friends. The group would ride north at night in two cars to Canton, where they picked up clothes, literature, and "different things" to help the movement. Fear of encountering law enforcement led them to various stratagems to disguise the cars they used.[23] They were some of "the church people in the struggle."[24] According to a woman who had been the financial secretary at the church, Longdale had secretly mobilized, relying on a group of "men who would hold on to this road: Cornelius, Walter, Frank, Jeff, and TJ protected this road. If they [outsiders, troublemakers] did anything on this road, they would make them sorry."[25] Residents knew they were being watched, and used every covert means at their disposal to keep the community safe. Eventually it proved to be not enough.

Longdale had been under active Sovereignty Commission surveillance since 1957, when rumors had first circulated about secret meetings, including the possibility of an NAACP cell, and the presence of the Evers brothers in the area. When Charles took temporary leave of Neshoba, MSSC agents were relieved, but still worried about the secret evening meetings. One agent questioned the head of the county's Chamber of Commerce about NAACP sympathizers in the area, and was assured there were none. Medger Evers came back to Neshoba regularly because of his job as state NAACP field secretary, dangerous work in tense Mississippi, though he traveled freely, collecting information on crimes against blacks, presumably hoping his very visibility provided its own kind of protection.

Medger Evers had been appalled by the death of young Luther Jackson in Philadelphia in 1959. Jackson, a former resident of Neshoba who had moved to Chicago, had been sitting in a parked car with a former girlfriend when police officer Lawrence Rainey—later famed for his ruthlessness—came by. Rainey pulled Jackson from the car, took him around to the back, and shot him dead on the spot, a murder that blacks considered a lynching. Shortly after, Rainey was elected sheriff of Neshoba County.[26] An uncorroborated report noted that "widespread police brutality was the most urgent civil rights problem in the state," a claim the FBI also made in 1964 when it searched for the bodies of the three slain activists.[27] The coroner's jury in the Jackson case agreed that his death was a case of "justifiable homicide," and Rainey was never charged.[28]

In the same year as the Denver Conference, 1960, Aaron Henry, a Clarksdale pharmacist, became state president of the NAACP, replacing C. R. Darden, a move occasioned by the worsening crisis, and the perception by black activists that the times called for more aggressive measures than those the NAACP had previously employed. Henry, like Medgar Evers, was willing to take the risks associated with moving the struggle forward. He initiated local protest movements that relied on the confrontational tactics of nonviolent direct action, which, though less dramatic than the Freedom Rides, nevertheless required the same level of courage.[29] Still, the violence against black activists went on, claiming the lives of not only the Reverend George Lee, but also Roy Melton, Vernon Dahmer, Lamar Smith, and in 1963, Medgar Evers himself, shot from ambush by Byron de la Beckwith.[30]

MAMML, ever at the forefront of the fight against the integration of Mississippi Methodist churches, was a part of the segregationist network that supported, and sometimes encouraged, these attacks on blacks, including their own black Methodist church colleagues. MAMML was willing to use questionable tactics to silence moderate clergy and to monitor churches, white and black, considered doubtful on racial matters. Its members believed the national denomination was out of touch with Southern culture, and that the local conference harbored closet moderates. To remove any hint of softness on the segregation issue, MAMML planned a conference coup to remove from office J. P. Stafford, the most visible lay official, an experienced lay leader, and a person MAMML considered too moderate. Mt. Zion was also a vulnerable target in this struggle because it was known to use literature and teaching material that came from denominational headquarters. Even Sunday school teachers were suspect.

The "Closed Door" Policy of White Churches

The drama over the moral dilemma facing the Methodist denomination was prominently played out in confrontations between highly placed leaders of the church, local and national, and Mississippi laymen, over access to worship in white Methodist churches by black Methodists and civil rights activists of either race. Galloway Methodist Church in Jackson, so large and imposing that it was referred to as a cathedral, and where John Satterfield once taught the Men's Bible Class, was a frequent setting for live demonstrations about inclusion and exclusion in the church. By 1961, both MAMML members and White Citizens' Council supporters had been elected to Galloway's official board and gained control of the votes. On June 12, the official board voted to tell its board of ushers not to allow anyone into the church who had the "purpose of creating an incident resulting in the breach of the peace," a policy decision to keep out blacks and civil rights activists.[31] Galloway Church ironically had taken its name from a Southern bishop once considered a moderate on issues of race.

In 1961, its senior minister was the Reverend W. B. Selah, a highly visible figure in Jackson, assumed by his congregation to be a proponent of the "Southern way of life," and a supporter of segregation. Yet when his official board told the church ushers to refuse admission to those who might "breach the peace"—a measure aimed at Freedom Riders and their associates—Selah made it known that he opposed the decision. A long-time Methodist, Selah was then seen as a racial moderate, and he strongly objected to the assertion of lay control over Galloway church, and the annual conference. The lay board overruled Selah's wishes, and Galloway Church was officially "closed" to blacks and their white supporters.

Galloway's closing coincided with the Jackson Campaign, a local, well-publicized civil rights action. Professor John Salter, from predominantly black Tougaloo College nearby, organized the campaign, to be joined shortly by the Reverend Ed King, the college's chaplain and a white Methodist minister. King was a Mississippi native prominent in the unfolding civil rights movement, a torment to segregationists and eventually a candidate for lieutenant governor on the Mississippi Freedom Democratic Party ticket, a mostly black new party. As part of the Jackson Campaign, King orchestrated "pray-ins" at area churches that announced themselves as "closed" to blacks and their civil rights colleagues. Warned by his friends to avoid the South after graduating from seminary at Boston University, King had ignored their counsel and eventually paid dearly for his convictions.[32] But in 1962 he was emboldened by the courage of the Freedom Riders and the intransigence of segregationist Governor Ross Barnett to work with the Jackson Campaign as it debated what kind of strategy to pursue, whether boycotts, lunch-counter sit-ins, or negotiations with the mayor. They decided on all three, as King continued his church pray-ins.

As this violence was escalating around the state, James Meredith applied to be the first black student at the University of Mississippi in Oxford. Accompanied by federal marshals and police officers, Meredith was greeted by a white mob prepared for action. In the "Battle of Oxford," National Guardsmen were called in to deal with the hostile crowd, but in spite of their presence, two people were killed and many were injured.[33]

The Meredith case and the ensuing "Battle of Oxford" impacted the struggle within Methodism, especially in the Jackson area. Local whites thought that the Jackson Campaign, especially the attempts by blacks to attend white churches, was the church counterpart to the showdown at Ole Miss, both examples of black assertions of entitlement. The moderate editor of the *Mississippi Methodist Advocate*, Sam Ashmore, thought otherwise, that the death and destruction created by the rioters at Oxford cried out for a compassionate, even apologetic, response from Methodists. He wrote an editorial intending to make his readers aware of their complicity in what had just happened at the university. "We in the church are to blame," he wrote, "because we allowed such a force of hate to build up in our state."[34] But instead of the acknowledgment of complicity he hoped for, he received criticism and charged comments, with no real sentiment for change.

Ed King continued the pray-ins at area churches from his base at Tougaloo College. Typically, King alerted ministers the day before that he was bringing a group of interracial worshippers to their church; lay ushers were therefore prepared with flashlights and other equipment to turn them away. It was a scene well covered by the media: young people, mostly black but some white, dressed in their Sunday clothes, prayed on church steps as well-groomed white men hovered over them in a threatening way. Galloway garnered most of the attention, although as other Methodist churches in the city adopted the exclusionary policies along with other Protestant churches, they too were included in the unwelcome publicity. When the chairman of the official board of Galloway announced in 1963 that "Negroes will not be seated nor allowed admittance to any church services," Reverend Selah decided that Galloway had strayed too far from denominational policy on race, and he resigned from the church.[35]

But in 1963 it could be a difficult thing to discern denominational policy on race. Historic professions about an inclusive church were ignored in the clamor over the future of the Central Jurisdiction. The General

Conference decisions in 1960 had pleased white Southerners at the same time they disappointed black Methodists and civil rights advocates. There was something incongruous about the national church being instructed in matters of race by a Jackson minister. But while the Reverend Selah's actions did not go unnoticed, the church doors remained closed. Ed King was voted out of membership in the Mississippi Methodist Conference that year, and his probationary status was terminated because of his civil rights activities. Subsequently he became the only white minister in the Central Jurisdiction.[36] His planned pray-ins continued with new groups of worshippers, some of them sent to jail for trespassing on church property. King was then involved in a very serious car wreck and badly injured, his face permanently disfigured in what he believed was deliberate action by the segregationist at the wheel of the other car in the crash.[37]

The Jackson Campaign was a part of a larger organized nonviolent protest against the segregationist policies of the city. Antisegregationist activity escalated as the boycotts and pray-ins continued and sit-ins began, resulting in students being arrested, with some held incommunicado for twenty-four hours. Mixed-race groups of clergy from outside the state tried to challenge the Methodist "closed door" policy, covered by much media attention as some of them were jailed. Before the Reverend Selah left Galloway, he announced his support for the signatories of the "Born of Conviction" statement, one of whom was his associate pastor, but his board said the views of their pastors were their own and not those of the membership. The Galloway board went on to affirm that "it did not consider segregation to be unchristian." In fact, the board stated, it was "a time-honored tradition," something every Methodist in Mississippi understood.[38]

The churches' "closed door" policy was managed by an umbrella group of unidentified segregationist organizations, whose members could be found listed in the records of the Citizens' Council, within MAMML, and even in branches of the Klan. The Mississippi Methodist Conferences, because of their history and stature, gave the segregationist insurgency strength and credibility. A cabal of right-wing forces employing tactics of intimidation prompted ministers to leave the state for assignments in safer territory, saying they were driven out by the "machine politics" found in the Jackson district and other areas of the state. It was influential laymen like John Satterfield and a few outspoken segregationist clergy who dominated the politics of the white Methodist Conferences. Within the national church, the Methodists for Church Renewal, a predominantly black group, organized in November 1963 with reform of the "closed door" policy in Mississippi at the top of its agenda. It also made contact with local black Methodists, intending to encourage them in their struggle, and to make them feel less isolated from the denomination. The group sent a few members to Jackson to test the policy, and they, too, were turned away at the door before being arrested.

Galloway Church replaced the Reverend Selah with the Reverend W. J. Cunningham. He was a Millsaps' alumnus who was aware of Galloway's problems but believed he could remedy them. He knew of Dr. Selah's struggle with his board over lay control of pulpit access, and the continuing "closed door" fight. After a stormy ministry of just over two years, he, too, resigned because of differences with the official board on these matters, his resignation becoming the price required for an end to the discriminatory policy.[39] While Cunningham was still at Galloway, the Methodist General Conference had made tentative efforts to support the church's besieged clergy and to challenge the "closed door" policy; its support however, did not extend to the desperate circumstances of area black Methodist churches. One of the most memorable events at Galloway occurred on Easter Day, March 29, 1964, when two Methodist bishops arrived to worship at the church. One of the men was Bishop James K. Mathews, who was white, and the other was Bishop Charles Golden, who was black. They were met at the church door and barred from entering. On the previous day, the bishops had met with the Jackson Methodist district superintendent—a person referred to as the "most powerful man in Mississippi Methodism" and the one responsible for running the district's "political machine"—who warned them that even his own bishop would be turned away if he tried to enter the church with "a nigra."[40]

Methodists and the "Closed Society"

In 1964, the General Conference that convened in Pittsburgh addressed a battery of racial matters, though not the basic sources of racism. Ed King and other supporters of integration picketed conference sessions, handed out literature, and held their own informational meetings. Bishop Gerald Kennedy, who had personal experience with Galloway Church, called on the church to remove all forms of segregation. Delegates who supported Kennedy's views appealed to the conference to intervene with the "political machine" that controlled the Mississippi Conference and intimidated critics.[41] Yet after much heated debate, the Central Jurisdiction was still in place at the end of the session, with only a planned denominational merger with the Evangelical United Brethren Church in 1968 offering hope that the CJ might be dissolved at that time.

The Southeastern Jurisdiction convened its own meeting of southern delegates shortly after the end of General Conference. John Satterfield was there, and through astute legal maneuvers he succeeded with a parliamentary sleight of hand to delay yet again the dissolution of the Central Jurisdiction. The delegates adopted a motion that said any future mergers must be "mutually agreeable to the conferences concerned."[42] It was clear that Southern white conferences were not likely to agree to receive a black church. Satterfield had concocted what black Methodists considered a "preemptive strike," proposing that the Judicial Council of the church first rule on the Southeastern Jurisdiction action before the question of merger could be taken up by the whole church. Once again, his measure postponed action on the Central Jurisdiction. According to W. Astor Kirk, the activist involved in the proceedings, Satterfield knew that his strategy had the support of New Yorker Charles Parlin—who had also ingeniously worked the parliamentary system of the conference to his favor—and was an ally in what Kirk called an "unholy alliance."[43] Further action to end the Central Jurisdiction would have to await denominational merger in 1968.

Not surprisingly, MAMML condemned the 1964 General Conference and the planned merger in 1968, and urged the Mississippi Annual Conference to abandon the Methodist Church. Mississippi acquired a new bishop in 1964, Edward Pendergrass, and he called MAMML's hand on its assertion that moderate conference policies were creating disaffected Methodists: Pendergrass said that threats and petitions sent to him by MAMML were false, illegal, and inconsequential.[44] At that point MAMML forfeited the support of the bishop and its members started to drift away, appearing less interested in matters involving the Methodist Church. In its years of greatest influence, between 1961 and 1965, MAMML contributed to the defection of as many as 5,000 members from Mississippi Methodist churches.[45] Large groups left Galloway and other Methodist churches to recombine as the Association of Independent Methodists, with a mailing list of 85,000.[46] The most significant characteristic of these new church groups was how un-Methodist they became; they were just as they described themselves, "Independent," essentially congregationally controlled conservative entities with no connectional ties.

One notable clergy defector from the denomination with future relevance to Mt. Zion Church was a young supply pastor, the Reverend Delmar Dennis. In 1963, Dennis ministered to the Pine Springs Methodist Church, as well as another rural congregation in the Meridian district, to which Mt. Zion also belonged. In February of that year he led the two congregations he served out of the denomination and into the independent Southern Methodist Church. Dennis would become better known to history later in his career when he served as chaplain of the Meridian and Neshoba Ku Klux Klan and became a friend of the state Klan head, Sam Bowers. He became an FBI informer and would testify as a surprise witness at the first trial of those accused in the 1964 Neshoba County murders. Thereafter, he lived the rest of his life in fear of Klan retaliation.[47]

By 1964, liberal Protestant churches and other religious groups had finally understood the urgency in the South, and offered support to civil rights programs with direct action campaigns. In June the National Council of Churches (NCC), a favorite target of MAMML, announced it was sponsoring a training program for students and seminarians willing to go to Mississippi to start Freedom Schools, the start of what became Freedom Summer. The program was described as a tutoring program for children, with a voting registration component for adults to aid them in registering to vote. Robert Moses, a commanding figure in the civil rights movement in Mississippi, made the prescient observation that Freedom Summer was likely to have casualties, and the casualties were likely to be white. White victims, he acknowledged, would draw the kind of political and media attention that black victims never would. The Delta Ministry was also started that summer, with the Reverend Harry Bowie one of its earliest recruits. The Methodist denomination became a major contributor, in terms of staff and financial support, to both projects; Freedom Summer and the Delta Ministry. The announcement of the two planned programs set off new alarms in the Magnolia State and produced an onslaught of media attention.

Mississippi had fast become emblematic of racial polarization in American culture. After Ole Miss history professor James Silver witnessed the rioting on his campus the night James Meredith came to enroll, he coined the term "closed society" to describe the lawless scene he saw. Mississippi, he feared, had become a police state. The "closed society" term caught on, aided by a media that seemed to sense its resonance in Mississippi life.[48]

Segregationists Prepare for Freedom Summer

As the news of Freedom Summer trickled through the state, segregation-ist groups geared up with an agenda of their own, one that resembled Freedom Summer only in its intensity. There was already a well-organized segregationist infrastructure in place, just waiting to be dispatched at any sign of movement activism. The size of the NCC army of volunteers plan-ning to enter the state was rumored to number anywhere between 100 and 1,000, leading segregationist organizations to develop tough strategies for dealing with the outsiders. There seemed to be an unspoken agree-ment that the Klan, with a growing membership following the Freedom Summer announcement, would take responsibility for the tough stuff, the violence and firebombing. The other groups would enlist supporters through ambitious propaganda efforts and active politicizing.

Right-wing Methodists, in MAMML or one of the other segregation-ist entities, arranged to have Myers Lowman from Circuit Riders return to the state for an extended speaking tour in the spring of 1964, his expenses shared by the MSSC and MAMML. Lowman had a reputation for being an effective advocate for segregation as well as a harsh critic of his own Methodist denomination. According to Stanley Dearman, who was at the time a writer for the segregationist *Meridian Star*, the tour accomplished Lowman's objective of targeting "the role of the churches in the race issue."[49] Lowman had access to a wide audience during his tour that spring. Through MAMML he had entry to Methodist churches, and through the MSSC he obtained admission to schools, fraternal groups, and general public audiences. He fueled the fires of segregation that roared through the surrounding communities. Mindful of the plans for Freedom Summer, MAMML invited Lowman to continue his extremist harangues in venues from Jackson to Meridian. His patrons scheduled talks for him in Meridian during the second week in June, where the *Meridian Star* had created an audience eager to hear him, an environment threatening to the new CORE group setting up in the city. MAMML claimed Lowman spoke to "almost 3,000 persons" on this particular tour.[50] With mem-bers of MAMML, the MSSC, the White Citizens' Council, Citizens for the Preservation of the White Race, the John Birch Society, as well as the Klan, filling the audience at these Lowman talks, Meridian and east cen-tral Mississippi provided an unhealthy setting for liberal idealists like the youthful CORE recruits who were developing plans for Freedom Summer.

8

Remembering the Neshoba Murders, 1963–1964

The problem of race is America's greatest moral dilemma.
MARTIN LUTHER KING, JR.[1]

Leadership in 1964 was complicit in what happened [in Neshoba].
DICK MOLPUS (FORMER MISSISSIPPI SECRETARY OF STATE), NOVEMBER 24, 2004

Collective memory is the way peoples or nations construct versions of the past.
DAVID W. BLIGHT, "IF YOU DON'T TELL IT LIKE IT WAS, IT CAN NEVER BE AS IT OUGHT TO BE"

Revisiting the "American Dilemma"

The year 1964 was the *annus horribilis* in Mississippi, a time of chaos and confusion for both blacks and whites in the state. Black activists, frustrated by their struggles of the last few years, were alarmed by the news of a reenergized Ku Klux Klan. Segregationists, for their part, had assembled a formidable coalition of religious and political organizations, which included most members of the two white Methodist Conferences. Mississippi had become home not only to the poorest people in the country, but also the worst racial crimes. It was a picture further corrupted that year by the actions of violent segregationists prepared to use any means—assault, arson, even murder—to preserve the Old South image they believed white neighbors shared and outsiders did not understand.

As white residents pondered the implications of Freedom Summer, they became enraged at the prospect of outside forces entering their state—invading it, they said—to bring changes that were alien to Mississippi's historic culture. Memories of the past, of how things used to be and ought to be, were on a collision course with agents of change. Divisions inside Mississippi Methodism continued, but without the church vocal opposition to desegregation and the segregated Central Jurisdiction was muted, because, in 1964 "things were going Mississippi's way," according to a critical member of the Mississippi Conference. Local black Methodists still protested that segregation in all forms was immoral, but the moral argument against discrimination had collapsed, as the state lived up to its designation as a "closed society." The dilemma was not between a moral ideal and a social reality, but between adherents of historical memory and tradition and those prepared to challenge the legitimacy of the old ways.

For black movement supporters, including the members of Mt. Zion Church, the arrival of outside volunteers was welcomed as fresh troops for the struggle. Despite the constant surveillance and escalating threats, black church members remained ready to accept the risks that came with supporting movement people, black or white, with food and housing. Within Mississippi the establishment offered no help in the intrastate battle: the justice system was corrupt; the mainline churches went quiet; the Democratic Party lost standing, and the Methodist Church, in the opinion of black Methodists at Mt. Zion and elsewhere, compromised its moral authority.

A Northern Methodist on Mississippi

On a cold January day in 1964—in the same month that the besieged black man Louis Allen was shot dead in Amite County—the Reverend Robert Raines, minister of the First Methodist Church of Germantown, Pennsylvania, reported to his hometown audience in Pennsylvania on a recent visit to Galloway Church, Jackson. His comments indicated what white liberals outside Mississippi thought was going on there. He was scornful of the conditions he witnessed in the Mississippi Conference. His stinging remarks about Mississippi Methodism first appeared in MAMML's monthly publication, seemingly an unlikely venue for a Northern Methodist's commentary on their local church, but the reality was that MAMML, too, criticized the local conference, if for entirely different reasons. MAMML's perspective on the conference said much about what was at stake in Mississippi.

Raines was reported in the MAMML article as saying that what he observed in Jackson was "the police state climate of Mississippi," the courage of black ministers, "a corrupt Conference machine run by the local

District Superintendent and a weak and cowardly resident Bishop." As a result of these dire circumstances, he said, the conference suffered the "continuing loss of the finest leadership."[2] At the heart of his comments was Raines's perception of a unitary state, where the police, the Methodist bishop, and the district superintendent worked in concert to maintain the status quo. Only the black Methodists and a handful of white moderates were willing to remain in opposition.

What Raines did not say, however, was that his own denomination, by taking its stand on the wrong side of America's racial fault line when it created the Central Jurisdiction, was also complicit in the sorry scene he witnessed. In Mississippi, Methodism was in disorder, and black Methodists and civil rights activists were barred from its churches. MAMML leaders found an easy similarity between Raines's criticism of their conference and attacks by other liberals, and so the journal simply quoted him verbatim, knowing its readers would make the necessary connection: another example of crazy liberal ranting. For MAMML, the problem with the conference was not that it was run by machine politics, but that it was wrong-headed.

A powerful synergy bound the divergent segregationist organizations together in the state. All had basically similar desires: to maintain the social structure of the recent past, to celebrate Southern traditions as they had existed since the antebellum period, and to ensure that they continued in the future. Except for the Klan, most, like MAMML, believed that their goals could be achieved without getting their hands dirty. Church support would, of course, enhance the credibility of the various agencies. Baptists predominated in the state, but theirs was not a connectional church, which meant that support came through the slow cultivation of individual churches. The Methodist Church was a conundrum for the state's segregationists; on the one hand, it had high-ranking powerful state leaders among its membership, and supported segregation by holding on to the Central Jurisdiction. For those reasons, some segregationist groups supported it. On the other hand, however, But outside the state it was frequently home to liberals like Raines who, like other Methodist progressives in the denomination, were also considered "soft on communism." There were other connectional denominations in the state, though smaller and less well known—the Roman Catholic, the Episcopal, and the Lutheran—groups only occasionally targeted for segregationist criticism.

At the time when the Reverend W. J. Cunningham served at Galloway Church, he was convinced that segregationist leaders had selected, then captured, his prestigious church for their base, later conspiring with his bishop, Edward Pendergrass, to get him dismissed for his opposition to the "closed door" policy. He had little regard for his bishop—Marvin Franklin at the time of Raines's visit—and would have shared Raines's designation of Franklin as a "weak and cowardly Bishop," although the bishop himself "was being pressured by whatever method, by the same invisible forces that had kept the largest church in his area a tight bastion of white supremacy since June 1961."[3] Through 1964, Galloway's "closed door" tactic spread to other communities, to cities and towns where the combined efforts of law enforcement and agents of the Sovereignty Commission enabled lay boards to keep it in place.

With most of the reasonable voices of the clergy gone from the state, only a few moderate newspaper editors remained to sympathize with the untenable position of the Methodist Church Raines described. They repeated the criticism of the church for having "laryngitis." Hodding Carter of the *Greenville Delta Democrat Times* was one such moderate editor still in the state who was willing to take on segregationist vilification. He was convinced that the White Citizens' Council used MAMML as their religious front to attack the church for what the group perceived as its twin ills, softness on communism and a lack of clarity about segregation. MAMML, he thought, had been "a persistent thorn" in the side for the Methodist Church.[4]

MAMML's right-wing positions lined up closely not only with other segregationist groups but also with the local media. The segregationist machine had almost exclusive control of the state's flow of public information. The *Meridian Star* was one influential segregationist organ, as was *The Clarion-Ledger*, owned by the powerful media moguls the Hederman brothers, whose interests also included television outlets and newspapers around the state. Hodding Carter of Greenville and Ira Harkey of *The Chronicle* in Pascagoula were notable exceptions.

The Challenge of Civil Rights

To activists in the state and those just arriving, it seemed that in early 1964 the federal government had forgotten them, and the Methodist Church had abandoned its moral arguments. President Kennedy's proposed civil rights measure stalled after his death. Although the Methodist Church remained officially committed to segregation, it invoked the same strategy of delay that the government relied on to avoid conflict over school integration. The FBI and the Justice Department, its agents said, would not protect any civil rights workers who went to Mississippi, lest it create the impression the state was unable to manage it own affairs. White residents of the Magnolia State might, therefore, anticipate the desired outcome: that things would remain as they had been; that the "Southern way of life" would prevail; and that the ferocity of the state's segregationist insurgency would persuade that year's Freedom Summer volunteers to go home or drop away in fear. Looking around their state, they might legitimately conclude that the power of Southern memory was stronger than civil rights activism. Mississippi was not going to secede; it would just get a firmer grip on its borders and keep out troublesome outsiders.[5]

When Freedom Summer volunteers arrived, they came armed with the conviction that they could make a difference in this very poor state, where inequality and discrimination were historically ineradicable. It was a tall order. To outsiders the connection between segregation and poverty was obvious, producing the greatest class divide in the country. Just 5 percent of Mississippi's farmers owned 50 percent of the land. Only 6 percent of the black population was registered to vote.[6] What the young activists of Mississippi Summer faced was formidable—centuries of memories and the heft of Southern culture. And the tactics they planned to rely on were those of nonviolent direct action, a strategy for those who believed moral integrity was more powerful than fists or guns.

The Summer Project in Meridian

Not the government or the church, it was the first Freedom Riders who convinced other civil rights activists that they might successfully challenge Mississippi traditions. The post-1960 activists in the state, increasingly young people, took from the riders' efforts the message that they were not alone in the struggle, and that nonviolent confrontational tactics possessed enormous power. They were ready to learn the techniques of nonviolent direct action and be part of a moral crusade. Black activists in the state knew from experience that confrontations over segregation could be ugly, but that was part of the message too; that when those who made sacrifices for ideals were harmed, their sacrifices would be an ennobling part of an essentially moral effort.

The black activists and their white colleagues in the CORE voting rights project that opened in Meridian in 1964 learned the same Gandhian approach to nonviolent direct action that was used by the Freedom Riders.

For most young protesters, it was a scary strategy for promoting social change in Mississippi's overheated environment, since it called for them to go into hostile settings and be provocative and confrontational, while staying mindful that their opponents knew they were unarmed and would respond nonviolently. The movement people were expected to have some experience with nonviolent philosophy and techniques, to understand the moral strength of their approach, and above all, to be brave. The Freedom Summer volunteers were given two weeks in Oxford, Ohio, to learn and practice. The summer-long program recruited scores of volunteers.

How would such a nonviolent movement fare in a contest with Mississippi's defenders of the "Southern way of life," with their deep reverence for military heroes? There would be many casualties among the volunteers.

One of the early volunteers was David Dennis, who became a CORE leader in Mississippi, although he was already a movement veteran even before the opening of Freedom Summer. In the fall of 1963, Dennis recruited another seasoned activist, Matt Suarez, to begin the work in Meridian on the voter registration program. To demonstrate the need for a voting education project, the Student Nonviolent Coordinating Committee and the Council of Federated Organizations (COFO)— the latter an umbrella group for the various civil rights agencies in the state—conducted a mock election that same fall, to provide evidence that black voters were eager to participate in a real election. The mock election, with Aaron Henry and Ed King as the candidates, produced 80,000 black votes, a clear indication that blacks wanted the vote and knew its power.[7] Suarez coordinated the project with the black leadership already active in Meridian: Charles Young, the head of the local NAACP; Albert Jones, a wealthy black entrepreneur; and the Reverend Charles Johnson, a feisty Church of the Nazarene minister. Young and Jones knew what was at stake in challenging the local status quo, and Johnson, new in town, learned quickly.

Meridian, the second-largest city in the state, provided rich soil for political protest in 1964. In the Mississippi context, the city was considered a "fairly liberal" place, where black neighborhoods, though lacking educational and financial amenities, could count on a core of leaders able to operate independently of the white community. Once Matt Suarez settled into Meridian, he sought the counsel of Jones, Johnson, and Young, and asked Sue Brown, the NAACP Youth Council president, to help him find recruits for the voting project. One of the earliest volunteers for the project was James E. Chaney, just twenty years old, who worked as a part-time plasterer. Chaney soon became an activist in the registration campaign.[8]

By that time the national media had decided to give front-page coverage to the events of the civil rights story, and was thus a new force and a significant addition to the emergent struggle. The revived White Knights of the Ku Klux Klan, with its eccentric leader, Imperial Wizard Sam Bowers, and its members in clownish outfits offering apocalyptic statements, provided fodder for the media. Bowers expanded the Klan by organizing a klavern in Lauderdale County, home to Meridian, and another in Neshoba County, where Lawrence Rainey and Cecil Price were sheriff and deputy, and where he had the help of Baptist preacher Edgar Ray Killen. While Meridian was not featured in national news stories about the movement, its racist newspaper, the *Meridian Star*, managed to grieve the local black population.[9]

When David Dennis took the measure of the ferocious segregationist opposition he faced in Meridian, he decided he needed additional staff to make the voter project a success, so he contacted CORE's New York office for recruits. By Thanksgiving, just days after the assassination of President Kennedy, Michael Schwerner and his wife, Rita, who had already applied to work for the organization, were informed by CORE that their applications to the Mississippi program had been accepted, and they were to leave for the field in January as soon as Rita had completed her degree at Queens College. White New Yorkers with a demonstrated passion for social change, the Schwerners were young, with Mickey twenty-four and Rita just twenty. Rita had trained to be a teacher, Mickey—as he was known—as a social worker, and in January 1964 they drove to Jackson to take up their work.

The chief planners for the proposed Mississippi Summer Project were Dennis and Robert Moses, both initially skeptical of the ability of these two white activists to work in the dangerous Mississippi environment. Their thinking changed when they realized that the plans for Freedom Summer were heavily dependent on white volunteers, most likely people even less experienced than the Schwerners, and they decided to go ahead with the appointment and assigned the couple to the Meridian voter project.[10] At the time, the Meridian CORE had a staff of eight.

The segregationist opposition in Meridian was not only well organized, it was backed by local law enforcement groups. The Schwerners had worked on campaigns for social justice in Brooklyn and Baltimore, and were thus hardly naïve about the difficulties they faced in Mississippi, although when assessing the challenge, they might have missed the depth of segregationist support in the community. They settled into the black section of Meridian, the only place the "outsiders" were welcome.

Mickey Schwerner, not a conventionally religious person, professed a deep commitment to equality and human rights. A product of the liberal Jewish tradition, he was seemingly unafraid of the dangerous conditions in which he was working. With Rita, he developed friendships in Meridian's black community, and with help from local volunteers, they set up a community center within weeks of their arrival.[11] Their attempts at church "pray-ins," however, were unsuccessful. Older residents, like Jones and Young, familiar with Southern culture, wondered if the young CORE activists might not be moving ahead too quickly. In fact, the Sovereignty Commission already knew of the Schwerners the moment they arrived.[12] The Sovereignty Commission noted the license plate on the Volkswagen Beetle they drove, and when they switched to the blue 1963 Ford Fairlane station wagon CORE acquired, commission agents shared with law enforcement throughout the state what would become a familiar license number, H25 503. Before Medgar Evers had been murdered, he had known the commission was watching him, and even knew the agent who tailed him. But Evers had a kind of mother wit about the rural South that Schwerner did not have time to develop, although ultimately even that did not save Evers.

Mt. Zion's Freedom School

Throughout the spring of 1964, Mickey Schwerner and James Chaney, by then close friends and co-workers, engaged in scouting efforts to find a suitable location for CORE's voter registration project outside Meridian. After conversations with Longdale's leaders, they picked out Mt. Zion Church as an ideal spot. The men saw the advantage of its rural location and also its connection to a network of rural black churches. Mt. Zion would be a place from which they could recruit other black Methodists in the area willing to take risks to register to vote.

Before the agreement between the men and Mt. Zion could be arranged, however, the congregation needed to vote on the proposal. During the two months before the congregational vote, in April and May, the two men met at night in the homes of various Longdale people, long-time residents like the Kirklands, the Coles, and the Steeles, to see if Mt. Zion's members would accept the hazards connected with having a voter registration project in their church. Church members knew their neighbors well enough to know there would be many supporters, but that there would likely be some dissenters who knew Sheriff Rainey had a reputation for shooting first and asking questions later. There was also the reality of the Klan lookout in the store at the end of Church Road. The risk was substantial.

On Sunday afternoon, May 31, with Chaney present, Dennis and Schwerner accepted Mt. Zion's invitation to explain the details of the project to the congregation. They described how the voter registration program would operate and answered people's questions: "Would there be teaching available for the children?" "What about instruction in learning how to type?" and so on. The visitors said that about a dozen volunteers, likely most from outside the state, both black and white, men and women, would be based in Meridian, with one or two assigned specifically to Mt. Zion. These outside volunteers would also be taking on risk. Meridian was an hour's drive away, and they would have to travel through Klan-infested countryside to get to Longdale. When the conversations ended and a vote was taken, a majority approved of the project.[13]

There were a few critics of the program in the congregation, but the long unflinching witness of the church was a factor in the decision to take on the risk. Members wanted to work for the franchise and other goals, rights their ancestors had once enjoyed but had been long denied. Relatives in the past had had the vote in the years surrounding Reconstruction, and there were members of the congregation who had worked for years to have it restored. The congregation was aware that a few weeks earlier, on April 4, the Klan had made its presence known by burning a dozen crosses across the county, including at the courthouse square in Philadelphia. The Freedom School offered the prospect of a better future, though it faced great odds. The local people did not know David Dennis or Mickey Schwerner; the men were strangers who were proposing to use Mt. Zion as a home base for a controversial voting rights project. Because of the constant bullying tactics of the voting registrar and his allies, the project was beginning with a base of only eight registered black voters in the county.

One significant stalwart of the congregation did not endorse the voting rights plan. Bud Cole was a reliable member of long standing at Mt. Zion, and had been a participant in the earlier meetings Schwerner and Chaney had had with several Longdale residents. But on the day when the church scheduled what was perhaps the most crucial meeting in its history, he decided to absent himself and tend to the needs of his farm.[14] Cole had heard of the tumult growing in Meridian, and like others in the congregation, knew that nearby resident Preacher Edgar Ray Killen was leading an active Klan chapter in Neshoba County. He did not know, nor did anyone else in the church, that Klan leaders Sam Bowers and Killen had already decided in early spring that Schwerner, or "Goatee" as they called him once he cultivated a beard, had to be "eliminated"; he was an irritant in Meridian, and a danger to the area if he succeeded with a voting project for blacks.[15] Bud Cole had worked hard to create a life for his large family, and he did not want to see them, or his church, put in harm's way. It would be easier to explain to his neighbors why he just didn't show up, rather than cast a "no" vote against the plan.

Other church people around the county shared Bud Cole's apprehension that active, visible participation in the movement held the possibility for disastrous consequences. Beatings and burnings in the area showed the Klan was active and growing, and for civil rights supporters to come forward to put their lives, their houses, churches and communities on the line seemed unwise. Cole was not alone in questioning the wisdom of testing Klan retaliation. The recent evidence of assault and arson combined in recall with vivid memories of Klan lynchings in the region.

The great majority of Mt. Zion's members, however, welcomed the movement and its representatives. As members of CORE, the workers were an integral part of the Mississippi Summer Project, with the National Council of Churches and constituent mainline churches, funding the Freedom Summer effort. Since the bulk of the budget came from organizations outside the state, Mt. Zion's members might reasonably have expected that the project would have steady backing. There were rumors of contributors from around the country promoting the program. Reliable outside funding likely factored in to the members' decision to approve the plan. The planners said the Freedom School would open in June, three weeks hence—though it actually did not open until September because of the events that subsequently unfolded during the summer. The Klan cross burnings in April had already raised tensions among Neshoba County's black residents. The increased level of Klan activity in Neshoba led movement activists to consider the county a "trouble spot," where segregationists used tactics like cross burnings to intimidate black residents.

As the COFO activists worked on the Freedom School, Mt. Zion people cultivated ties to the young people, inviting them to stay and eat in their homes. For whites in Neshoba, however, COFO was anathema, its very name having the sting of a curse. Longdale residents therefore had to work clandestinely with various COFO projects, including the secret nighttime drives to Canton, to learn what they could about the summer plans. The rumor had it that a thousand volunteers would be coming to Mississippi. The prospect was reassuring, since it seemed an army was required to combat the combined forces of segregation. The summer volunteers, mostly students, came to Mississippi after the two-week training period at Western College for Women in Ohio, where they learned the philosophy and techniques of nonviolent direct action from experienced workers like Schwerner, and even Chaney, a relative newcomer.

Two Sundays after the May 31 meeting to approve the Freedom School, the Reverend Frank Jordan, the circuit pastor for Mt. Zion, took his turn leading the worship services. With four Methodist churches on his circuit, Jordan had to limit his time at Mt. Zion to alternate Sundays. Typically, at the end of a church service, he left Mt. Zion quickly to get to his next assignment, so he was not on the scene the day of the congregational vote on the Freedom School. He surely knew of the major decision the church members had made. As they often reminded him, it was their church more than his, and they would still be there long after he had gone. The vote to participate in the Summer Project had been their choice.

The Conspiracy Begins to Unfold

Mt. Zion's minister was usually paid his honorarium in the week following his sermon at the church. The church prided itself on staying current with all its expenses, assessments, and bills. On occasion a second Sunday collection was taken to ensure sufficient funds were at hand. On Tuesday evening after the Reverend Jordan's earlier Sunday appearance at the church, the finance committee typically gathered at Mt. Zion to look over its budget and count the money in the small treasury. It was the usual group that came together to conduct a routine business that Tuesday night, June 16, 1964, eight adults and two children. Both adult Steeles were present, Cornelius and his wife, Mabel, and their children; the Coles, Bud and Beddie; the Rushes, Georgia and son John; and two friends of the Steeles, Jim Cole, and T. J. Miller. Of the group, it was Cornelius Steele and Beddie Cole who were most involved with the movement and in touch with COFO activities.

When the finance committee meeting ended, the members left the church in opposite directions around the circular driveway; the Coles and the Rushes headed one way on the driveway, and the Steeles and their friends the other. Someone had forgotten to turn off a light at the church, so Mabel Steele sent her young son John back to turn it off. But in a blinding flash, the group realized it was being confronted by a mob of white men, some hooded, some not, all of them well armed.[16] The attackers had flashlights they shone on the church people, and with the blinding lights, the surrounding darkness, and the group's robes, the people leaving the church could not be certain who their attackers were. But Neshoba County was a small place, and people of both races encountered each other on many occasions. Despite the flashlights and the robes, Mabel Steele was fairly certain she recognized local law enforcement officers among the group waiting to grab them.[17]

Cornelius Steele was in the first group to leave the church, and the first to be stopped. He was ordered to turn off his car engine, as the mob began to assault the rest of the church people. An unseen interrogator reportedly said they were looking for the "white boys," and when Steele told him there were no whites present, he was warned to keep his distance from them or else "we can't help you."[18] Fifty-eight-year-old Bud Cole, on the other side of the driveway, later said he was asked much the same question, and when he replied they had no white guards, he was slammed on the back with what he said was a "heavy instrument," knocked to the ground, and kicked by his attackers until he lost consciousness. Then some in the group turned on Cole's wife and asked what she had in her purse. She was convinced, she said later, that they were trying to beat her husband to death. She told them her purse contained only Sunday school literature, though she worried that some of her COFO material might be in it. As one of the men raised an arm to hit her, she asked if she might say a prayer, and the attacker, a policeman, allowed it. Her prayer that night has become a notable part of the record of the event. On her knees, she said she prayed, "Father, I stretch out my hand to thee, no other help I know, if thou withdraw thyself from me, O Lord wither shall I go."[19] The attackers then beat the Rushes along with the Coles. Two shots were heard in the distance. Either Beddie Cole's prayer was answered, or the shots in the night were a warning to the mob that someone was coming. The assailants fled, and with Bud Cole seriously injured, the Mt. Zion people got in their vehicles and headed home.

Sometime after arriving at their homes, the residents reported hearing a car speeding along Church Road. Then they saw the night sky lit by fire, and when they looked out they saw their beloved Mt. Zion Church burning to the ground. No one from Mt. Zion reported the event to the police, but when reporters eventually came by, the people who had been attacked told their stories.[20]

Working Together: COFO and Mt. Zion

At the time of the attack, the organizers of the Freedom School at Mt. Zion, the Schwerners, James Chaney, and David Dennis, were out of the state, the Schwerners and Chaney in Ohio preparing for the Summer Project, Dennis in Louisiana. All the participants in the Ohio sessions were told about life in Mississippi and the rigors of the civil rights work there. They did role playing, and engaged in mock confrontations with rabid segregationists. After the young people listened to these mostly informational talks, they were called to an elevated level of attention by Robert Moses and others who said there was a real possibility some of them could be killed.[21] John Doar of the Justice Department reminded them it was not the federal government's responsibility to protect them in the work they were taking on. Jail, beatings, death, were all possibilities, speakers said, but only a handful of volunteers found the warning a reason to leave. Black Mississippi attorney R. Jess Brown gave the mostly white audience practical advice about life in his home state, where he said there were only two racist classifications, "Niggers and nigger-lovers. And they're tougher on nigger-lovers."[22] Bob Moses and others involved in the summer project understood that white casualties would generate national media and political attention.

During their time in Oxford, Schwerner and Chaney met a young volunteer who seemed right for their team in Meridian, perhaps even for leading the Freedom School at Mt. Zion. The young man was Andrew Goodman. Like the Schwerners, Goodman was from New York, and like Rita he was a student at Queens College. He was just twenty, had attended very progressive New York schools, had participated in demonstrations, and like the others, had a passion for social justice and change. During his time in Oxford he had entered—enthusiastically, it was said later—in the training sessions that week.[23] He was initially assigned to Vicksburg, but at Mickey Schwerner's request, he decided on Meridian. All the volunteers on the Oxford campus heard Bob Moses solemn warning; "Don't come to Mississippi this summer to save the Mississippi Negro. Only come if you understand, really understand, that his freedom and yours are one."[24] It had the ring of a moral crusade for an inclusive society. It was not long after their arrival that Mickey got word of the disaster at Mt. Zion, and with

James Chaney, Andy Goodman, and a few Meridian colleagues, they drove back to Meridian on Saturday morning. Rita Schwerner remained behind with the program in Oxford.

The Klan Conspiracy

When Bud Cole was asked why he hadn't reported the fire at the church and the assault on him and the other members—and he was often asked—his reply was always the same: why would I? Who would I report it to? The police were involved. He had been the one who suffered the most severe beating in the attack, left with injuries that would last his lifetime, making it impossible for him to walk again unaided. But word of what had happened leaked out gradually over the next days and weeks. A cover-up was already taking place after the fire.[25] The Klan had devised a plan to kill Schwerner, ending the possibility of a Freedom School at Mt. Zion. Because the events of that night were never officially investigated, what is known about them comes from a variety of sources: the memory of victims, from other residents of Longdale, from white Philadelphians like Florence Mars, and from participants-turned-FBI informers at the trial of other members of the Klan attack. The evidence is not precise, but there is a sameness about the core elements in the event. The FBI file for Mississippi Burning—labeled the MIBURN files—holds some information about the Mt. Zion beatings and church burning, but because the files are heavily redacted they are only minimally useful. In fact, over fifty black churches were burned that summer.

Evidence gathered from among these sources name Preacher Edgar Ray Killen as the local Klan organizer who presided over a meeting of the combined Neshoba and Lauderdale Klans in the old Bloomo School the night of the attack. Witnesses at trials for those accused in the attacks, trials that were held in 1967 and 2005, said there were about seventy-five to eighty Klansmen present, most of them from Neshoba and representing nearly the whole of the membership. Killen's conduct of the meeting, they said, was interrupted by former sheriff "Hop" Barnett, who said that on the way to the gym he noticed "heavily guarded" activity at Mt. Zion Church. He was contributing to the steady Klan surveillance of the church.[26]

Barnett's announcement convinced the Klansmen that Michael Schwerner, at the center of their conspiracy, was at the church. Killen called for volunteers to go investigate.[27] Heavily armed, a group of Klansmen left for Mt. Zion. About an hour later they reportedly returned, with Wayne Roberts, an ex-Marine among them, proudly displaying a bloody fist that he said he acquired when beating up some of the black Methodists outside their church. Roberts boasted that they "were well beaten and well stomped, except for one old negro woman," who was in fact Beatrice Cole, the wife of Bud Cole.[28] The Klansmen learned that neither Schwerner nor any other whites were at the meeting. The group acted with the complicity of local law enforcement, notably the sheriff and his deputy, identified by some of the Mt. Zion people.

According to later trial testimonies about the crime, most of the Klansmen returned to the Bloomo School after the assault to give their report, with Billy Birdsong of the Lauderdale Klan complaining that the Neshoba men had not done their full share of beating. What happened next can only be surmised. According to some accounts, a few Klansmen either remained in Longdale or drove back later, and after a few drinks—in "dry" Neshoba County—decided the surest way to capture Mickey Schwerner was to burn the church he was planning to use as a Freedom School. Forced to search for a can of gasoline, they spread it around the building, and sometime between 10 p.m. and 1 a.m. set the church ablaze.[29] Although no one was ever named as the person who burned the church, the burning fit easily into the larger Klan conspiracy to kill Schwerner and end the Freedom School.

Reports of the beatings and burning slowly dribbled to outside sources, but the members of the Mt. Zion community understood the dimensions of the tragedy; this was not a time to be hopeful. Their church had been destroyed, members of the congregation had been attacked, and the loss of community independence was equally lamentable. Longdale had been invaded. They knew it was futile, as Bud Cole had said, to report the events to local law enforcement, since not only would there be no investigation, there quite likely could be retaliation for even suggesting whites were involved. There was an FBI agent in Jackson, but even had the Bureau taken an interest in the crime, it might well be the case that the agent was a white Southerner with very little interest in an attack on a small black community.[30] With no one to whom they could report the attack, there seemed no possibility of any justice forthcoming.[31] Longdale residents cared for their injured, and made plans to hold a church service on Sunday in the smoldering ruins of Mt. Zion Church. White Neshobans paid little attention, except to regard it as a sign of a troubled summer ahead.

Killing the Dreamers

On July 19, 1964, a federal civil rights bill finally passed the Senate, due to President Kennedy's work on the measure the year before, and then to the jawboning efforts of his successor, President Lyndon Johnson. Given the heated state of affairs at the time, the response to the bill was predictable. Southerners opposed the measure, 54 to 46 percent. Mississippi was even more fervently opposed: there, 96.4 percent of white voters opposed the new Civil Rights Bill.[32]

It was while this groundbreaking legislation was still working its way through Congress that Mickey Schwerner and the others in Oxford, Ohio, learned that the site of their voting rights project had been destroyed. Perhaps all of them, but particularly Mickey, felt culpable given the turn of events, because it had been he and Dennis and Chaney who had persuaded Mt. Zion's congregation to sponsor the school. If Bud Cole felt vindicated because of his concerns, he never let on; years later, former deputy sheriff Cecil Price, presumably a "changed man" after years in prison, approached Cole and asked if he could forgive and forget, to which Cole responded "I forgave you long ago."[33]

Once back from Ohio, Andrew Goodman, new to Mississippi, sent a postcard to his parents which was destined to become a treasured document. He wrote: "PM June 21 1964 Meridian, Miss. I have arrived safely in Meridian, Mississippi. This is a wonderful town and the weather is fine. I wish you were here. The people in this city are wonderful and our reception was very good. All my love, Andy."[34] The reception had been with newfound friends in the black community in Meridian. The card arrived at his parents' home on June 24, after the Goodmans had met with President Johnson to learn that the Ford station wagon that had carried their son to Mississippi had been found, abandoned and burned. News of the group's return to Mississippi had preceded them via messages sent by an "Agent X," appointed by the Sovereignty Commission to infiltrate the meetings in Oxford and keep Schwerner and Chaney under surveillance.[35]

The day Goodman sent his family the postcard, his first real day in Mississippi, was a Sunday and it was Father's Day. Since he had been lined up to run the voter registration project at Mt. Zion Church, he went with Schwerner and Chaney to Longdale to check the damage to the church and its members and to offer comfort to the residents. Even for Mississippi it was a tense time. News of the impending passage of the Civil Rights bill, combined with preparations for the start of Freedom Summer, had

increased segregationist agitation. It was a hazardous time for an interracial group to travel through the rural countryside to Longdale. When Sue
Brown of the Meridian COFO office was later asked why the men had not
postponed their trip until a calmer time, she said, "Our work was NOW.
Freedom NOW."[36] The three men set out for Longdale up Highway 19 with
Chaney at the wheel of the station wagon, all of them promising to be back
by four in the afternoon.

They would never return.

Once in Longdale, they visited with Ernest Kirkland, a young man
involved in planning for the Freedom School. They met in the afternoon
about one, and after talking with Kirkland they went to comfort those hurt in
the Klan attack.[37] No one in Longdale expressed any doubts that was a Klan
operation, meant to prevent the voting rights project from going ahead. The
victims also had picked up from the attackers the information that the Klan
was looking specifically for Schwerner; in Klan literature he was referred to
as a "commie," a "mixer," a "Jew boy," and someone who wanted to change
the fundamentals of their lives through the black voting project.[38]

The three men visited with Cornelius Steele to get his version of the
event, but he had nothing new to add. Kirkland remembered they stopped
by to see J. R. Cole and George Lewis, and looked unsuccessfully for
Georgia Rush, who was away. In the small, sun-baked houses they visited,
they were offered hospitality by the saddened members of Mt. Zion, who
spoke of their heartbreak at the destruction of their church and their loss
of a sense of autonomy; despite all their safeguards, they had proven vulnerable to a Klan attack and could be again. Then the three went to look at
the remnants of Mt. Zion, its ashes still giving off smoke five days after it
was torched.[39] Finally it was time to leave.

They headed back to Meridian taking a longer route along Highway
16, which required them to cross the city of Philadelphia.[40] Chaney was
again the driver, and if he had been speeding, he slowed down—too late
as it turned out—when he recognized a highway patrol car on the side
of the road.[41] Local law enforcement had secretly received word from
an unknown informant that the men had been at Longdale, news possibly passed on by someone who had seen them at the ruins of Mt. Zion.
Deputy Sheriff Cecil Price on patrol recognized CORE's blue Ford station
wagon and gave chase. By the time he stopped them, they were at the
side of the road in front of First Methodist Church with a flat tire. It must
have seemed to them the worst of bad luck to have their tire go flat with
a Mississippi sheriff in pursuit in the hostile environment of Neshoba

County. Keeping the car in good repair was a priority for CORE, and the Ford had had two new tires installed only two months earlier.[42]

Deputy Price arrested the three; Chaney for speeding, Goodman and Schwerner for "investigation." The Klan had been searching for Schwerner for at least a month, and now it had him. A carefully developed conspiracy that had been weeks, if not months, in the planning, might now achieve its objective. At first Price was unsure of his captives; he initially described one—likely Chaney—as George Raymond, a well-known and assertive black activist, but he quickly realized he had found the real treasure when he recognized Schwerner.

Under police custody, the three men were segregated, as Neshoba custom required. Patrolman Wiggs of Philadelphia put Chaney in his police car and took him to the jail. Another highway patrolman, Earl Poe, testified later that he took Schwerner and Goodman to jail in his patrol car.[43] Poe recalled that as Schwerner got into the back seat, he noticed Poe's gun resting there, and Schwerner handed it to him: said Poe, "I guess that's the first time a prisoner ever handed me my own gun."[44] Schwerner might not have considered himself a "prisoner" at that moment—he was arrested for "investigation"—but the arresting officers, especially Price, knew that he was a marked man, and that Chaney, a black man, would likely receive a different treatment from the others.

A momentous chain of events in American history began to play out. The participants—the policemen, and the young activists—brought very different histories and values to the event. It apparently did not occur to Schwerner to hold on to the gun as he sat in the back of the patrol car; he was a nonviolent man, and no one would use a gun against him because he was trying to help people to vote. What was his crime? From what he knew of Southern history, it could be for riding in a car with a black man, or for visiting the black community of Longdale. But in his tradition—and was it not universal?—those were not "crimes" that would call for the use of a gun. But Price, and perhaps Poe and Wiggs as well, knew that Schwerner would not see the next morning's light, and likely neither would Chaney and Goodman. Considered outsiders, though Chaney was actually from nearby Meridian, they were identified as troublers of local tradition and the "Southern way of life."

The men were taken to the Philadelphia jail where they were booked by jailer Minnie Herring, who listed them all as "Negroes," and put them in separate cells: Goodman and Schwerner in one, Chaney in another. No speeding ticket was issued; speeding did not typically call for jail time.

Poe and Wiggs told their supervisor, Inspector Maynard King—later remembered as an FBI informant—of the arrests, although many people who saw them trying to change their flat tire already knew they were in jail. They were arrested at about 4:20 in the afternoon, well past their scheduled time to be back in Meridian. Nervous co-workers in Meridian eventually started making phone calls to locate them, and were told by the Neshoba jailer that they were not in her jail. At the same time, the well-rehearsed Klan conspiracy was put into play. As part of that plan, Goodman, Chaney, and Schwerner were released from the jail around 10:30 at night into an environment dark and hostile.

It was while the motorcade of Klansmen headed back to Philadelphia that Killen explained for the first time that he had arranged for a bulldozer to cover the bodies of the three jailed men. This was apparently the first indication that the Klansmen were not to beat up the three, but kill them, although talk of "eliminating" "Goatee" had circulated at Klan meetings since early May.[45] If anything were to go wrong with the plan, Killen imagined he would be the first one questioned, so he arranged an alibi. According to trial testimony, after the three civil rights workers left the jail, Killen was dropped off at a funeral home to pay his respects, creating what he believed was the perfect alibi, in the unlikely case he should ever need one. But he and his fellow Klansmen were confident they were safe, since every white person in town was assumed to be a segregationist and therefore opposed to Mt. Zion's Freedom School. They would never need an alibi.

They could count on the cooperation of local law enforcement who, according to trial witnesses, were complicit in the conspiracy. Deputy Sheriff Cecil Price was the most active participant, chasing down the three men, taking them off to jail, and then pulling them over after they had been released. Sheriff Lawrence Rainey would also be charged with being part of the conspiracy, but since he was able to place his whereabouts the night of the murders at his wife's bedside in a Meridian hospital, he was acquitted at trial. Nevertheless, the success of the conspiracy depended on the cooperation of local lawmen. Hop Barnett, the former sheriff, had been at the courthouse to welcome the Meridian Klansmen as Killen gave them their instructions for the night's work.

In 2005, at the trial for the chief conspirator of the 1964 events, Edgar Ray Killen, witness testimony revealed the extent of the plans the Klansmen had arranged to get rid of Schwerner and the others. Witnesses told of a conspiracy, rooted in a desire to protect the "Southern way of life," to close down a school for black voters and those who were planning it. Killen was named the chief conspirator, who thought there would be negligible costs to the perpetrators for the crime. Witnesses commented on the swiftness with which Killen put his plan into operation while the three men were in jail on trumped-up charges. He drove from his home near Philadelphia to Meridian to line up volunteers willing to beat up the three—or "tear up their butts"—after they were released. Killen's description had made it clear that the plan involved violent action, yet ten men had responded to his call for help, leaving their ordinary lives and Father's Day celebrations behind to join in the attack.[46] Before they left Meridian, Killen had told them to get special gloves from the hardware store.

The three men were released from the jail late at night. They went straight to their car without stopping at the neighboring Benwalt Hotel to phone their COFO colleagues to tell them their whereabouts. At that moment, immediate escape from Neshoba probably seemed the safest plan, and so with Chaney driving, they headed south on Highway 19 back to Meridian. About nine miles outside of Philadelphia, Deputy Price once again pursued them, and when the flashing red light of the police car went on, Chaney decided to pull over rather than attempt flight.

Reportedly a small convoy of cars—at least three—soon appeared outside a local grocery, where Price and the other conspirators shared last-minute details. Price loaded the three men into the back of the police car and headed back toward Philadelphia, followed by the others, until they reached Rock Cut Road, "a graded clay road," where the cars turned off the highway into the blackness of the countryside and stopped.

After the Klansmen were gathered at the roadside, the rest of the conspiracy played out. Schwerner, according to all witness testimony, was the first of the three to be yanked from the police car, his killer the burly Wayne Roberts. His final comment, made to Roberts, was "I know just how you feel, sir," words even Killen remembered. He was shot in the heart at point blank range. Goodman was the next person pulled from the car and was also shot at close range, in the abdomen. Chaney was the last to be taken from the car, and he attempted to run, but was felled by three shots and died with the other two. A privately ordered autopsy, unlike the official state one, claimed that Chaney had been badly beaten before being shot, although another report from the FBI said that the severe damage found on his body could have been caused by the bulldozer when the bodies were covered up.[47]

James Jordan, one of the participants who later turned witness for the state, named those present that night as Deputy Sheriff Price, Wayne

Roberts, himself, and six others: Travis and Horace Doyle Barnette (some-times spelled Barnett), Jimmy Snowden, Jimmy Arledge, Billy Wayne Posey, and Jerry McGrew Sharpe. Killen was not named.[48] When Doyle Barnette later admitted his part in the killings, he gave essentially the same account as Jordan, although he made Jordan a more active partici-pant than Jordan had claimed for himself.[49] Jordan and Barnette were both from the Lauderdale Klan, and according to FBI Agent Joseph Sullivan, the officer eventually placed in charge of the investigation, if the "Neshoba Klavern carried out the murders on their own, they would also certainly have gotten away with it."[50] Sullivan was convinced that no white person in Neshoba County would have ever given up evidence about the conspir-acy. The Klan operated in a culture of impunity.

After the men were killed, the remainder of the plan unfolded much as it had been conceived. The bodies were loaded into the back of their Ford station wagon and the caravan traveled to a remote construction site where a dam was in the process of being built. The dam site was huge and empty of water, and the three bodies were placed at the bottom—or at least fifteen feet down, according to testimony—and when a bulldozer arrived nearly on schedule, the bodies seemed permanently covered. Olen Burrage, a wealthy landowner who had arranged for building the dam on his property, now allowed it to be turned into a cemetery.[51] The conspira-tors were certain that the dam would forever cover their crimes, and their neighbors would forever keep their secrets.

Other men died in the tumult that was Mississippi in the sixties. The remains of Charles Moore and Henry Dee, also killed by the Klan, were uncovered during the search for the bodies of the three.[52] None of the other deaths involved such an elaborate conspiracy, nor did they involve the killing of white men. The deaths of the Neshoba Three—the audac-ity of the killings and the extent of the cover-up—revealed the extent of cultural support for the segregationist network, its reach and its certainty of white community cooperation. At the time it seemed an audacious response to the moral crusade for an inclusive society.

FIGURE 1 Road sign entering Neshoba County, one of 82 counties in the state

FIGURE 2 New highway memorial sign for the three murdered men; it, too, has been vandalized

FIGURE 3 Timber-lined road into Longdale

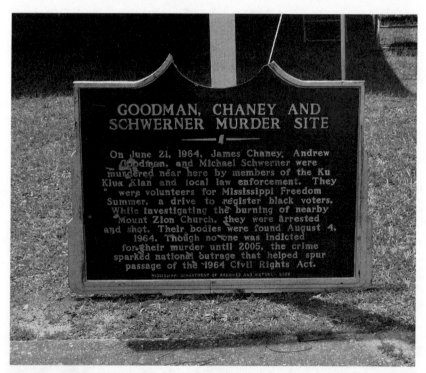

GOODMAN, CHANEY AND
SCHWERNER MURDER SITE

On June 21, 1964, James Chaney, Andrew
Goodman, and Michael Schwerner were
murdered near here by members of the Ku
Klux Klan and local law enforcement. They
were volunteers for Mississippi Freedom
Summer, a drive to register black voters.
While investigating the burning of nearby
Mount Zion Church, they were arrested
and shot. Their bodies were found August 4,
1964. Though no one was indicted
for their murder until 2005, the crime
sparked national outrage that helped spur
passage of the 1964 Civil Rights Act.

MISSISSIPPI DEPARTMENT OF ARCHIVES AND HISTORY, 2006

FIGURE 4 Defaced memorial sign for Goodman, Chaney, and Schwerner in front of Mt. Zion Church

FIGURE 5 Mural in downtown Philadelphia celebrating the Neshoba County Fair and the Choctaw Fair

FIGURE 6 Obbie Riley, Neshoba County district supervisor and lay leader at Mt. Zion Church

FIGURE 7 Arecia Steele, long-time member of Mt. Zion Church

FIGURE 8 Freddie Grady and Jennifer Riley Hathorn, descendants of early settlers and members of Mt. Zion Church

FIGURE 9 Sign at the entry to Church Road pointing to the church

FIGURE 10 Jewel McDonald, member of Mt. Zion Church, the Philadelphia Coalition, community activist, and relative of family members assaulted by the Klan the night of the church burning

FIGURE 11 Leroy Clemons, President of Neshoba area NAACP, community activist, participant in efforts promoting racial reconciliation

FIGURE 12 Stanley Dearman, former editor of *The Neshoba Democrat,* member of Philadelphia Coalition

FIGURE 13 James Young, two-term mayor of Philadelphia

FIGURE 14 Dick Molpus, former Mississippi secretary of state, and one-time gubernatorial candidate

FIGURE 15 Dick Molpus and author

FIGURE 16 Rebuilt Mt. Zion United Methodist Church

FIGURE 17 Cemetery adjacent to Mt. Zion Church. At the fiftieth anniversary ceremony Dick Molpus said that if ever a person found their spirits flagging they should walk around this cemetery and they would be revived

FIGURE 18 Jerry Mitchell, investigative reporter for Jackson Clarion-Ledger

Source: Dave Anderson

PART THREE

Mt. Zion's Witness

Creating Memories

9

Morality and Memory in Neshoba in the Sixties

But I say to you, the citizens of Neshoba County are no more responsible for these deaths than were the citizens of the City of Dallas, Texas were [sic] responsible for the death of the late president.

"DISTRICT" JUDGE O. H. BARNETT, *NESHOBA DEMOCRAT*, FEBRUARY 4, 1965

This case was the high water mark of armed resistance to integration. It was terrible. But it took something like this to stop it.

STANLEY DEARMAN, FORMER EDITOR, *NESHOBA DEMOCRAT*, INTERVIEW, MAY 14, 2002

An essential characteristic of collective memory is the cultural authority attached to it.

W. FITZHUGH BRUNDAGE, *WHERE THESE MEMORIES GROW*

Making Memories

"Never, never, never I say, cuz the Ku Klux Klan is here to stay." These words from a peppy little ditty popular in the South during the 1960s affirm an explicit commitment to segregation, while also implicitly endorsing Southern tradition and old values. Because their past held so much that was idealized, white Neshobans could hardly conceive of exchanging it for a discordant future. Yet during the 1960s, Neshoba's defenders of tradition were under pressure from messengers of change who challenged the old memories and even questioned the moral values associated with them.

White Mississippi Methodists claimed their place on the side of Southern traditions. On the national level, the Methodist denomination, by contrast, recommitted in 1968 to the values of an inclusive society, which strained the ties with its Mississippi constituency. In Neshoba County the contest between tradition and change can be seen in the two community celebrations held each summer since 1965. The first one is the grand and historic Neshoba County Fair that since 1889 has gathered large crowds of almost exclusively white celebrants; and the other is the Mt. Zion Church commemorative service of remembrance, begun in 1965 for the martyred civil rights workers and their mission that attracts a majority-black assembly. (There is also a third festival, the Choctaw Fair that brings together mostly Choctaw participants.) The two are actually both commemorative ceremonies, the first of the traditions of the white Old South, and the second a witness to the local black experience, including the cost of the denial of justice, and the need for recommitment to work still undone.

The nation first encountered the determination of white Neshobans to hold on to their collective past during the ongoing media coverage of the search for the bodies of the slain civil rights workers. The white community threw up borders around itself as protection against the intrusion of "outsiders"; media representatives, FBI agents, and 400 sailors dispatched by the president. They presented a silent front to these visitors, except to acknowledge that they had no knowledge of the dark events of the recent past. "How was it possible that no one in this small community knew anything about this brutal affair in which so many people were obviously involved?" was the question FBI agents repeatedly asked. White residents of Philadelphia showed little sympathy for the murdered men, who were regarded as intruders bent on a mission to change age-old customs.

It was inevitable that the two communities of white Neshoba and black Longdale would regard the events of Freedom Summer differently. Mt. Zion mourned the murdered men even as it looked for public ways to honor them as well as their mission. White Neshoba, believing it was challenged by black assertiveness and government mandates, responded to the new demands with "strategic accommodations" that required only minimal, largely cosmetic, alteration to existing social norms. Its major strategy was simply to ignore the "outsiders," to assume a collective silence, and deny any association with the murders or those who carried them out. The culture of impunity allowed law enforcement to act on behalf of the white community, and to defend its claims against involvement with the recent calamitous events.

Even before the discovery of the bodies of the three men, most residents of black Longdale, long experienced in the ways of the local sheriff and police, had feared Goodman, Chaney, and Schwerner were dead. Neshoba County was known as an unforgiving place for civil rights workers, and movement activists knew almost instinctively that the three had been murdered. CORE's David Dennis was certain of the outcome from the moment they failed to show up on time in Meridian; he remembered later, "I had no doubt they were dead."[1] His original plan had been to go with them to Longdale, but because he got sick he went instead to his mother's home in Shreveport, thus adding self-recrimination to feelings of anger and grief. He was painfully aware that he had been the one to introduce the men to the voter registration project. Years later he wondered if his more extensive experience working in the South might have led him to make different, safer choices than they had.[2] CORE's national director, James Farmer, acknowledged his agreement with Dennis and the Longdale people when he told the press gathered in Neshoba, "I think there's almost no hope that they are alive."[3]

According to records from the trials of the participants in 1967 and 2005, the Klansmen were confident they had executed the perfect crime and could count on community support to keep the conspiracy quiet. Mike Hatcher, a former Meridian policeman, said at the subsequent trial of the Klansmen that as early as the day after the men disappeared, an eager Edgar Ray Killen had come up to him at work to say, "We got rid of the civil rights workers," and he confirmed that Schwerner's last words to his assassin were, "I understand just how you feel, sir."[4]

It was not long after the murders, however, that Mt. Zion people decided it was not helpful to dwell on what had been lost or capitulate to Klan terror. Instead they would create positive meaning out of what were certainly disastrous events. The beginnings of plans for a commemorative service slowly filtered through the congregation, until by the following spring they had evolved into an announcement for a public remembrance event to which the Reverend Martin Luther King would be invited. For the church planners it was important to commemorate all that had happened—the burning, the beatings, and especially the murders—through a memorial service to be held annually at Mt. Zion Church on the date closest to the killings, or Father's Day. The men were martyrs, the Longdale people believed, killed for a cause they all shared. Since memorializing martyrs is never limited to a single ceremony, neither would the celebration at Longdale be a one-time event, but continue as long as there were people willing to recall their lives and beliefs.

An annual memorial service was also an opportunity for Mt. Zion members to create a "usable past," one shaped by their own recall of the past and not handed down from regional Southern versions of how things were. Mt. Zion could, and did, choose to integrate their remembrance by inviting whites as well as blacks, and created an agenda that corresponded to their own needs and values. Typically only community elites organized such services of remembering or forgetting, making them the sole producers of the history of record. In this case black residents of Longdale would decide what would be remembered. Black memory until the sixties had been a private and internal affair, "whereas white memory had been both public and [presumably] universal."[5]

The memorial service was meant to be a reminder of not only the men but also of the values they represented: equal justice, schooling for everyone, and the goal they had set for the Freedom School, namely voting. Over the years, the annual event became a form of public history, a means of allowing a small black community like Longdale to get its message out. As W. Fitzhugh Brundage has noted, "No black community ... [has been] too small to nourish an ambitious commemorative tradition."[6] These ceremonies, usually Janus-faced, tended to look toward the past with its sufferings and loss, but also to contemplate a future that held new promise for those willing to work for it. Mt. Zion's services not only remembered the unnecessary loss of three young lives, but served as a reminder to all of the community and those in attendance of the continuing injustices visited on the black community. Within a few years the memorial service grew into an event with regional, occasionally national, interest that drew a substantial number of representatives from the media. Neshoba County's white community never created anything comparable to commemorate what happened at midnight in the woods outside Philadelphia.

White memory of what happened, in fact, was a study in contrast. Its memory was enshrouded in silence and denial; white Neshobans could not honor Goodman, Chaney, and Schwerner because to do so would elevate the cause they represented. As ever in the history of martyrdom, there are the victims, and then there is the passion associated with their witness, the cause for which they died. Mt. Zion honored both the messengers and the message while white Neshoba maintained stony silence regarding both for forty years.

From the very beginning, white residents denied that the events—the killings of outsiders and the firebombing of the church—had any major significance. Florence Mars said that her neighbors were convinced it was all a hoax contrived by the activists themselves.[7] Mississippi's Senator James Eastland said essentially that to President Johnson on June 23 when Johnson informed him of the disappearance of the men: "I don't believe there's three missing. . . . I believe it's a publicity stunt," said Eastland.[8] When Johnson phoned him back to say the burned-out Ford Fairlane belonging to CORE had been found, Eastland still insisted that in Mississippi in 1964, "There's no violence or no friction of any kind." The kind of cultural memory that had shaped his life allowed him to reject even physical evidence that contradicted his beliefs.[9] The hoax story filtered as fact through the white community until ultimately the bodies were discovered and the myth lost currency. Local whites were anxious to have the tumult of the recent past behind them, and the recovery of the bodies forced them to acknowledge it again. The only acceptable response was to close themselves off entirely to the outsiders investigating the case. Some said there was a whispered rumor that since the activists were intruders in east central Mississippi, they might just have got what was coming to them.

The Forty-Four Days

With no cooperation from the local white community, it took forty-four days to find the bodies of the murdered men, a search that prefigured the history of the next dozen years and more. Collective silence was at the core of the community's resistance, considered the best defense against intruders looking for answers. The Klansmen had placed the bodies in a place so unlikely, so inaccessible, that they believed the men would never be found, and with no bodies there could be no case. The anxiety that pervaded white Neshoba was likely behind the whispered memory that "it is not a crime to kill a nigger" or those who consort with them. The deaths of the three quickly assumed political as well as racial overtones, and cast into the public limelight the talkative Baptist preacher Edgar Ray Killen, a boastful man familiar to most Neshobans. As early as the day after the murders he was telling friends about the seemingly successful conspiracy. He could confidently assume that his listeners agreed with him that it was good the troublemakers were gone, and some nameless someones had seen to the task.

There had been many people privy to the plans to kill Schwerner. There were the eighty men present at the Klan meeting at Bloomo School the night Mt. Zion burned to the ground and marauding Klansmen searched for Schwerner. Some of those at the school surely shared the plans for the conspiracy with their family and friends. Those white Neshobans who were party to the plans and their consequences shunned the media as well as the FBI agents working on the case.

The hoax story was still current even as President Johnson ordered 400 sailors to the area to search for the bodies. What was now a crisis in Mississippi was the first domestic emergency of Johnson's administration, and given the extent of media attention it attracted, the unsolved murders appeared to be turning into a national disaster. Johnson's plan was to be nominated handily at the Democratic convention in August and then coast to victory in November. His phone records show that by the end of June he became heavily invested in events in Neshoba, whether because of a desperate political need to put this behind him or because of a personal conviction about bringing justice in a high-profile civil rights case. He directed J. Edgar Hoover—not known as a friend to civil rights activists—to concentrate the resources of the FBI on a search for the bodies.

The involvement of Hoover's office in the search eventually required calling up its questionable "Top Echelon" program, a closely guarded secret resource that had been in existence for some time. The "Top Echelon" branch relied on hardened criminals to provide information about organized crime figures or groups like the Klan or the Mafia in exchange for the bureau's turning a blind eye on their deeds.[10] The bureau worked quietly with criminal informants, using methods that, if known, could raise questions about FBI conduct and the fact that perhaps the president and the bureau chief were engaged in the case. It also emphasized the difficulty of penetrating the community code of silence. In the early days of the search, before agents confronted the wall of white silence, the bureau had relied on traditional measures, offering rewards for information leading to the discovery of the bodies; first $10,000, then $25,000, and then reportedly $30,000. But these well-tried techniques produced no results; no leads to the bodies. Agents combed neighborhoods, promising immunity as well as reward money, and came up with nothing.

Then on August 4, forty-four days after the men went missing, on the Old Jolly Farm owned by Olen Burrage, the exhaustive search came to an end. Bureau agents moved a dragline on to Burrage's property and within a few hours first the stench of rotting flesh and then the bodies themselves gave notice that the three men had been found.[11] Locals were stunned that the agents had accomplished such a thing. At the burial site, Agent Jay Cochrane and his bureau colleagues had moved with a purposefulness and certainty that was breathtaking. On that vast stretch of earth that was the dam, how did they know just where to place the dragline, where to search, how deep to dig? After forty-four days of fruitless looking, they had found the precise spot they were seeking. Joe Sullivan, the chief FBI inspector on the ground, was the only one apart from Hoover and a few close aides who knew exactly how the bureau had finally gotten the information about the exact location of the bodies. Without that help, the men would have remained missing, as so many other lynch victims had in the past. Sullivan and his bureau partners vowed that they would never tell who gave them the needed information. And they never did.[12]

Yet someone obviously did reveal where the bodies were buried, a secret Klan participants had been sworn to take to the grave with them. The likeliest clues about the discovery have filtered through the Neshoba County rumor mill, and from the person who has been most diligent in resolving cold civil rights cases, investigative journalist Jerry Mitchell of the Jackson *Clarion-Ledger*. After years of working on the case, beginning in 1989, Mitchell concluded that a local white Neshoban did offer up the information to the bureau, and that the bureau had indeed worked with Mafia members to solve civil rights cases, but not likely the one in Neshoba. There had been a "Top Echelon" connection, just not here.

Reporter Mitchell's inspiration for tackling the case, he once said, came from viewing the 1989 movie version of the bloody events in Neshoba, rightly named *Mississippi Burning* as fifty black churches burned that summer. Filmed in Neshoba twenty-five years after the murders occurred, the movie contributed a sensational new perspective on how the bodies might have been located, and provided new support for believing in the pervasive white conspiracy of silence. The *Mississippi Burning* movie depicted a man who was clearly a town leader being kidnapped by a thuggish-looking guy who took the captive to a shack, and there he brutalized him and threatened him with castration. The torture treatment is depicted as successful, with the hired gun getting the information he was sent to find, which he then shared with the FBI. The account aroused titillating speculation about what had been required to crack the case in the face of solid white resistance.

A Historical Mystery: The FBI and the
Mafia in Mississippi

The story regarding how the bodies were discovered—as told by film-makers, journalists, and historians—and what the FBI's role in it was, is a revealing sidebar to the main history of the civil rights struggle in Mississippi, and adds to the belief that extreme measures were considered necessary by everyone involved to penetrate the veil of white resistance. And in the mystery surrounding the search for the bodies, the mission of the three men—restoring the voting rights of the black residents of Mississippi—got lost. The FBI's inability to crack the case through conventional means left unanswered the question of how Agent Sullivan finally broke the case. There had to be an informant; the mystery for white Neshobans then became not who were the murderers, but who cooperated with the FBI.

The story of how the remains of the three men were found, while an interesting historical question, reveals both the significance of the case to the FBI and the solidarity of the white Neshoba community. It also shows President Johnson's intense concern with the case. As Agent Sullivan had noted, the bodies would never have been found if all the killers were from Neshoba. Finding the bodies ended the "hoax" story, and surely confounded Klansmen who were certain that, despite knowing moles had infiltrated their organization, no white person would ever disclose what had happened.[13]

Most in the public saw President Johnson's involvement with the case as connected to his political future, lauded by supporters, and dismissed as "politics as usual" by critics. When the Democratic National Convention convened on August 25, 1964, just three weeks after the bodies were discovered, issues of race and civil rights dominated the party agenda. The Mississippi Freedom Democratic Party (MFDP), newly organized around the principle of equal rights for all and numbering mostly blacks in its membership, planned to challenge the seating of the regular delegates from Mississippi. When Johnson got wind of their plans, he proposed an alternate idea to the MFDP delegates: they could have two at-large seats and the president's pledge that future conventions would not accept segregated delegations. MFDP representatives rejected his counteroffer, but the success of the bureau in finding the bodies still allowed the president to present himself as a friend of civil rights. Because of the passage of the Civil Rights Act that summer, outlawing segregation in public accommodations and employment, Johnson knew he would never get the votes of white Mississippi in any case; they would be lost to the Democratic Party for the foreseeable future. Johnson the Southerner, and Democrats as well, became the new "outsiders" to Mississippians.[14]

The seeming failure of a Johnson-Hoover alliance to persuade white Neshobans to cooperate in the search fueled the possibility that the FBI had in fact resorted to extraordinary methods. That potentiality prompted journalist Fredric Dannen to write, "The FBI resorted to extreme measures in its war on the Ku Klux Klan, and turned to informants in the Mafia and organized crime during the 1960s."[15] The record shows a marriage of con- venience between the FBI and the Mafia in the 1960s contracted to solve civil rights crimes, although there is no clarity about just what cases they worked on together. Dannen was not alone in claiming an FBI Mafia-Klan connection in the Neshoba case. When FBI Agent Anthony Villano wrote about contacts he had with crime figure "Julio," who he pictured as a likely Mafia hitman and also a federal informer, Gregory Scarpa. A member of the Colombo crime family, Scarpa was described as a gangster, racketeer, and a murderer—known to the bureau as "informant NY-3461," according to Dannen—who in 1964 had a mutually advantageous relationship with Villano.[16]

The Mafia's Scarpa appeared as a central figure in the government's deal- ings with Mississippi civil rights crimes. More details about his involvement with the FBI as an undercover operative surfaced after his 1994 death, when his long-time girlfriend, Linda Schiro, testified at the trial of an accused FBI agent, Lin DeVecchio, who was once a Scarpa handler. According to the testimony Schiro gave at the trial of the agent, she and Scarpa had traveled to Mississippi because Scarpa had agreed to get information for the bureau regarding the location of the bodies of the three men. She was clear that Scarpa's role had to do with the Neshoba case. (According to her account, which DeVecchio said he "did not believe," she and Scarpa flew to Mobile, after which Scarpa went on to Mississippi alone.[17])

Scholars detached from the case and presumably more objective still believe it possible that the bureau used the Mafia during the years of movement struggle. Historian Taylor Branch and legal scholar Howard Ball suspect that organized crime figures did play a role in the FBI's battle with the Klan, although precise evidence of the connection is not available in public records. Ball's thesis has Gregory Scarpa in Neshoba as a partici- pant in the bureau's plan to get information from a suspect, who was likely subjected to torture.[18] Branch explains that when Inspector Sullivan was called from the field in Neshoba, there were rumors at bureau headquarters of a "major break" in the case, including rumors of "raids to shove condom-wrapped shotgun shells into the rectums of hostile Klansmen."[19] At the time he wrote, Ball conceded that the identity of the person who passed on the information to the FBI "remains a mystery to this day."[20] The mystery could be solved if the FBI released the full MIBURN files, an improbable development. Inspector Sullivan and his close associates kept their promise to hide the identity of the informant, although after fifty years, that informer, is now likely dead.

A number of Neshoba residents, as well as Jerry Mitchell, have privately agreed for some time that one of Neshoba's own broke the white conspiracy of silence. Most evidence points to Mississippi Highway Patrolman Maynard King, who died in 1966, as another mysterious "Mr. X," who, after several late-night conversations with Inspector Sullivan, was stirred by conscience to reveal the location of the bodies. Since King himself had not been part of the Klan's inner circle, he had to have received the information he shared with Sullivan from a participant, who wanted a part of the reward money but not any notoriety. With King the most likely "Mr. X," his unnamed source who passed on the information is known only to any surviving participants and perhaps the FBI. Names of possible informants that have been tossed around include Klansman Pete Jordan, former Philadelphia Mayor Clayton Lewis, Sheriff Rainey, and bulldozer operator Herman Tucker.[21] Yet throughout the twentieth century white Neshobans refused to believe that one of their own would have led agents to the burial site. Except for Maynard King, whose actions seem prompted by a sense of duty and morality, money seems finally to have been the incentive to break with tradition and cooperate with the FBI.

The Neshoba County Fair: Cultural Symbol

Six days after the bodies were found and the Neshoba case was no longer headline news, the annual Neshoba County Fair opened on time as usual. The fair, an annual event held on the outskirts of Philadelphia, has been called by many the "Neshoba Metaphor," a visible symbol of all that is valued in local tradition. It has also been termed a Confederate reunion, a place where collective social memory is renewed and restored. At the fair the historical memory of the region's public life is annually reshaped for present relevance, endowing it with a power for the celebrants to remember their collective past.

The sociologist Emile Durkheim once referred to such events as "collective effervescence," a special time set aside for building ties of trust, and for collecting "tribal members . . . together for a period of ceremonies, dances, and festive meals" to feed collective memory.[22] In between these banner celebrations, he suggested, there are a variety of local rituals, songs, stories, even tales passed from parents to children, that fill the empty places between the commemorative occasions.[23] The Neshoba County Fair has a powerful hold on the memories of whites in the region for far more than its entertainment value: it is a time and place to rejuvenate emotional ties to values the celebrants hold dear, including segregation and states' rights autonomy along with good old-fashioned hospitality.

For many it is a unique celebration, surpassing even Christmas in its community significance. Until recently, apart from the murders, it was the only thing most people outside the region knew about the county. A repository of white collective memory, it connects the life of the area, and showcases white values. Understanding the place the fair holds in the life of the community helps explain the deep bond of loyalty that made possible the sustained conspiracy of silence, and Edgar Ray Killen's confidence that he could depend on community support.

The fair has been a museum for the preservation of Old South customs. Since 1954 and the *Brown* decision, blacks have rarely attended the fair except as workers, essentially boycotting it. In the twenty-first century, as a result of the 1965 Voting Rights Act, black political candidates seeking office have learned to take advantage of the political forum the fair affords all office seekers, and they too campaign there.

The Neshoba County Fair—or simply The Fair—advertises itself as "Mississippi's Giant Houseparty", while *Southern Living* magazine lauded it as "the sweet spot of all that is sacred in the South."[24] And despite the horrific events of the summer of 1964—or perhaps even more because of them—fairgoers came out in the same large crowds as before. Every year it is the signature county event. Businesses, excepting food services, close during fair time, and the fair has the reputation of being "*the* political forum for the state." It is the oldest campground fair in the country, and during eight days every summer is home to residents of 600 cabins, 200 RVs, and unknown thousands of daytrippers. Its appeal goes well beyond Neshoba County; many who once had ties to the area return to it from all around the world. Part camp meeting, part gambling hall and race track, part hospitality center, part political campaign, part fraternity, the fair is most of all a family reunion for a large extended family.

And quite a reunion it is. Mississippi native and long-time New Yorker Willie Morris was convinced that "there is no county fair in America quite like the Neshoba County Fair." The ability of fairgoers to celebrate in 1964 as if it was business as usual testified to his judgment.[25] For Florence Mars, the 1964 fair "'almost' seemed the same," although she suspected that with the "hoax" story demolished there was added tension in the air. Still, she gloried in memories of fairs past: "The most wonderful event in my life every year was the Neshoba County Fair, held in late summer."[26] Morris had the same feeling, despite the fact that the fair was held in the "hottest and rainiest part" of the summer; it remained he said, the "penultimate" Mississippi experience.[27] At the 1964 fair, a plane flew low over the crowd and dropped pamphlets from the White Knights of the Ku Klux Klan. The leaflets noted the group's good works, and the foolish assumption that the Klan had anything to do with the murders of the three men, whom they identified as "Communist Revolutionaries." The pamphlets directed readers to the Klan's Christian witness; "We are under oath to preserve Christian Civilization at all costs," it read.[28]

At the fair, white Neshobans were able to enjoy traditional foods and reminisce, but it was the hospitality and sociability they spoke most about. That is typical of what occurs at fairs nationwide according to those who have studied them, and who point out that fairgoers value most the opportunity for socializing and celebrating.[29] But the Neshoba County Fair stands out even among other state and county fairs for its emphasis on rekindling ties of family, friendship and tribal attachment, all vital to the preservation of regional traditions and Southern collective memory.

While there is a resemblance between the Neshoba County Fair and other fairs, what people note as different is the intense level of emotional investment participants bring to it, like a religious revival possessed of sacred meaning. As with an Ole Miss football game, the fair contributes to Mississippi's reputation as "The Hospitality State." Yet however great the pleasure the fair has provided participants, its ethnocentric folkways—which even some Neshobans call tribal ways—have troubled small numbers of residents of the area. A few especially observant white residents of the region began to understand the fair as the symbol of James Silver's "closed society" that it is.

To these white Neshobans, who enjoyed the "Giant Houseparty" quite as much as their neighbors, the fair helped perpetuate that very label concerned Mississippians were trying to get past; the inward, conspiratorial sense that at least since 1964 was associated with the area. In it own celebratory way, these observers said, the fair managed to chain Neshoba to a tragic past, to the separate, segregated patterns that got in the way of a more open future. Its folksiness and ebullient hospitality ironically encouraged clannishness and inwardness rather than openness.[30] To the white critics of the fair—and by extension the segregated traditions of the Old South—people with long roots in Neshoba County, because of the deep emotional ties residents had to the summertime event, it was unlikely there would be any meaningful change in the near future. The scion of one of the old lumber companies remarked that when he looked around the fairgrounds and realized that no blacks owned any of the coveted cabins, it was for him an epiphany.[31] For this small group of white Neshobans, meaningful cultural change would not come until fair sponsors realized that profound adjustments to fair traditions had to be made, or until the fair itself died a natural death.

The fair served as a barometer of racial dynamics in Neshoba, while simultaneously offering a statement about white Southern collective memory. According to a reporter from a Jackson newspaper, as late as 2010 virtually everyone in attendance on the day she was there was white. As the nonwhite member of a mixed-race couple, she said she "was uncomfortable because I didn't belong."[32] In a rough estimate of the crowd, she claimed to see only "20 blacks and zero Asians."[33] She was among those who thought describing the fair as the "Neshoba Metaphor" was apt. It is so embedded in the hearts of white Neshobans, it becomes the incarnation of their values, culture, and family feeling. Understood in this way, it corresponds with the sociological understanding of *Gemeinschaft*, or that form of association that brings individuals together in a strong primary relationship, in a collective sense of loyalty to entities that are racially and ethnically homogeneous.[34] Fair cabins are passed down in families and are treasured family possessions. Hospitality is the norm, and even the woman reporter who felt that she "didn't belong" was invited inside to eat with a family she did not know.

Confirmation of the fair's significance was reinforced in 1980 when Ronald Reagan campaigned there at the start of his bid for the presidency. Calculating a Southern strategy in his run for office, Reagan accepted an invitation to speak at the fair. Although his appearance has been described—especially by Mississippians—as the opening of his campaign, it was rather the "first stop after the Republican convention, not the official kickoff."[35] On August 3, 1980, Reagan made his case to 30,000 fairgoers, endorsing conservative politics and states' rights, concepts appealing to white Neshoba County residents, but not to many other voters around the country. The speech resonated with local white values, especially his assertion that "I believe in states' rights," an evocative phrase that probably cost Reagan votes nationally. Given the intensity of the cultural associations Mississippians have with the fair, Reagan's statement of belief could sound like a religious commitment offered at a holy place.

To most Americans outside of Mississippi, Neshoba held a different set of associations, notably the murders of the civil rights workers and the state's long reputation for harsh racism, assumptions Reagan likely knew. Within two days of his fair appearance, Reagan was in New York City speaking to the Urban League, where he reminded listeners of his firm commitment to the rights of black Americans, which sounded very much like an effort to repair any negative press criticism resulting from his Neshoba address.[36] He won Neshoba County by a generous margin in the general election, and he also won Mississippi, despite the fact that his opponent was an incumbent and a Southerner as well. Reagan had tapped into local memory by implying sympathy with white Neshobans' views on race. Voters across the nation who warmed to his ideas about the economy were perhaps unfamiliar with what he had said at the Neshoba County Fair.

The fair revealed the wide gap on racial matters between the white establishment in Neshoba and the black community of Longdale that had been in place for generations: race still trumped all other considerations of worthiness. It was a display of white privilege where blacks had historically been low-paid workers. It was a noisy, fun-filled, but meaningful experience for the whites who attended. Its counterpart in the black community of Longdale was the annual June commemorative service: church-based and dignified, a contrasting celebration of values in a very different context.

10

Truth and Tradition in Neshoba County, 1964–1967

Custom is just as real as law and can be just as dangerous.

TONI MORRISON, *HOME*

What stories are we prepared to tell, and what stories are we willing to hear, without transforming them into preferred narratives that make no demands on our comforting illusions?

EDWARD T. LINENTHAL[1]

The End of Freedom Summer

By the end of August 1964, Neshoba County had accumulated an awful racial toll: the hulking shell of a burned-out church; an assault on five black Methodists; and the murders at point-blank range of three civil rights workers. Yet in the Mississippi context, these were not crimes. Fifty black churches had been burned during Freedom Summer, and many more than five blacks were beaten, but there was no investigation of these serious offenses, and Mississippians, black and white, knew there would not be. Then what about the murders? Was there to be a meaningful search for the killers, whom everyone suspected, or actually knew, to be Klansmen? Again, in the local context, as journalist Bill Minor observed, a white man in Mississippi had never been convicted and sent to prison on charges of assaulting blacks. Had anything of substance really changed because of Freedom Summer or were Southern traditions as firmly entrenched as ever? As Senator James Eastland had demonstrated in his conversation with the president about the burned-out Ford, it was possible to invoke a Southern traditional explanation even when faced with contrary physical evidence.

"This is a Terrible Town"

The young people of COFO were determined to demonstrate to white Neshobans that the civil rights movement did have bite, that it was still active and impassioned, and that the tragedies of the past few months were not in vain. So on August 13, just as the Neshoba County Fair was moving into high gear, a group of blacks and a handful of whites deemed that the time had come to open a COFO office in Philadelphia. They occupied space in a hotel once owned by Charles Evers, and with a limited staff, and a small supply of guns, they resumed the business of civil rights activism.

Except for Florence Mars and a few others, white Neshobans harbored an intense dislike of COFO members, who were very open about their goal of changing the status quo. Mars was one of very few white Philadelphians in contact with the group, largely young, self-confident activists whose positive, assertive attitude challenged white preconceptions of what constituted appropriate social demeanor between the races. The young people were criticized for their dress, their casualness with the opposite sex, their "Bolshevik" politics, not to mention their views on integration. Mars said they were thought of as "the embodiment of evil, of everything white Mississippians found despicable. The word [COFO] itself was poison and in many caused a powerful feeling of revulsion. COFO workers were called "'nigger-loving, race-mixing-beatnik agitators,' and were considered to be an abomination, filth, the scum of the earth.'"[2] White Neshobans evidenced no new desire to achieve racial harmony as the result of Freedom Summer. Nightly, groups of local toughs harassed the small contingent of civil rights workers by driving around the hotel, honking horns, and shouting epithets, intent on provoking an altercation.

Racial tensions were high in Philadelphia after the murders. The police department, in a city of just over 5,000, added between fifty and sixty new recruits to its force as auxiliary members, most presumed to be Klan members.[3] City residents knew them to be either Klansmen or sympathizers, and their appearance—low-riding helmets on their brows, belts holding live ammunition and guns—gave Florence Mars the impression of "Nazi storm troopers."[4] Their presence in such large numbers was meant to project the image of white solidarity, hoping to intimidate black residents.

White Neshobans maintained their silence with FBI agents, now trying to collect evidence for a trial of the alleged killers. With the face of white resistance in place, it seemed to black residents little had changed.

The summer of the murders, Martin Luther King came to the area to comfort the people of Longdale for their personal suffering and for the loss of their church. Mt. Zion people received him warmly, but outside Longdale even the presence of FBI agents could not guarantee his safety; it was dangerous territory for him. In a brief talk to the congregation he took note of their courage: "I rejoice," he said, "that there are churches relevant enough that people of ill will will be willing to burn them. This church was burned because it took a stand."[5] Mt. Zion was already developing plans for a new church, and the conversation had begun about a commemorative service to keep alive the memory of the recent tragic events.

Dr. King visited Neshoba again two years later to participate in a variety of locally planned activities related to the civil rights movement. He was asked to participate in the commemorative service at Mt. Zion, now in its second year, and to worship with the congregation in its newly rebuilt church. He was also going to join with COFO loyalists at their outpost in Philadelphia in a march of solidarity to the courthouse. At the last minute, his plans changed, due to a shooting attack on James Meredith, now an Ole Miss graduate, on the second day of what was to be a solo walk from Memphis to Jackson. With Meredith hospitalized from the shooting, other civil rights activists, notably Dr. King, pledged to continue the march through Mississippi without him. On June 21, the anniversary of the Neshoba murders, King and about twenty others left the line of the Meredith march and detoured to Philadelphia so he could keep his commitments to supporters there.

Among local activists expectations ran high that the presence of high-visibility leaders like Dr. King would contribute to the symbolism of the day, as well as aid their efforts there. Instead, what King and the other visitors encountered in Philadelphia was a portrait of white rage, as crowds of segregationists alerted to his arrival gathered on the sidewalks to shout epithets. King presented a bold front as he and a small group of COFO activists gathered from many places—Longdale, Independence Quarters in Philadelphia, and more distant locations—walked the route up the hill to Courthouse Square. As they walked, whites cursed and jeered, taunting King in particular, and seeming eager to do him violence. The expanded auxiliary police force did nothing to restrain the crowd. Deputy Sheriff

Cecil Price allowed the riotous conditions to continue, but took the opportunity to seize one of the marchers, the Reverend Clint Collier, and jail
him on an old traffic charge. What Robert Moses had called "the heart of
the iceberg" had not thawed, and Philadelphia again took on the appearance of a white police state.

As the marchers made their way back to Independence Quarters at the
bottom of the hill, the crowd surged out of control, throwing bottles and
stones, revving their cars at the marchers. In the midst of this chaos, King
passed a judgment on the town that would haunt it for decades: "This is
a terrible town, the worst I've seen," he said, before adding, "There is a
complete reign of terror here."[6] He managed to extricate himself from
the threatening mob and get to the commemorative service at Mt. Zion,
but too late to participate in the service. He promised his friends and supporters in Longdale he would return in three days with a larger group of
marchers. Derided in the white-controlled city, he was embraced in the
black town. It was an experience he would explain later that was almost
as overwhelming as the very worst encounter of his career, the march in
Chicago.

He kept his promise to return, and with additional supporters in
the ranks, he walked the route again, when a still angry, but smaller,
crowd jeered and threw bottles and eggs. Clint Collier, released from jail,
dodged the missiles as he led a prayer before the white mob, now mod-
erately restrained by auxiliary policemen who had been put on notice by
the governor. One of those with Dr. King on the march was the youthful
SNCC leader Stokely Carmichael, who, when he witnessed the fury of
the mob, called back at them with slogans of Black Power, which in that
volatile scene seemed to have greater relevance than King's nonviolent
message.

The Klan was very much present that day as the marchers walked
past, some disguised as auxiliary policemen and others just young
toughs. The local Klan was smaller in size now because its members
knew that FBI moles had infiltrated the ranks, but despite that it still
had muscle and the unspoken approval of the community. Many "ordinary" men in town were part of the auxiliary police. While the rest of the
country showed signs of acceptance of at least parts of the Civil Rights
Acts, Mississippi seemed eager to accept John Satterfield's translation of
the Supreme Court's "all deliberate speed" to mean "not yet." Churches,
most restaurants and public accommodations, remained shuttered to
black residents.

Evaluating of the Bystanders: Innocent or Responsible?

The actions of the wild mob that day spoke of a white community still tied to a past that did not readily welcome "outsiders" or accept black residents as equal partners in a social contract. White Philadelphians showed they were as willing as ever to condone or ignore illegal acts against black residents, that the strained racial relationship was "intractable." Many, probably most, in the crowd were "ordinary" white citizens of Neshoba, who did not throw stones or bottles or even taunt with ugly names, yet stood outside the line of the march lending support to those who did shout and throw bottles and cans. Behavior of that sort, a form of passive encouragement, has provoked latter-day observers of once-divided societies to question what constitutes individual or group culpability, and what is simply a cultural remnant of "the way things used to be."[7] Should "ordinary citizens," who do no violence yet maintain their silence in the face of social evil, be considered complicit in a collective cultural conspiracy or as innocent bystanders? Without expecting residents of troubled societies to sacrifice themselves and their livelihoods in a threatening environment, can persons maintain reasonable personal morals without becoming complicit in the evils around them? The actions of the white crowd that day in Philadelphia were produced by a cultural racism that was protected by law enforcement. They resemble in kind, though not degree, the behavior of those who, when feeling threatened, close ranks and "seek security in narrower, more localized identity groups."[8]

A number of students of mob action have reflected on the kinds of conditions most conducive to the sort of behavior on display that day in Philadelphia. Is it possible, or is it necessary, to determine "responsibility-ascription" among the "ordinary" white citizens on the street during Dr. King's visit? Antje Du Bois-Pedain, arguing from the perspective of South African apartheid, has maintained that determining responsibility is vital if justice is ever to be achieved. She has observed that the issue of responsibility is more than an "idle concern with moral truth for its own sake," but ideally is generated by "self-inspection and practical action [for] redressing the injustices of the past," including accepting a role for oneself. Some responsibility for the racial hatred on display that day can be traced to decades of malicious race-baiting politicians whose careers thrived on white supremacist passions. Ultimately, however, Du Bois-Pedain argues, it is necessary for participants, even if only observers, to ask themselves why they contribute to the maintenance of an unjust system.[9]

Daniel Jonah Goldhagen is another scholar who examined the role of "ordinary" citizens, setting out his thesis in a very controversial 1996 book called *Hitler's Willing Executioners*. Goldhagen also considered the role of bystanders and their connection to injustices in their society.[10] According to him, German brutality against Jews had historical roots, traceable to a long-standing tradition of anti-Semitism in Germany.[11] Those who did the killing of six million Jews, he said, were not coerced, were not only Nazi soldiers, but were people influenced by their culture to believe that Jews should not live among them.[12] German collective memory of the role of Jews had replaced history and shaped their present. Goldhagen indicted "ordinary people" who collaborated with the regime. Indeed, he argued, even the churches were complicit in the anti-Semitism that made geno- cidal killing possible; it can be seen, he said, in "the moral bankruptcy of the German churches, Protestant and Catholic alike."[13] A more recent scholar, Susannah Heschel, similarly described the close connection between German Protestantism and the Nazification of virtually all aspects of church life.[14] Despite the condemnatory language of Goldhagen's book, his work was actually well received by a German public who found a mea- sure of relief in his discussion of how it might be possible to "come to terms with the past" of German history.[15]

Goldhagen's broad brush does not allow for much detail to consider responsibility in the context of the police state Mississippi had become, although there are structural similarities common to other highly con- trolled societies. White Neshobans responded to the injustice around them by refusing to talk about it, by covering it with a cloak of silence. By so doing, through denial, they created an acceptable solution to "coming to terms with the past" that worked for many decades after the murders. Eventually twenty-one men (later eighteen) were arrested in connection with the killings, though they were hardly the only ones responsible for Mississippi's racist crimes. The cultural climate in place since slavery days supported racism and white supremacy.

Determining responsibility has also become the goal of those who pursue cold civil rights cases, not just of the Neshoba Three but others. Their job is to identity the victims, and where possible, the perpetrators. The past can have a real face when the victims and the victimizers are identified. That reality was particularly evidenced in the trial testimony of Carolyn Goodman, mother of Andrew, who humanized her murdered son for a Mississippi jury as she spoke of his youthful interests and his delight in being in Meridian. Jerry Mitchell of the Jackson *Clarion-Ledger* accomplished a similar objective when he wrote in his columns about past racial victims, the alleged nature of their "crimes," often shockingly trivial, and bestowed on them a human recognition most never had in life. The media and popular culture can potentially contribute to the process of overcoming their audiences' historical amnesia, as Goldhagen observed about Germany's reception of such offerings as *The Diary of Anne Frank* and *Schindler's List.*[16] Similarly, despite the sensationalism of the film *Mississippi Burning*, it introduced the possibilities of the extremes of racist behavior to new audiences of viewers emotionally distanced from them.

Forces inside and outside the county's borders prodded white Neshobans, so long involved in the "closed society," to gain a measure of self-awareness. A writer once described Philadelphia as a "strange, tight little town, loath to admit complicity."[17] Accepting collective responsibility for past misdeeds is a difficult yet necessary task if a community is to "come to terms with the past." Reconciliation requires accepting that complicity rests not only in the doing of violent deeds, but also in knowing of them and remaining silent. The Klan group that met at Bloomo School that June night to plot the conspiracy was too large to keep an explosive secret in an area the size of east central Mississippi.

The Search for the Klan Killers

The collective silence of white Neshobans extended beyond the search for the bodies to the search for the killers, and beyond that to government efforts to try the perpetrators. As was the case when the FBI searched for the bodies, the state of Mississippi made clear it would not cooperate with attempts to find the killers, letting the job fall once again to a federal agency. Local whites nevertheless complained about the process, because the effect was another show of power by outsiders coming in to their state seeming to attempt to run their affairs.

The federal government and the Justice Department were thus assigned the conduct of the case. Chief FBI agent Joe Sullivan, previously in charge of finding the bodies, began searching for evidence for the case, combing Neshoba County for any information he could find, traveling the roads of Longdale. On one of his Longdale trips he met with Bud Cole, and was surprised to learn from him that he had never reported the beating he had endured the night the church burned. Cole then gave

Sullivan a lesson about black life in Neshoba County. He explained that he was certain law enforcement agents had been involved in the events that fateful night and it would be foolish to protest; typically the sheriff and his deputies came to Longdale only when they wanted to pick up liquor and parade their authority.[18]

The government's plan was to have Sullivan collect as much evidence as he could, then share it with Justice Department attorneys who would try the case. They would have to rely on an old Reconstruction measure, the 1870 Enforcement Act, to charge the offenders with conspiracy to deny persons of their civil rights.[19] Mississippi had never convicted a white person for murdering a black person, and it was clear no state court was about to challenge that precedent in this case. Although a murder had obviously been committed, the perpetrators would not be charged with murder. US attorney general Nicholas Katzenbach had said publically that the killers of the three men would "never be brought to trial because no Neshoba County jury would convict them," an assumption with which the state's attorney general, Joe T. Patterson, took umbrage; Katzenbach had never submitted his evidence to a Neshoba County jury and he could not know the outcome.[20] In this game of legal show-and-tell, Katzenbach was relying on past experience in Mississippi, and Patterson was trying to smoke out the evidence Katzenbach had in his possession.

In time the FBI and Justice Department attorneys believed they had in their possession enough evidence, slim though it was, about brutality against blacks, the church burning, and the murders to subpoena one hundred witnesses to appear before a grand jury. The large pool of witnesses, it was hoped, would reveal members of the Klan, and encourage informers to come forward with pieces of information.

No evidence was produced regarding the church burning, the beatings, or other brutalities, but the conspiracy charge was eventually sustained. What supported the conspiracy charge were the two confessions the FBI had received from former Klansmen and testimony from two informers. Before the end of the year, the FBI had confessions from two men who were actual parties to the murders, James Jordan and Horace Doyle Barnette. Both were Klansmen from neighboring Lauderdale County, who had accepted bureau offers—money, relocation, and reduced sentences—in exchange for information about the crime. The bureau was also in possession of information received just two days after the murders from a Neshoba County resident, Buford Posey, who told agents he was certain Edgar Ray Killen and the sheriff's office had committed the crimes.[21] Posey was considered eccentric by his neighbors, largely for his views on civil rights, but Sullivan used the information to put additional pressure on Sheriff Rainey and his deputy. In addition, the two informers were well known in the area: the Reverend Delmar Dennis, once a Klan chaplain and dissident Methodist minister, and Carlton Wallace Miller, a policeman.

The extent of the evidence allowed the bureau to bring a case against twenty-one individuals, charging them with conspiracy to deny the three movement workers their civil rights. Harold Cox of the Second District of the US Court of Appeals, a known segregationist and close friend of Senator James Eastland, was the federal judge in the case. President Kennedy, in deference to Eastland, Cox's law-school roommate, had appointed him to the court.

Among those actually indicted were five members of law enforcement who were charged with acting "under color of law." In addition to Sheriff Rainey and Deputy Cecil Price, they included Philadelphia policeman Richard Willis, patrolman Otha Neal Burkes, and former and future sheriff Ethel Glen Barnett, known as "Hop," all lawmen familiar to the residents of Longdale.[22] The others indicted in the conspiracy were named in Jordan's testimony: Bernard Akin, Earl B. Akin, Jimmy Arledge, Edgar Ray Killen, Billy Wayne Posey, Horace Doyle Barnette, Travis Barnette, Sam Bowers, Olen Burrage, James "Pete" Harris, Frank Herndon, Wayne Roberts, Jerry Sharpe, Jimmy Snowden, and Herman Tucker.

Over the following ten months charges against the accused men bounced around in the courts. US commissioner Esther Carter dismissed the charges against them on December 10, 1964, and in February 1965 Judge Cox reaffirmed her decision, except in the cases of lawmen Rainey, Price, and Willis. The dismissals convinced the federal government of the need to take the case outside the state and to the Supreme Court, where in *United States v. Price et al.*, the Supreme Court in March 1966 decided unanimously that it "did not agree with Judge Cox."[23] The Supreme Court's decision allowed the prosecution to return the case to Judge Cox's District Court, where on February 26, 1967, eighteen Klansmen were finally indicted on charges of conspiracy to deny the victims their civil rights. The trial was then postponed until October.

When the proceedings began in October, they were held at a court in Meridian, with the entire legal community of Neshoba County at the disposal of the defendants. John Doar of the Justice Department presented the government's case. In a significant concession, Judge Cox agreed to Doar's request that the jury pool be drawn from throughout the southern

Mississippi district rather than just the area surrounding Neshoba, an admission that it was highly unlikely the government could find twelve local jurors inclined to convict. Doar knew that he was viewed as an out-sider, and carefully presented a subdued argument. He had the confes-sions of the Klansmen and the testimony of the informers to work with, although even those statements could seem unpersuasive to the local community. Prominent local attorney Laurel Weir of Philadelphia argued for the defendants. Early in the trial he botched his case by asking CORE activist, the Reverend Charles Johnson of Meridian, if it was not true that he and Schwerner had tried to get black men to rape one white woman a week during Freedom Summer. Even Judge Cox was outraged. He asked where the question had come from, and Weir answered that it had been passed to him from Edgar Ray Killen.[24] Cox warned Weir that he would not tolerate such a line of questioning.

National newspaper coverage of the long-delayed trial showed images of the defendants that soon became iconic: relaxed and looking con-fident, Sheriff Rainey and Deputy Price smiled for the cameras, surely mindful of the fact that Mississippi had never convicted a white man for the murder of a black person, or for a federal civil rights violation. The men seemed assured of community support and acquittal. When the jury delayed in reaching a decision, Judge Cox issued a "dynamite" charge, a judicial imperative, which had the desired effect of yielding a decision on October 20, 1967. The result was surprising and unexpected; seven of the men were found guilty: Cecil Price, Sam Bowers, Wayne Roberts, Jimmy Arledge, Jimmy Snowden, Billy Wayne Posey, and Horace Doyle Barnette. Others, who seemed just as culpable, Sheriff Rainey, Preacher Killen, Olen Burrage, and Sheriff Barnett, were allowed to go free. The seven who received guilty verdicts, an outcome that upended an historic tradition in the white community, began serving their sentences of from three to ten years in 1970. Upon their release, all returned to the area. At the trial's end, Judge Cox had referred to the murder victims as "one nigger, one Jew, and a white man."[25] Sam Bowers, the head of the Klan and one of those convicted, said much later in an interview he believed was sealed and con-fidential, that he didn't mind going to jail because "the main instigator of the affair," Preacher Killen, would leave the court a free man. "Everybody, including the trial judge and the prosecutors and everybody else knows that that happened," he added.[26]

The conviction of the seven was major news. A Mississippi jury had ordered white men to prison, not because they had committed murder, but because they had deprived two white men and a black man of their civil rights. Journalist Bill Minor, an observer of all things political in Mississippi, wrote in the *New Orleans Times-Picayune,* "Never in this century has a white man in Mississippi been convicted and sent to prison for a federal civil rights violation."[27] Rita Schwerner, Mickey's widow, said the case received widespread attention because it involved two white victims and that the sons of black mothers would never have received the same attention.[28]

The Longdale people understood her meaning only too well; all of the historical evidence was on her side. The conviction was no guarantee of future justice in the courts for Neshoba's black people: the outcome was largely the result of the great media attention given to the murders, and the fact that, as Schwerner said, there were two white victims. The verdicts did not turn on any major systemic change in the justice system, but rather on the personal qualities of the victims. It did, however, reveal a cultural shift from the time of Emmett Till's 1955 trial, when jurors took less than an hour to decide the innocence of his lynchers.

By the time the trial ended there was evidence from around the country that the Civil Rights Act and the Voting Rights Act had begun to make a dent in segregation. The Magnolia State, which described itself as the "last bastion of white supremacy" and defender of the "Southern way of life," provided the evidence that the struggle for civil rights and equal treatment before the law still had a long way to go there to change white cultural traditions.

Mt. Zion Rebuilds

Even before the murderers had gone to trial, Mt. Zion had rebuilt its church right on the site of the old one. It was a very public statement to the community that their visible witness would continue as before, that they would not be chased away. There had been no investigation of the crimes that occurred within Longdale and no likelihood there ever would be. Their response to the injustices of the past was to maintain a public presence, in their new church building and in the annual commemorative service. Their commemorative services were their way of communicating collective values, as the Neshoba County Fair was for the white community.

The new church was paid for with funds from a variety of sources: from church members; from the Central Jurisdiction of the Methodist Church; from the Committee of Concern, an interdenominational group in the state; and from civil rights supporters around the country. The Methodist

Church, the denominational parent of Mt. Zion, extended the church a substantial loan. A few white residents of Philadelphia, mostly Methodists, offered their labor and their resources to assist with the rebuilding, among them lumberman Pete DeWeese and the Reverend Clay Lee, the new minister of the white Methodist church in town. The volunteers were then cautioned away, they said, by anonymous threats to burn their mills and the new First Methodist Church if they offered help.[29] Cornelius Steele, head of Mt. Zion's building committee, suspected there was another important reason for the lack of local help. Steele believed that white aid was contingent on a promise from Mt. Zion that it would never use its facilities for anything but locally defined religious purposes.[30] Mt. Zion had been born and come of age in a political milieu, and it was not about to accept such a limitation on how it expressed its faith. For them, faith and works went together.

The white community did have a fund-raising effort of its own, evidenced by contribution jars at shops in town, soliciting donations to the legal defense fund of anyone charged with criminal behavior against civil rights activists during Freedom Summer.

The Struggle for Inclusive Schools and Churches, 1964–1974

*The Negro in The Methodist Church could not with
prudence be a part of such a struggle for desegregation in
the community life . . . and at the same time not favor or
urge the same reform within the Church.*

DR. JAMES P. BRAWLEY, Central Jurisdiction

*White Mississippians obviously believed implementation
of the* Brown *decision with "all deliberate speed" meant
something longer, something much longer.*

BOLTON, Hardest Deal of All

A "Coalition of Conscience" or a Conspiracy of Evil

The events of Freedom Summer did not relieve the crisis within
Mississippi Methodism. The General Conference of the Methodist
Church had announced that at the next quadrennial session, in 1968, the
segregated Central Jurisdiction would be abolished, when merger with the
Evangelical United Brethren was accomplished, although even with that
development, ending the CJ in Mississippi seemed an unlikely prospect.
Decisions by denominational hierarchy did not resound in the Magnolia
State. Mt. Zion Church would continue within the Central Jurisdiction for
what appeared an indefinite future, if John Satterfield and the white leadership of the Southeastern Jurisdiction were to have their way. All areas of
the state were embroiled in racial conflicts related to the implementation
of the Civil Rights Act and the *Brown* decision, and the Methodist struggle
was another dimension of this larger conflagration.

It was in the public school system, in the years between 1964 and 1974,
that the fight to end segregation was most intense. Within Mississippi,

the school and the church were bound together like conjoined twins, mutually reinforcing each other, the custodians of history and memory. Decisions by the courts on individual cases, even historic ones that saw a white man sentenced to prison for an offense against a black man, did not carry the same kind of institutional heft as changes in the churches and schools, the places where ideas were planted, values generated, and lasting friendships were made. At least until 1963, white Mississippians believed they could keep both institutions, the repositories of history and memory, under local control. The outside monitors of racial compliance in the schools, the Supreme Court and the federal government, had said desegregation should be accomplished with "all deliberate speed," and the Methodist General Conference, after much debate, used virtually the same language to describe the timing of voluntary merger between the Central Jurisdiction and white jurisdictions. White Mississippians believed compliance in their churches and schools was voluntary and under local control; John Satterfield thought that accepting mandated desegregation in the church was "immoral." Timing, for these people, depended on the consensus of local folks to entertain a fundamental change in their culture. With no evidence of a willingness to change, it seemed conflict was inevitable. The debate over voluntary versus mandatory had huge implications that involved more than playing for time, and included a basic difference over states' rights and federal control.

As a result of their reading of the "deliberate speed" decision, white schools and Methodist churches in the 1960s felt no need to enroll black children and adults who sought to study in desegregated schools and worship in inclusive churches. Black residents, by contrast, believing that the law and institutional rulings required timely compliance, demonstrated new assertiveness of their right to be treated equally by schools and churches. The pray-ins protesting the "closed door" policy at Galloway Church continued under the Reverend Ed King's direction. The "closed door" tactic was copied by other Methodist churches in Jackson and around the state, in what looked like a united plan to keep black worshippers out, whether the worshipper was a student, a minister, or a bishop. But activists kept coming to the church doors. Other nonconnectional churches, like the Baptist, followed suit and closed their doors.

The denomination's expressed willingness to continue the Central Jurisdiction in 1964 bought time and settled nothing, except to preserve the impression of moral support for segregation. The confrontations over an inclusive church in Mississippi looked harsh and ugly, but were less vicious and less numerous than the schools fight. Public schools were in almost every town in the state, and should whites ever be forced into a single school system, it would have the effect of persuading them "they would have to leave the United States . . . since it would be the end of the world . . . and a way of life," according to historian Neil McMillen.[1] Race-baiting governors, in particular Ross Barnett, who was considered the greatest champion of segregation in the state, and whose legal adviser was John Satterfield, had a talent for fanning the flames of racial discord. Taylor Branch, who studied racial matters in Mississippi, reported on a Barnett appearance at an Ole Miss–Kentucky football game in 1962, a time when private negotiations were underway to register James Meredith at the university an extension of the schools fight. Publicly urging opposition to Meredith's enrollment at Ole Miss, Barnett once appeared at center field and shouted three simple statements: "I love Mississippi" to which the crowd roared in response; then "I love her people!" which led to another roar; and finally, "I love our customs," which yielded a response that was "enough to ignite pre-battle ecstasy. People were ready to die."[2] Barnett's rabid racism contributed to the segregation fight at the public school level as well as the university, turning the school struggle into "the hardest deal of all."[3] In the schools contest, the most visible clash of Old South memory and modernity was on display.

Black Mississippians, as those at Mt. Zion, were at least as invested in the importance of schools as whites. In Longdale, where the community supported the church and the school, residents were proud of both. Mt. Zion's members, as blacks elsewhere, placed a high value on education as a vehicle for escaping segregation and widening their world beyond the "closed society." They accepted segregation as the only option open to them in the white-controlled society. Tithe money supported Mt. Zion School as well as the church. Residents were therefore understandably angry when Longdale lost control of its school in 1949–50 when the county school board took over its operation. The school remained an essentially private school, supported by the local residents with only minimal funds from the county. The school board appeared motivated by a desire to supervise not only the curriculum but also the teachers, to monitor what they might say about controversial matters such as voting. Some of the parents of the school children were among those who regularly showed up to attempt to register to vote. The school treasurer, who was still Ross Jones, reported no difficulty collecting contributions to the school budget from residents; should there be a modest shortfall in any given year, he likely supplemented the budget himself.[4] The school continued to operate until

integration arrived and the doors were closed, the building ultimately suc-
cumbing to weather and disuse.

Everyone agreed, however, from politicians to parents, that all educational opportunities available to black children in the state were inad-
equate; schools were often little more than shacks, poorly supplied,
underfunded, and taught by black teachers with only minimal access to
education themselves. As late as 1950, black teachers, though they were
courted by higher salaries to keep segregation in place, still earned 39
percent of what white teachers did.[5] Parents knew that education was the
single most life-changing gift they could give their children. In Longdale
education through the high school level was a gift only few parents could
afford, since in the absence of a local high school, it meant sending a child
away to board in Meridian, home to the nearest upper-level school. Finally,
in 1970, in *Alexander v. Holmes*, the Supreme Court ruled that Southern
states could delay school desegregation no longer, and that integration
must occur "at once." Mississippi's officials were put to the test to figure
out how to make accommodations to the new ruling without changing
their old social patterns.

The "at once" decision placed responsibility for its implementation in
the hands of school officials and school boards. Although white schools
in this very poor state were not much better off than black schools, white
residents were convinced that their schools were superior simply because
they were white. Even with inadequately educated white teachers and
undersupplied white schools, white parents believed that the quality of
"whiteness" made their facilities better. They were not prepared to abandon them without a struggle. It was often heard said that they could not
imagine their young children going to school with young black children,
much less having white adolescent students at the same prom as black
teenaged students.

However robust the fights at the doors of Methodist churches to keep
out black worshippers, they could not compare with the physical assaults
on black schoolchildren, and the teachers and parents who supported
them. The school fights were local town fights, and they reportedly encap-
sulated a "sacred set of absolute meanings and stories, possessed as the
heritage . . . of a community."[6] Mississippi was one of the strongest hold-
outs against school integration—helped in its stand by the legal skills of
John Satterfield, who lobbied in Washington for separate schools. Not coin-
cidentally, the Northern Mississippi Conference was the very last in the
nation to abandon the segregated Central Jurisdiction, when Satterfield's

legal maneuvers no longer worked there he was nothing if not tenacious in his battle against desegregation. In 1966, prior to the "at once" decision, when black children in Grenada attempted to attend the local white school, they were set upon by white mobs that beat them with ax handles and metal pipes.[7] The deep-seated anger that exploded in these school confrontations belonged primarily to the parents rather than the students.

In the white Neshoba school district, the public animosity over integration was directed at the school board rather than at the eligible black children. The school board had the duty to respond to the 1970 Supreme Court ruling. Aware it would have to make some accommodation to the Court decision, the school board devised a compromise plan it labeled "freedom of choice." An earlier response, called a "financial equalization program"—providing equal resources to black schools and white—had gone nowhere, and thus the freedom of choice plan replaced it. Under the new proposal, a handful of black children would be admitted to white schools, which could then claim to have reached "partial" integration. Supporters of the plan said it was unrelated to racial considerations and was rather a kind of home-rule "free choice" program.

Some forty years later, a handful of black students who were involved in this early freedom of choice trial, spoke of their experiences with it. Their recollections produced a common conclusion, and that was that despite the shoving, name-calling, fighting, and ugly scenes they experienced, they were not personally demoralized by the experiment with change.[8] They were convinced that progress came at a price, and they were willing to pay it. Others reported bitter confrontations that had parents contemplating bringing a court case. For those who remembered the experience as challenging but not demoralizing, their responses may have to do with their being the children of motivated parents, usually a mother, who wanted her child to "be somebody." Other black parents, however, found it too trying to send their children into a hostile environment, and kept them out of the program. There were only about ten families in the initial experiment willing to expose their children to what they viewed as the punishing environment of a white school. One of those who did go in 1967 was sixth grader James Young, who in 2009 would be elected the first black mayor of Philadelphia.[9] A white woman on *The Neshoba Democrat* office staff said that in that same year "5 or 6 [black] kids" were in her junior high school ninth grade class, and she, too, recalled the fighting. Black students, she said, were required to go "back to their own school" to graduate.[10] A freedom of choice plan was adapted for the high school as well, and it called for three black students to enter the white school, where the jostling and name-calling were also present, and where students had books knocked from their hands.[11] Fighting seemed to be a regular part of the school day, but Neshoba County successfully accomplished full integration in 1970 without the horrific mass violence that had occurred in nearby Grenada.

Full compliance with federally mandated school desegregation arrived in Neshoba in January of that year, when black schools in the city and county were shuttered and closed down, although the cost had been high. Without the black schools for the black children, school integration became inevitable. Beginning in 1966, the community's level of anger was directed mainly at the school administration, as residents shouted their way into board meetings and wrote nasty letters to *The Neshoba Democrat*. School Superintendent Jim Hurdle, the man at the top, absorbed the heat and seemed to stay the course, despite having his house shot into and his family subjected to obscene and threatening phone calls. *The Neshoba Democrat* headlined the struggle, with broad coverage at the start of a new school term. Superintendent Hurdle went on television to announce that because of the support of fair-minded local citizens, full integration would occur in January 1970, as the law required. The harassment directed at him was relentless, and he threatened to resign unless it stopped. To no avail: in September 1968, short of his goal, he took his own life.[12]

Once full integration became a reality, black students were the minority in the formerly all-white public schools, and it was not a simple adjustment for them to make. They were in a new environment, in a place where they had not been invited. A black woman who was in tenth grade at the time remembered that "people around here were not too happy with the idea [of accepting black students]" in the white schools.[13] The fighting went on, and segregation was the norm for after-school activities, including team sports, dances, proms, as well as baccalaureate services.[14] With the black schools gone and no alternative to mandated integrated schooling, the community resorted to ingenious means to maintain as many of the old ways as possible. There were two school systems in the area: one for the city of Philadelphia, which became 70 percent black, and the other for Neshoba County, which was 70 percent white. There was also a kind of internal segregation within the schools. It was reportedly the students, more than parents, teachers, or administrators, who regularly sorted things out. A major consequence for black residents was that with the closing of schools like Mt. Zion, black teachers and administrators lost their jobs and were not readily rehired by the white or integrated schools.

Nevertheless, beginning in 1970, a larger percentage of black children and white children went to the same schools in Neshoba County than was true in most Northern communities.

Methodist Merger at Last

School integration opened the way for the Mississippi Methodist confer-ences to move ahead with plans to be racially inclusive. Unfortunately, the two white Methodist conferences—Mississippi and North Mississippi—had no leading counterpart to the courageous Superintendent Hurdle, no one out front willing to say the time had now come. As with the school system, the Mississippi Methodist conferences relied on outside pressure before accepting the inevitable. White leadership had been compromised by the racial strife of the 1960s, including the "closed door" policy of the churches and support for the Central Jurisdiction; young white ministers were effectively driven out of the state, to areas presumably less conten-tious. Among the black clergy in the Methodist Church, however, there was a core group of assertive young ministers for whom the bruising bat-tles over integration were a kind of basic training for the real work ahead. They were the clerical counterparts of the movement activists, and they made little distinction between the challenges they faced in their churches and those they found in their local communities.

The Reverend Henry Clay was one such example of a clergyman in the Mississippi Conference of the Central Jurisdiction who regarded his minis-try as a service to both church and community. Through much of the 1960s he was the minister of St. Paul's Methodist Church in Laurel, which just happened to be the base of the Klan and the home of its leader, Sam Bowers. A tall, slim man with a remarkable sense of presence, Clay was also a semi-nary graduate with well-honed interpersonal skills; after the 1970 merger he would eventually go on to work in the conference administration. As a young minister in Laurel in the sixties, he did not allow the nearness of the Klan or its imperial wizard to interfere with his ministry to the com-munity. In 1963, he invited Metropolitan Opera star Leontyne Price to give a concert at St. Paul's, which was her home church, before an audience he insisted would be integrated. Pictures of the large, racially mixed crowd made national news. The action also made Clay a marked man locally. He learned just what that meant in July 1966 when he took his family to a fast-food restaurant—after the passage of the Civil Rights Act—and they were stopped at the door of the eatery by a "big burly white guy," who told them to "go get served as colored." Undaunted by the confrontation, Clay reported the incident to the Laurel police chief, and together they went back to the restaurant so Clay would be properly served. When the white man guarding the door still refused to move, the police chief called for backup, and the man finally moved aside, but not before saying to the Reverend Clay, "Sambo, I'm gonna get you." Four days later Clay's parsonage was shot into at midnight, shattering glass in the house and in his car. Clay reported the offense to the FBI, and the white man subsequently admitted that he had interfered with the minister's civil rights.[15] Experiences like that, as well as visits from Sam Bowers, prepared him for administrative work in the Mississippi Methodist Conference of the United Methodist Church. Other clergy with similar experiences also wound up as district superintendents or in other conference leadership positions.

In the white conferences, which had a small supply of talented clerical leadership, lay people determined many of the important decisions, such as the long-delayed merger question regarding the CJ. When Bishop Pendergrass became the conference leader in 1964, he accepted segregation as his predecessor did, and neither of them had any inclination to adopt a denominational plan for merger. The majority of the white laity were in agreement with him. The churches were not public institutions, white members argued, and no federal agency could tell them how to manage their affairs.

But in a connectional church like the Methodist there was an outside agency, the General Conference, which set denominational policy and had the constitutional authority to initiate change. The General Conference that met in 1956, the first after the *Brown* decision, indicated support for the Court's decision in the case and introduced civil rights issues as a major item on the meeting's calendar. Unable to carry the vote on the CJ, delegates who endorsed an inclusive church constituted a vocal presence at General Conference sessions. A delegate from East Tennessee once commented that since so many black clergy and laypeople subscribed to denominational literature, it was only fair and just that more blacks be hired to work at the denomination's publishing house.[16] The delegates also gave similar attention to the future of the Central Jurisdiction, with those from outside the South admitting it was a moral stain on the denomination. Still, all they could agree upon was that it should be abolished with "reasonable speed," language that Attorney Charles Parlin believed was entirely appropriate because, since General Conference was not a "military" church, it could only "recommend."[17]

By 1963, however, with no progress toward voluntary mergers, Floyd H. Coffman, a Methodist layman and a district judge in Kansas, noted in a letter to Bishop Clair of the Central Jurisdiction that "no transfers have been accomplished in this quadrennium."[18] It was clear that the "voluntary transfers" of black churches or conferences into neighboring white conferences had not occurred under the so-called Amendment IX definition of voluntarism. Most individual black churches and conferences were, themselves, unwilling to take action alone, believing that a kind of "freedom of choice" strategy would weaken the impact of a denominational announcement officially bringing the Central Jurisdiction to an end. At the 1964 General Conference, delegates urged the churches to implement voluntary transfers, while black delegates continued to press for a date certain, suggesting 1972.

Without a consensus, the General Conference called a special adjourned session in 1966, where the fate of the Central Jurisdiction would be decided. The majority of the delegates to that session finally agreed it was necessary to abolish the Central Jurisdiction. Once again, John Satterfield spoke for the minority, and in an emotional appeal that noted his family attachment to Methodism going back generations, in which he referred to a copy of denominational Minutes in his possession that included a copy in his own possession of denominational Minutes from "1773 to 1813" that once belonged to his great grandfather, he argued that if the meeting affirmed a date certain, "you will destroy the Church in many areas."[19] In Mississippi, Methodists found it "hard to hold the line," he said, the MAMML argument in favor of defecting from the denomination obviously fresh in his mind. He cited evidence that everyone present likely already knew, that the vast majority of black Methodists were in the South, and a majority of their churches were in the Southeastern Jurisdiction. In Mississippi alone, there were 357 black Methodist churches in two conferences, Mississippi and Upper Mississippi, and 1,062 white, divided between Mississippi and Northern Mississippi.[20] The numbers, presumably meant to reveal a significant black presence, were designed to support his contention to delegates from outside the South that there is a "tremendous difference in your area and in ours." He recognized that progress toward merger had taken place outside the South. In fact, on June 25, 1964, at the Northeastern Jurisdictional Conference meeting in Syracuse, two annual conferences and a bishop from the Central Jurisdiction were transferred into the Northern Jurisdiction, the "first such transfers in history," according to a denominational news release.[21] Further individual conference transfers were subsequently announced for Minnesota,

Wisconsin, Ohio, Illinois, Indiana, Iowa, and Michigan. It appeared as if the denomination was revisiting the regional conflicts of 1939 and even 1844.

In 1968 General Conference said "no more" to Mississippi's delaying tactics. The decision made it impossible for Mississippi's Bishop Pendergrass to continue to oppose merger and still remain in the church, although John Satterfield suggested that as a sign of protest, the Mississippi Conference might withhold its funds from the General Conference. The message from General Conference to the two white Mississippi conferences now became an integral part of a larger denominational plan for restructuring, one that would create the United Methodist Church out of what had been the Methodist Church and the Evangelical United Brethren. The General Conference announcement did not mean that local congregations would be integrated, but that conference leadership would be desegregated, as in those conferences that had already undertaken merger. With the merger, black and white bishops and district superintendents would serve where they were assigned, regardless of the race of the constituency they served. Meetings of conferences and committees would be held in black churches or white, and parity in salaries and pensions became the goal of the new denomination. Even at late as 1970, however, this was not an arrangement white Mississippi conferences were willing to accept, not without at least attempting to arrange an alternative. With the help of John Satterfield and the Southeastern Jurisdiction, they hoped to be able to create a homegrown solution to church integration.

For white Mississippi Methodists, acceptance of the end of the Central Jurisdiction meant more than conference merger, it also meant continuing affiliation with a national church many laypeople said was out of touch with the needs of the Magnolia State. They opposed an ongoing relationship with the National Council of Churches and the Delta Ministry, both perceived as too left-leaning, and whose support depended on generous contributions from the Methodist denomination.[22] These two large organizations were representative of the high tide of Protestant liberalism in the 1960s, and they were objectionable to substantial groups of white Methodists in Mississippi.

Bishop Pendergrass contributed his own unpleasant personal experience with the NCC and the Delta Ministry in 1966 to the general mood of alienation expressed by his constituency. He reminded them of a trip he had taken that year to the offices of the National Council in New York City to present the case for his conference. He felt he had been personally insulted while he was there, suggesting that his treatment reflected NCC attitudes toward his Southern constituency. His expectation was that his visit would sensitize the executives of the National Council and the Delta Ministry to the fears and tensions of the Methodists he served, people consumed with anxiety over integration and anticommunism. Instead the trip had gone disastrously for him. While he was away, Clint Collier, planning a run on the Mississippi Freedom Democratic Party ticket, used the opportunity to picket the bishop's Jackson office. And when he was in New York, Pendergrass felt snubbed; no arrangements had been made for his stay, and officials kept him waiting a very long time in the hallway.[23] When white Mississippi Methodists learned of this experience, they expressed outrage at the shabby treatment by Northern liberals: obviously, their hospitality was no better than their politics and theology. Surprisingly, later in that year, for no clear reason, the bishop announced that his state would make a grant to the Delta Ministry. Bishop Charles Golden, who was the black counterpart to Bishop Pendergrass in the Central Jurisdiction, and like virtually all members of the Central Jurisdiction an enthusiastic supporter of the Delta Ministry, was at a loss to explain his colleague's action, as were most other local Methodists.

The reality was that laymen like John Satterfield in the Southeastern Jurisdiction of the church exerted more influence over Mississippi Methodists than Bishop Pendergrass. Satterfield had argued all along that the basis for merger, if it occurred, had to be "moral" and "voluntary," not "political" and "mandatory." Southerners, he believed, should have the option to set their own "target date" for merger.[24] He convinced his own conference that the planned merger with the Evangelical United Brethren was wrong, and pressed the argument for a voluntary merger. An out-of-touch hierarchy that did not understand Southern mores and seemed disinclined to learn, he believed, should not control his conference and his jurisdiction.

When the General Conference next convened, in Atlanta in April 1972, a majority of delegates voted to end voluntarism and agreed all mergers must be completed by July 1973.[25] Satterfield objected, but this time to no avail. Denial and delay would no longer work in the denomination, just as the Supreme Court no longer accepted it for schools. The white Methodists of Mississippi were still not ready to capitulate to the denomination's demand. Some simply left the denomination for other variously identified locally controlled Methodist congregations with loose ties to the Association of Independent Methodists.[26] And conference officers in the state just renamed the Central Jurisdiction the Former Central

Jurisdiction without making any other adjustments. Unknown malcontents, Methodist or not, made nighttime raids on the properties and parsonages of black Methodist ministers, as had happened to the Reverend Henry Clay.[27] Bishop Pendergrass, fearful that he could face a major secession movement and loss of church assets if the Mississippi Conferences continued to refuse the General Conference decision, at last assembled a biracial committee in 1972 to plan for merger. Millsaps College in Jackson, a Methodist institution with a national reputation, had been admitting black students since 1965, a move that showed the significant difference within the conference between racial moderates like those at Millsaps and the majority of conservative segregationists like the bishop.

Bishop Pendergrass's dilemma was how to support his own Mississippi segregationists and still respond to the denominational order for merger. If he continued to side with the segregationists and Mississippi failed to implement merger by 1972, an outside board of bishops would come in and create a plan of its own. The bishop explained the obvious to his members: it would be better for them to create their own merger agreement than to have one imposed on them. When his appointed merger committee failed to act, he proposed that blacks and whites meet separately and each group draw up its own merger plans, and use them as a basis for compromise. The black committee members did their work; the white members waited, and asked to see what the others had done before drafting their own proposals. The black members refused to reveal their work; they did not want to put forward a proposal before they had assurance that the white members were invested enough in the process to draft a proposal of their own.[28]

In August 1972, when Bishop Pendergrass retired, Mack B. Stokes, with a ministerial degree from Candler School of Theology and a PhD from Boston University, became his successor. He was also a friend of John Satterfield. Apparently a gracious man even by Mississippi's high standards, he waged a charm offensive to convince lay people—as Bishop Pendergrass had tried unsuccessfully earlier—that it was better to design their own merger plans than to have them imposed by "outsiders." His efforts succeeded, and in November 1972 the Mississippi Conference approved merger, and shortly thereafter in 1973 the North Mississippi Conference became the last in the country to do so.

It remained to be seen what Mississippi Methodists, black and white, lay and clergy, would make of their new relationship. The Reverend Henry Clay, the Reverend W. B. Crump, and other black clergy served in administrative posts in the conference, creating situations where black clergy presided over gatherings primarily white, and vice versa, a novel and uncomfortable situation for both groups. Black ministers confessed to feelings of trepidation on such occasions, which almost inevitably took place in white neighborhoods. W. B. Crump, who along with Clay and C. E. Appleberry would later serve as district superintendents, remembered the anxiety he felt when he entered a white church once closed to him.[29]

The years following merger were a time for testing. The local culture had become less threatening to its black citizens, less abrasive, but most whites were not accustomed to sharing their facilities with their black co-religionists. Integration existed on the administrative level, while at conference and district gatherings the races tended to remain separate. The most disturbing evidence that everything was not proceeding smoothly was the steady decline in membership; memberships declined in white churches, but more significantly in black churches, along with a loss of black clergy.[30] Although the denomination had promised that black clergy and administrators would have meaningful positions in the new United Methodist Church, black leadership was absent in the most powerful positions in the church. There had been systemic change, but it was more cosmetic and administrative than personal and congregational.

For many Mississippians in 1980, the new decade promised a fresh start, including the election of the moderate William Winter as governor. The year also witnessed a turning point for Methodist denominational policy makers, when Central Jurisdiction issues no longer dominated the agenda of General Conference. At the same time, two formidable figures in local Methodist affairs, layman John Satterfield and the civil rights activist Bishop Charles Golden—formerly of the Central Jurisdiction—ended their service to the church. Bishop Golden retired after serving a conference in the Western Jurisdiction of the now-integrated denomination. John Satterfield, who had opposed most of Golden's ideas throughout his career, died of a self-inflicted gunshot wound. It was said of Satterfield that in his last year, after trying without success to meet with his new bishop to discuss his views, he recanted his segregationist stance and said, "I was wrong." Bishop Clay Lee, a personal friend, also said Satterfield had not been well.[31] Satterfield and Bishop Golden had witnessed major structural changes in the church: both with roots in Mississippi and distinguished Methodists, they were polar opposites in their views and had no cause for personal interaction during their careers. They represented the two sides of Mississippi. Although Golden and Satterfield cherished the denomination, each had his reasons to be critical: for Golden, it had been the lack of acceptance for black laypeople and lack of opportunity for black clergy; and for Satterfield, it was the perceived liberal and intrusive policies of the national church. Black clergy and members continued to leave along with many whites, as Methodism followed other mainstream Protestant denominations down a steady path of decline. Church growth in the future could be found in inclusive congregations, with many members born in other countries, and in 1980 Mississippi did not have an inclusive culture.

For Mt. Zion Church in Longdale, denominational merger meant that its delegates to conference could now attend sessions along with whites, where they would be the minority. Delegate Arecia Steele from Mt. Zion, a daughter of Methodism, enjoyed the "fellowship" at conference sessions, even as concerned black delegates worked vigorously to get their candidates elected to denominational boards and committees.[32] A new administrative structure meant that Mt. Zion would now pay its assessments to the Mississippi Conference instead of the Central Jurisdiction, and the United Methodist Church would be the new holder of the deed to the property. Women remained the mainstay of the congregation as many men went off to other destinations: better jobs, the military, and sometimes prison.

The annual commemorative service at Mt. Zion continued to grow in size and stature after the merger. It attracted people concerned about civil rights issues along with politicians from around the state and nation. White Neshobans were heard to wonder aloud why the Mt. Zion people "didn't just get over it." As with the Emancipation Day ceremonies in the nineteenth century that once celebrated black freedom, the annual June festivities recalled another moment in the black freedom struggle. It was a significant achievement for Mt. Zion to continue this public statement in an environment already well saturated with remembrances of Confederate heroes. The United Methodist Church, just like the nation, had split regionally over the issue of its black members, and had reunited in 1939 when it placed reunification over the interests of black Methodists. The future would determine the authenticity of the inclusive denomination created in 1968 nationally and in Mississippi in 1972.

12

"A Tight Little Town" Tackles Its Future, 1980–2000

We deeply regret what happened here 25 years ago. We wish we could undo it.

DICK MOLPUS, Mississippi secretary of state, 1989

Mississippi doesn't do race anymore.

GOVERNOR KIRK FORDICE, 1992

MISSISSIPPI WAS A latecomer to the unfolding drama in the twentieth century referred to as "The New South." This newer South was a region that not only advertised its good weather, it invited out-of-state visitors to become residents, and planned for a climate of improving race relations and economic opportunity. By 1980, people of both races in the Magnolia State gave indications of believing a more promising future lay ahead, and some white Neshobans joined in the process of creating the New Mississippi. The tumult of the 1960s and 1970s was behind; the schools were integrated, Methodist conferences merged, and it was time for Mississippi to enjoy the new prosperity lighting up areas of the South. In the last two decades of the twentieth century Mississippians did, indeed, try to leave behind the remnants of the "closed society," but the effort, burdened by old memories of the past, though tempting and even financially agreeable, called for more experience with modernity than the presence of new gambling money alone could provide. Old South customs, rooted in segregation and white supremacy, would yield slowly, and required learning to live with new forms of community.

It had taken bitter battles for Mississippi to arrive at the place where it might consider community in more inclusive terms. The public schools, nominally integrated, appeared to a casual observer as more inclusive than many outside the South. And the United Methodist Church acknowledged with its new name its place on the side of an inclusive society, including Mississippi. There had also been the precedent-breaking decision in the civil rights case that indicted eighteen Klansmen and sent seven to jail. As a sign of the old days, however, ten or more Klansmen connected with the case still walked freely on the streets of Philadelphia. A majority of white Mississippians was also confident there were political opportunities for them ahead in the developing Reagan revolution. Reagan's campaign, following the lines of Nixon's Southern strategy, announced its states' rights goals, which encouraged supporters to believe that a Reagan victory would reshape old political alliances in Mississippi.

People at Mt. Zion Church observed a noticeable relaxation in racial tensions. The Klan as a discrete entity was gone, its leadership declawed when Sam Bowers went to prison and its chaplain turned FBI informer. Black residents were sensitive to breaches of the Civil Rights Act and attempts to return to Jim Crow behavior, and they said so. An increase in the Neshoba black population—which added 1,000 new residents since the previous census—revealed the names of new black voters on the rolls.[1] But Longdale and Mt. Zion were still the preserve of black residents, as Philadelphia churches and historic city neighborhoods were for whites. As Neshoba adjusted to the full implications of the Civil Rights Act, the inclusive goals of Freedom Summer still seemed a long way off. Racial separation trumped inclusion every time, making it seem that white memory of "how things used to be" contained a longing for how things should be again.

In 1980, black and white voters in the state countered the national Republican trend when they elected as their new governor a seasoned white moderate, the Democrat William Winter. When Governor Winter entered office he brought with him a youthful administrative team referred to as the "The Boys of Spring." His supporters viewed the election as an encouraging sign of forward movement on race issues, although in 1980 it was too soon to tell if there was sufficient social support to sustain it. Mississippi observers knew that the state had an uncanny ability to disappoint, that whenever a break-through seemed possible, a crisis emerged that was resolved by reverting to tried and true Old South methods. It was as if Mississippians had a masochistic longing to remain forever in last place among the states. Yet between 1980 and the end of the century there were encouraging signs that a shift in racial attitudes was in the making, and the shift was shaped by important local actors: recently enfranchised black voters, moderate white politicians, journalists, editors, Choctaw entrepreneurs, and even a football player. Historic reality and Southern memory still coexisted in tension, amenable, it seemed, to lasting change only when persuasion was accompanied by outside pressure.

Politics Are "Winterized"

William Winter's election did, indeed, seem to bring a breath of spring. The governor promised to deliver on programs that would enable the state to become what it ought to be, rather than reproduce a broken image of how things were. During the campaign by a politician who was once a quiet segregationist, Winter made a commitment to bring progress, mobility, and opportunity to the state, with a heavy emphasis on the need to overhaul the educational system. His young political aides, these "Boys of Spring," reaffirmed the sense that this administration really was a new beginning. They saw themselves as agents of reform, who would commit to the Winter legacy by running for public office on their own at a future date.

Winter's years as governor have been remembered mostly for their educational improvements, largely because of the new policies he put in place. Old timers in the legislature, used to being in control, were reportedly left breathless by the governor's reach and boldness. For at least a dozen years after his election, politics in the state were "Winterized," before they were overwhelmed by Reagan-style conservative measures and by politicians like Republican Kirk Fordice, who would campaign for conservatives in 1991. The reform politics of the Winter era instituted a number of significant lasting changes which lasted well beyond his term in office, having an effect even on the tenacious problems identified with Neshoba County.

Winter's major achievement was a reform bill targeting education, passed at a special Christmas legislative session in 1982. Black residents of the state, always supportive of educational reform, were strong backers of the governor's educational objectives. His bill mandated statewide kindergartens, teaching assistants for the lower grades, compulsory attendance, teacher pay rises, training programs for administrators, and an accreditation system for the public schools. The funding for the new program was expected to come from increased sales and income taxes.[2]

When five members of his administrative team were subsequently elected to statewide offices on their own, it appeared the Winter reforms would endure. The list of aides who followed him into various public offices was impressive: Ray Mabus was himself elected governor in 1987; Dick

Molpus was elected secretary of state in 1983, and again in 1987 and 1991; Bill Cole was elected state treasurer in 1983; Marshall Bennett was also elected as state treasurer in 1987, 1991, 1995, and 1999; and Steve Patterson was named state auditor in 1991 and 1995.[3] The elections of these men, moderates all, was an encouragement to black voters that their votes had made a difference, and that the slightly less restrictive social environment might be accompanied by important policy changes. Whites were not oblivious to the changes black votes brought. The political heirs of Governor Winter were essentially fiscal conservatives and social moderates who wanted to bring progress to the state without the old race-badgering tactics.

One of the members of the Winter team had a personal influence on developments in Neshoba County, and that was Philadelphia native Dick Molpus. Molpus was the son of one of the Neshoba County timber families and was elected to state office under three governors. While he was secretary of state, Molpus continued Winter's emphasis on public education, renegotiating undervalued state leases to raise $24 million for schools. He also managed to achieve sweeping lobbyist reform, election law improvement, and mail-in voter registration.[4] In addition, he made clear he was troubled by Neshoba County's unresolved civil rights crimes, and he had the political visibility to make the issue a priority.

Dick Molpus: "We Are Profoundly Sorry"

In 1989, while secretary of state, Molpus was asked by the planning committee at Mt. Zion Church to be the featured speaker at their annual commemorative service. It was announced as a particularly significant event because it was the twenty-fifth anniversary of the murders and the church burning. The occasion would prove to have far-reaching consequences for Molpus, for Neshoba County, and for its black residents in ways the secretary could not have anticipated. He was very aware of Neshoba's troubled legacy from the civil rights era, and the fact that it still impacted everyone in the county. In keeping with the importance of the event, the church had invited family members of the victims to attend, along with notables in state politics and civil rights. Molpus convinced then-governor Ray Mabus to join him there, despite the governor's misgivings once he learned what Molpus's topic would be. Also invited to the service was a group of church people from Philadelphia, Pennsylvania, who had been in contact with the Philadelphia, Mississippi, community, through a program known as Philadelphia-to-Philadelphia. The connection with this liberal Northern group was not a popular one among local Neshoba whites.

Mt. Zion had been organizing the annual commemorative services since 1965, and its members reserved the right to plan the format, which included choosing the speaker. The ritual for the service had not changed much over the years; the event memorialized the victims and honored the values for which they died. It was the chief event on the church calendar. The event's planners knew of Dick Molpus's ties to family and business in Neshoba County, and they knew as well that he was a Democrat. They thought of him as a neighbor, though not necessarily as their advocate. As a native son, he was the right choice, they believed, to address what was expected to be an unusually large crowd.

Molpus had moved to Jackson when he was elected to public office, but his roots, he said, were still in the county. He knew of its awful celebrity, that it continued to be identified as a "terrible town" because of its violent past. The local audience knew him as friend and now as secretary of state.[5] His unique status conferred both an opportunity and a responsibility; it was an opportunity to speak to locals as one who knew them and their hurtful past, but there was also a responsibility to remind them that their continued denial of their history was harmful, to themselves as well as to those victimized by the events of 1964. One of his aides later commented that, like his mentor William Winter, Molpus thought the business of government was to make things better, and that office holders should bring a sense of moral commitment to their task, not just blindly, but from the perspective of "enlightened self-interest."[6] This was such a time.

It was a large interracial crowd at Mt. Zion Church that Molpus addressed from the back of a flatbed truck on the day of the commemoration. Reporters and observers estimated that between 400 and 500 people were gathered on the lawn of the church, about 100 of them media people.[7] At the time forty years old, Molpus was no longer a political novice, so he knew there would be some risk involved in attempting to speak for his white neighbors, especially if his address were to contain words of apology to the families of the 1964 victims. Yet that was his intention, to speak on behalf of the white Neshoba community, many of them friends. To the gathering of Neshobans and victims' families he said, "We deeply regret what happened here 25 years ago. We wish we could undo it. We are profoundly sorry that they are gone. We wish we could bring them back. Every decent person in Philadelphia and Neshoba County and Mississippi feels that way. The nation and the world thinks of the events of

1964 in Philadelphia in historical terms and the deaths of these dedicated
young men as a pivotal event in a great national movement. Of course,
this is true—but it is not the whole truth. Today we pay tribute to those
who died."[8] Molpus admitted that his apology did not present "the whole
truth," that the facts of the beatings, the church burning, and the continued denial of equal justice to blacks were missing, but for the moment it
was enough. Apology was a new word in the national political vocabulary,
and one quite alien in Mississippi.

Members of Mt. Zion were as surprised as the rest of the congregation
by Molpus's words, by the apology and the reference to a "great national
movement." White Mississippians never referred to the civil rights movement in such a way. From the time of the lynching of the three men (and
into the twenty-first century) no political voice in Mississippi was raised to
condemn the murders and endorse the goals for which the men had died.
Molpus was the first and only one to do so. Before the commemorative
event, he had spoken with a group of local residents, mostly white busi-
nessmen but also several Choctaws and African Americans—including
the important county agent Ivory Lyles—who constituted a collection of
friends and supporters of his who affirmed that they were happy to "do
this for Dick."[9] Molpus may have assumed that the support of this group
of locals indicated how the crowd at Mt. Zion would receive his speech.

The Molpus staff had persuaded Governor Mabus that it would not be
politically damaging for him to be there, but Molpus had not been as exact-
ing in calculating the political consequences for his own career.[10] His friend
Florence Mars was in the audience, and she feared that in trying to do the
right thing, he had gone "too far in his apology," that he was ahead of popular sentiment, not just in Neshoba but also around the South. His speech
was emotionally charged, a challenge to the gods of thunder, and they did
not disappoint; rumblings of disagreement came quickly.[11] Molpus himself
had predicted that his words would be upsetting to some in the crowd, that
he would "piss some people off."[12] His speech owed something to being a
Winter disciple, and his belief that Winter's policies had been absorbed by a
generous section of the electorate. But what he said that day was primarily a
product of his own convictions, that the unresolved killings were an enduring tragedy for everyone—for family members and for Mississippians, black
and white. Even with hindsight, knowing the consequences for himself, he
has said he would do it again. It was time to right an injustice.

Those who knew him described Molpus as a man of principle. A close
friend thought the best description of him was as a "social gospel Christian"

who, rather paradoxically, believed religion had no place in political campaigns. At the time of the speech, he was a state leader who wanted to circulate the message that racial change was taking place in the country and it was time for Mississippi to get on board. Unfortunately he failed to anticipate the broad his speech would have.[13] The public response to it brought into sharp relief the continuing line of political separation between the two Mississippis. It revealed the sharp distinction between Old South and New South values, and located Molpus decisively in the ranks of the New Mississippi. Florence Mars had been right; most of the white people in his audience that day were not ready to hear his indictment of their continuing denial of the murders and the significance of the civil rights movement. The question for them remained as it had always been: what had the tragedy of 1964 to do with them? To whites in the audience, as well as those who later heard reports of the speech, the civil rights workers remained outsiders who arrived in their county uninvited. Molpus' listeners did not believe they were complicit in the death of the men and they owed no apology. Reaction to the Molpus speech made it clear that white Neshobans accepted no role in, or responsibility for, what had happened. As a result of the speech, Molpus found his political base shifting to slippery ground.

In 1995, he finally learned the full political cost of the speech, particularly the apology, when he decided to run for governor. At the time, the emergent Republicans were looking to consolidate their power and they were eager to face an opposition candidate they figured might play to their strength as states' rights conservatives. In the gubernatorial race, Molpus faced Kirk Fordice, the Republican incumbent, in a campaign characterized by wicked race baiting by Fordice, a campaign that fulfilled the prediction of Molpus's friends that his Neshoba apology would cost him politically. Neshoba's racial wounds had not healed, and Molpus's words had reopened them. Although the language of the candidates tended to be encoded, the campaign was fundamentally about race, often a slugfest between a conservative and a Mississippi-style liberal. Constance Slaughter-Harvey, an African American attorney who had served as assistant secretary of state under Molpus, had urged him not to run because she foresaw a bloody campaign that would be especially difficult since Molpus "would not fight dirty."[14] Molpus based his campaign hopes on a coalition of voters made up of African Americans, progressive whites, and even working-class whites, collectively a paradigm for the "other" Mississippi.

Prior to the election, some Molpus supporters had believed they saw signs that Mississippi was finally modernizing, that the phoenix was at last rising from its ashes, and Molpus would have a chance to usher in the new Mississippi. But the strength of old values was too strong. Among colleagues in the Winter-Molpus camp were Molpus friends who had a facility for understanding developments in terms of the confluence of events, when "the stars were aligned," and "everything just came together," and this seemed to them such a moment. The right constellation didn't happen in this election, and the historical moment for a moderate alliance looked lost. However, the moderate moment did not leave with a whimper.

From the beginning of the gubernatorial campaign, Molpus realized the apology would be an issue, so he redoubled his efforts to defend the principle he believed was embodied in the apology, which was not just to win. The Fordice/Molpus campaign from the outset was a clash between Old South memory and New South reality. The candidates were from totally opposite positions on the political spectrum. Fordice was a businessman, conservative, outspoken, and rough around the edges, trailing a messy personal history, although his campaign ran on a faith-and-family mantra. Molpus was an experienced politician, a moderate who believed there was "a special place in hell reserved for politicians who campaign on the Bible and religion."[15] The Fordice strategy was to hammer away at Molpus's Neshoba apology, which the Republican candidate did to his best advantage right in Neshoba County itself.

Fordice clearly chose the "famous" Neshoba County Fair as the perfect venue to try to humiliate Molpus. The debate at the fair between the two has often been cited by those in attendance, especially journalists, as high political theater: famous son of good family meets high-spirited good ole boy, the patrician versus the street fighter, although what was at stake was far more than style. Rumors had been circulating for some time that the governor's forty-year marriage was in trouble, a fact he alternately confirmed and then denied, but the hint of marital problems allowed personal matters to enter the overheated campaign. When the moderator of the "Great Debate," Sid Salter, asked Fordice how he reconciled his strong support for family values with his 1993 statement that he and his wife suffered "irreconcilable differences," possibly because of another woman, he responded, "When any of y'all get in that shape and get 'em all educated . . . all that, you come and we'll have that argument then."[16] To which his opponent responded, "You're pointing your finger at me? I don't owe an apology in this state. It's you that owes the apology for that."[17] Molpus then continued, "Your private life does not interest me. Your public life is what appalls me."[18] After which, it was reported, Molpus backers went wild, yelling and cheering. In fact, both candidates had packed the audience with their supporters, with local candidate Molpus enjoying a slight edge. The men were said to have "slugged it out" before a crowd of 3,000, the two speakers waving their arms, as sweat poured down.

The debate, at the Neshoba Fairgrounds in the heat of summer, was a telling moment about where things were in the evolution of Mississippi politics. Touted as the debate of the century, it was transmitted live within the state, which enabled viewers to see that the audience was as much a part of the proceedings as the two men. When the moderator asked the candidates about reopening the 1964 civil rights case, Fordice answered, "I don't believe we need to keep running this state by Mississippi Burning and apologizing for 30 years ago. This is the '90s! This is now! We're on a roll! We've got the best race relations in the United States of America, and we need to speak positive Mississippi."[19] Seemingly unmoved, Molpus stood by his apology of 1989, and said "Mr. Fordice, I apologized . . . to the mothers, fathers, brothers and sisters of those three young men who lost their lives in Mississippi! I apologized then, and I make no apology to you about that."[20] Molpus went on to charge that Fordice had vetoed a telecommunications bill that provided set-aside contracts for women and minorities, to which Fordice responded by pointing at the audience of 3,000 people and saying, "these people don't understand set-asides." The comment set the crowd to hooting.[21] Fordice came back with a charge that Molpus was a flip-flopper on the grocery tax, which allowed Fordice supporters to follow a prearranged plan to clap their flip-flops in the air.[22] When the speeches ended, Fordice said to Molpus, "I want you to shake hands like a man instead of grinning like that." To which Molpus answered, "I'm going to tell the truth, and you may think its negative."[23]

A majority of the news writers who covered the event focused on the circus-like atmosphere, except for an editorial in the Jackson *Clarion-Ledger*, which praised it as a valuable public service, when candidates were able to meet head to head unscripted.[24] Columnist Bill Minor, who regularly wrote an "Eyes on Mississippi" piece, said of the event, "Never in 47 years of going to the Neshoba County Fair have I seen such a show as the GREAT DEBATE between Gov. Kirk Fordice and Secretary of State Dick Molpus last week. They should have charged admission. I thought way back that Molpus was going to be too gentle to get into a roughhouse with the blunt-spoken, hip-shooting Fordice, and the Neshoba debate seemed to be pretty much the case." But Minor thought that a debate coach would judge Molpus the winner, though it was Fordice who established "a rapport with the red necks" in the audience and appealed to "latent prejudices within a lot of whites in Mississippi."[25] Another reporter likely spoke the truth when he said, "They don't like each other. They don't agree with each other politically. And when both view the other, they see the antithesis of everything they believe in from the standpoint of public policy and the practice of governing."[26] It was a verbal battle cheered on by swarms of partisan fairgoers.

When the votes were counted, Molpus had lost. His campaign advisor Bob Lyle offered a number of reasons: Democrats were leaving the party over Bill Clinton; Molpus was facing an incumbent; and the "Mississippi Miracle" known as casino gambling had helped the state economically. But an untold number of white voters, Lyle said, wanted to "punish" Molpus for the 1989 apology.[27] Molpus even lost the vote of his home county of Neshoba, where many whites were especially angered by his suggestion that they were somehow complicit in the Klan murders. On the other hand, blacks voted for Molpus in Neshoba and across the state, demonstrating yet again the affinity between their values and the kind of socially progressive policies he represented. He received less than 20 percent of the white vote. Since the white voters had chosen Fordice, the conservative Republican over Molpus, the moderate Democrat, what had looked to some as an emergent moderate alliance appeared to crash and burn. Could a "revolution go backwards?"

The Phenomenon of Marcus Dupree

While politicians in Jackson, like Governor William Winter, had earlier puzzled over how to define what constituted racial progress in 1980, a young black athlete demonstrated how it could look on the ground, on a Philadelphia football field. School integration had finally admitted talented black athletes into the previously all-white schools, and Philadelphia High School was glad to claim an exceptional black player, Marcus Dupree. In 1980, Philadelphia's folk hero was not the newly elected Governor Winter, who promised significant statewide change at a price, but young Dupree, whose prowess on the field was loudly cheered by an inclusive football crowd, a scene that augured well for the town's future.

He was a young phenom, someone who caught the attention of anyone remotely interested in football, and in the process became a political actor on the local Neshoba scene. A leading sports newspaper, *Inside the Blue Chips*, commented on his physical gifts: "Marcus Dupree is without a doubt the number one player in the United States. His size, 6'3", 222, and

4.3 speed are simply amazing."[28] A white political alderman in Neshoba boasted of a fairly typical Dupree win for the school: "He took a kick on his own forty-yard line, moved left to the fifty, was trapped near the sidelines, then circled back to his thirty. The hapless defenders, as they grabbed at him, came up with handfuls of his jersey. Finally, as he raced down the opposite sideline for a touchdown, he did not have a jersey left, only shoulder pads."[29] During his high school career, "Dupree managed eighty-seven touchdowns and 5,284 yards rushing, an average of 8.3 yards a carry. He had scored fourteen touchdowns in his last three games."[30] When Florence Mars looked back on her town's history some two decades later, she considered that in 1980 Dupree likely did as much as any civil rights measure to bring greater racial harmony to Neshoba County.[31] Dupree's outstanding success in football turned out cheering multiracial crowds of fans, boosters of the young black man. As a result of his talent, Dupree became the most highly recruited high school football player in the nation. His national popularity offered a new sense of pride to a community that had long labored under the burden of a "terrible" racist past. He was a special kind of "Mississippi Miracle," celebrated in Philadelphia in public ceremonies, in parades in his honor, and in local news coverage. In 1980 it was a first for a local black man.

The experience was extraordinary for Neshoba County as well as for the young man himself who shouldered a heavy symbolic weight. Football itself was an important part of the symbolism. Football holds deep significance in the South, a region that some have said literally worships the sport. The coach of Alcorn State once reportedly observed, "In the South [football] is a religion, and Saturday is the holy day." Willie Morris thought so too, and wrote an entire book devoted to the spectacular career of Marcus Dupree, in which he explained that "Friday night was still, as it was in my boyhood, the holy night."[32] The public adulation conferred on Dupree came from all the races in Philadelphia. Born a month before the civil rights killings, Dupree was a member of the first class to go all the way through integrated schools in the city with some of the same kids. He was one of the "born frees," seemingly as popular with white teammates as with black. In his final appearance as a player in Philadelphia, he led his team to victory in a game played in Warriors Stadium at the Choctaw reservation, before a crowd described by Morris as, "the most distinctive . . . I have ever seen . . . four thousand or so people seem[ed] almost an equal mix of whites, blacks, and Indians."[33] In the way that superhero athletes can do, Dupree's achievements were embraced by the whole community, leading a television

sports producer to declaim: "It would be naïve to believe that Marcus sin-
glehandedly gave rise to a 'New South.' But it would be cynical to disbelieve
that he did help change the lives of the people of a small town with a hor-
rible past."[34] A local celebrity, Dupree looked like a portent of what a New
South, a New Mississippi, at its best might be. But his playing career after
high school took unexpected turns, and by 1991 he appeared burned out
physically and perhaps emotionally too, worn down by the expectations
loaded on him by his community and by some inept coaches after he left
Philadelphia. His moment in the sun was over, although Willie Morris continued to be in the grip of the promise once offered by the young star.

The major credit for Marcus Dupree's "Jackie Robinson" kind of historic
contribution to Neshoba County belongs, of course, to Marcus Dupree. But
it is credit to be shared; with the "outside" justices of the Supreme Court
who, in the *Brown* decision, mandated school integration, and with courageous local people, like school superintendent Jim Hurdle, who was willing
to accept the burden of enforcing the law. Marcus Dupree's football talents
would have gone largely unnoticed a decade earlier had he been limited
to playing at a blacks-only high school. His was a significant contribution
to Neshoba County's public history, a black hero, bringing racially mixed
crowds together to support the same goal, a moment when all Neshobans
could see the value in an inclusive society. His achievements impacted the
local community in other ways as well, as *The Neshoba Democrat* integrated
its reporting, devoting full sports-page coverage to his remarkable playing
and the public events honoring him. The Dupree performance encouraged
moderate Neshobans of a certain age—largely those born in the decade
after the Second World War—to anticipate a "generational change" as the
young people of their own children's age, also educated entirely in integrated schools, ushered in a new era of cooperation.[35] The segregationists
had been right in predicting that schools, if integrated, would be the first
place the races would come together.

Still, the tension between old memories and new realities continued.
Vestiges of Jim Crow remained, as in a local restaurant that in 2002
retained the outline on the wall of plaques once designating areas "white"
and "colored."

Mississippi Burning

The opportunity for interracial community that Marcus Dupree's success
created began to fade in the local area following his graduation and his

departure from Philadelphia. The collegial relationships that formed around his football prowess derived from his remarkable celebrity, although there were some institutional changes that were enduring, as at the newspaper.

Yet a potent force originating from outside the area reminded Neshobans that their tarnished image was not an ephemeral thing. They alone did not control their community's legacy, particularly its racism, and its influence on the present. In 1988, when the Hollywood movie *Mississippi Burning* went into wide release, its retelling of the 1964 killings emphasized the culpability of local residents. The film's title was borrowed from the FBI code for the investigation, and it appeared at a fortuitous moment, as other public flares lit up the country sky to republicize Neshoba's unflattering past. Described by its makers as a work of fiction, the movie gave all the appearances of being an historical docudrama. Filmed in Neshoba County, it portrayed highly charged scenes of intimidation, lynching, and arson. Dick Molpus said he saw the film just before accepting the invitation to speak at Mt. Zion's twenty-fifth-anniversary commemoration, and found it deeply moving, a reaction that was shared by journalist Jerry Mitchell, who said viewing it produced an epiphanic moment for him. Admirers and critics came away with vastly different reactions, but one thing the film did do was to thrust Mississippi once again into a harsh national spotlight.

Though it was fiction, the movie introduced younger audiences to issues that had informed the civil rights movement. The story was painted with broad strokes: all whites appeared mean, narrow, and when not openly racist, certainly segregationists; while blacks were depicted as victims, cowed, abused by whites in law enforcement and in the community generally. The film introduced the link to the Mafia—a Gregory Scarpa stand-in—through a brutish character sent to Neshoba to extract information for the FBI from a terrified white man. It showed a horrific lynch scene and endless images of fire burning through churches and homes. The FBI agents emerged as the real heroes, dedicated to solving the crime even if it took highly questionable means. Nominated for numerous awards, highlighted on the cover of *Time* magazine, the film was attacked by critics for its sensationalism and savaged by those who took offense at its portrayal of tired old stereotypes; the ignorant white racist and the pious, self-effacing black. Yet because of its graphic images and dramatic storyline, the film found a large audience and the subject of civil rights gained new currency. In much the way that *Schindler's List* introduced younger Germans to a visceral portrayal of Nazism, one that suggested public culpability—at least morally if not criminally—*Mississippi Burning* portrayed white responsibility for the events of 1964 to young Americans. By incriminating the sheriff and other law enforcement in the area, it offered a vivid description of the limits of legal justice for blacks in ways that written accounts rarely could. It showed white Neshobans generally as complicit in an environment of hate and fear.

The history was inaccurate—though it did not claim to be history—but it put faces on the perpetrators of racist crime as well as those who were the victims of racist abuse. An unfortunate meaningless ending simply compounded the film's imperfections. Black audiences criticized the level of passivity imposed on their Southern kin, as Longdale residents Freddie Grady and Jennifer Riley Hathorn had said in our very first conversation. Nevertheless, despite its flaws it became a catalyst for conversation among a new generation of Americans about the unresolved murders in Neshoba County. For white Neshobans, it meant revisiting the crime and hearing again the scorn heaped upon them, stirring emotions many probably hoped had been put to bed.

Texas native Jerry Mitchell of the *Clarion-Ledger* said the film made him aware of just how compliant Mississippians were generally, and Neshobans particularly, in supporting the murders and the aftermath. It encouraged him to begin investigating cold civil rights cases, he said, such as the murder of Medgar Evers.[36] It was Mitchell's investigative work on Evers's killer, Byron de la Beckwith, that led to a new trial and the disclosure that Beckwith's defense money was mysteriously channeled through the Mississippi State Sovereignty Commission. It gave Mitchell investigative credentials as well as greater publicity, as a Mitchell-like character was portrayed in a movie about the Evers's case. He wrote regular front-page stories about movement events in Neshoba from the civil rights era, providing names and dates that the filmmakers did not possess. He discovered clues that had been overlooked and found forgotten witnesses. His columns, along with the movie and Dick Molpus's apology, all coming at the end of the decade of the 1980s, revived the case most white Neshobans tried to ignore. The worshipping community at Mt. Zion Church, for decades their commemorative services the lone witness to the events, became a primary resource for those now interested in the history.

The Neshoba Democrat

Not everyone in Neshoba County kept current with Jerry Mitchell's columns, although virtually everyone knew the stories in the most recent issue of *The Neshoba Democrat*, the weekly paper that had been offering up news of the community since 1881. Like many weekly papers in small rural areas that aid community cohesion, it was a good barometer of local priorities. Before the 1980s few blacks were mentioned in the paper except as perpetrators of crimes. It was an important departure from the past when it began giving extensive coverage to Marcus Dupree's victories. Another notable marker in its history was the hiring in 1966 of Stanley Dearman as editor; a journalist with a more moderate voice than the region was accustomed to hearing.

Dearman joined a proud journalistic tradition at *The Democrat*. The paper had in the past employed Turner Catledge, who moved on to become managing editor of the *New York Times*. Catledge once observed that the two papers were much the same, except for the "size of the figures."[37] Their missions, he thought, were similar: they served as mirrors for readers about "what was happening in the day and [to make] a record for those who chance[d] this way in years to come."[38] Catledge lost his enthusiasm for his old Southern newspaper after friends complained that *The Times* published too much about "The Troubles," and he offered that "the town had let me down."[39]

What Catledge described was an old-school notion of the role of a local paper in a country town, that it was similar to a diary and a social calendar, an approach Dearman gradually changed. Dearman thought a local paper, especially one that served as the major—and for many the only—print source for news of the world, had an editorial responsibility to help its community understand its role in a broader context. As he grew into the job, he became willing to uncover the tortured corpses of the past and write about them for his readers. He retained the neighborliness of a local paper, but his editorial policy was more open and progressive than his predecessors. He took on the county ban on alcohol consumption, arguing that it was wrong, hypocritical, and dangerous. Everyone knew that Neshobans drove to the county line to buy their liquor. And while the county's official position prohibited the production and public consumption of alcohol, the penalties were selectively imposed on moonshine makers, many of them black, and on public drinkers.

Dearman eventually rolled out bits of Neshoba's segregationist history. He joined the paper after the 1964 beatings and murders, but before the 1967 trial that put some of the perpetrators in prison for several years. Slowly his editorials began to explore the need to reexamine the case and to bring to trial all those involved in any way with the crime. The murders and equal justice for black Neshobans were separate issues for him, as they were for almost all white Mississippians, and the paper reflected that. Nevertheless, years later he said that resolving the murders had a "metaphysical sense" for him; it was all "about justice." Yet in his role as editor he received more criticism and harassment about his views on alcohol consumption, he said, than about the murders, an indication of the secrets Neshoba was most eager to protect.[40]

Dearman editorialized about the case periodically, although in his early years on the job it seemed hopeless to think that anything he wrote would ever bring Killen, Posey, Price, Burrage, and the others to full justice. The Dearman years were nevertheless marked by greater openness in the paper than had been the case in the past. He provided the community with more details about its hidden past, commented on the achievements of black residents, though withal he possessed that rare journalistic skill of being able to introduce bits of new community history without disturbing the politics of most of his readers. His editorials about the 1964 case grew sharper and more urgent as the decade of the 1980s came to a close.

The Advent of Casinos

While the majority of Dearman's editorials mirrored community values, reporting about Choctaw plans for legalized gambling, which would bring in outsiders who smoked, drank, and bet, would appear to challenge the beliefs of many of his readers in this Bible Belt state. But casinos became an important addition to the county beginning in the 1990s, through the efforts of the Mississippi Band of Choctaw Indians and their enterprising chief, Phillip Martin. Although not new in the state, gambling had previously been confined along the riverbanks and the Gulf Coast. Martin had bigger plans for the Choctaws.

Chief Martin possessed high energy and the imagination of an entrepreneur. Born in the area, he joined the military as a young man, and was appalled when he returned home to discover that Choctaws still lived in dire poverty. The tribe had lost its claim to the land in the 1830 Treaty of Dancing Rabbit, and by the 1960s many on the reservation were sharecroppers on land they believed rightly belonged to them. Martin was soon elected to the tribal council, and then became its president, where he created a policy that called for federal legislative measures to create new economic opportunities on the reservation. He began with manufacturing.

In addition to his entrepreneurial skills, Martin was an astute and energetic leader, who learned how to be a Washington lobbyist in order to secure government support and find willing investors for his projects. By 1979, he had arranged with Packard Electric, a division of General Motors, to open a plant in the county, with other corporations lined up. The chief later claimed that between 1979 and 1985 he and the tribe had created 4,000 permanent, full-time jobs on the reservation, hiring not just Choctaws but other people in the area.[41] There was a clamor for the new jobs at the reservation as small farming all but disappeared, leaving only the lumber industry to pick up the slack.

Legalized gambling had started in coastal riverboats parked in June 1990, after the legislature had given its approval.[42] Although seemingly out of sync with local religious values, gaming was soon known as the "Mississippi Miracle," and it made Mississippi the third-largest gambling-revenue-producing state in the nation in less than a decade, behind only Nevada and New Jersey. One explanation for its remarkable growth was the fact that the general electorate as a whole was never asked to vote directly on the matter. In counties where casinos were proposed, the county electorate was told about the economic benefits casinos would bring, and the communities inevitably approved the necessary measures. In the beginning, politicians were willing to support gaming where it already claimed a place, along the Gulf and lining the Mississippi River, but were reluctant to agree to its expansion. That changed as the money flowed in: money spoke with a loud voice in this impoverished state. By 2002, thirty casinos—not including the Choctaws—employed 32,000 workers, generated 2.7 billion dollars in revenue, and paid over $32 million in state taxes.[43] Many religious leaders and their organizations opposed casinos—which also served alcohol—on moral grounds, while others opposed them for different reasons, some that resembled the comment made by Nobel Laureate Paul Samuelson, that gambling involved "simply sterile transfers of money or goods between individuals, creating no new money or goods . . . its main purpose is to kill time."[44]

Despite the criticism, Chief Martin recognized the economic gain attached to casino gambling and lobbied for high-stakes gaming in flashy casinos on the Choctaw reservation. The chief approached the federal government, and also the legislature and the governor, arguing that Choctaw gaming would be different from that in the rest of the state because the casinos would be on Indian-owned land, and besides it would be discriminatory to deny gambling to the Choctaws since it was practiced elsewhere in Mississippi to great financial success. Following intense lobbying by him, in 1992 he reached a tentative agreement with the new governor, first-term Republican Kirk Fordice.

Fordice proved to be the flip-flopper when it came to gaming. Issues related to race actually dominated his administration, although he famously said "Mississippi doesn't do race anymore." Black legislators didn't like him, and legislative fights over race-related matters were reminiscent of the battles during Reconstruction and later Jim Crow. But he conveyed an image of a rough-hewn politician white Mississippians identified with— as his reelection campaign with Dick Molpus showed—and they accepted his rugged speech, his religious convictions, his racial choices, and even his troubled personal life. They were therefore willing to go along with his opinion when first he said he opposed gaming and casino gambling, and then in his second term reversed himself and agreed to the entreaties of Chief Martin and others, people who often showed up on lists of contributors to his campaign coffers. Martin apparently made a convincing case for the economic boost gambling could provide to Neshoba and east central Mississippi, leading the governor to sign an "Accord between the Executive Branches of the Governments of the Mississippi Band of Choctaw Indians and the State of Mississippi" on November 25, 1997.[45] It became the pivotal document that opened the way for Choctaw gaming, beginning in Neshoba and growing from there.

The Choctaws once employed the subsequently discredited Washington lobbyist Jack Abramoff to argue their case, but Chief Martin proved to be the more effective negotiator. Dick Molpus recalled running into the chief at Reagan Airport, surprised to see this normally conservatively dressed man in full Indian regalia; beaded shirt, a belt, and even a headdress. When Molpus commented that he had never seen the chief dressed that way, Martin reportedly said, "I don't usually dress this way, but they eat it up in Washington."[46]

When the gaming resorts opened in Neshoba they produced a dramatic change in the local landscape. The Silver Star Hotel was the first to open in 1994, followed in 2002 by the Golden Moon. It was a jolt to the senses when drivers rounded the piney woods outside Philadelphia suddenly to encounter enormous Las Vegas–style entertainment centers. The casinos produced an obvious economic boost, but also a change in a sociological sense. They attracted a clientele from around the southeastern states that was new to Neshoba, people eager to spend their time gaming with a drink in one hand and a cigarette in the other. As the largest employers in the region, casinos became a source for newfound wealth. Choctaw people were the biggest benefactors of this revenue, enjoying the new schools, hospitals, roads, utility services, and other amenities that appeared on the reservation territory. But non-Indians also enjoyed economic gains, either by working at the casinos or in one of the ancillary services that sustained them, although often it was part-time, late-night work in jobs that were unable to lift temporary employees above the poverty line. In fact, critics of the casinos cited this plethora of low-wage jobs as a reason to oppose them, since for many of the workers employment did not provide a living wage. But for devotees of the casinos, it was like having the Neshoba County Fair open year round. Everyone was welcome. "Y'all come" was the message, inviting guests to dine in one of the many restaurants, play golf, relax at the hotel, and of course, gamble at the tables. Although local religious groups continued their protests, the Choctaw bonanza was not to be denied.[47]

The Neshoba population at the turn of the twenty-first century was roughly 30,000, distributed among 19,500 whites, 6,000 blacks, and 4,200 Indians. The Choctaws therefore represented only about 14 percent of the local population, but they had lit up the local economy, not just through hiring and trade, but by paying taxes based on a negotiated arrangement. Most financial arrangements were private Choctaw matters, so their books were usually opened only when outside auditors asked to see them. Soon the tribal leaders expanded their manufacturing projects into overseas locations, opening two plants in Mexico. By 2002, the casinos had replaced timbering as the major industry in Neshoba.[48]

Choctaw entrepreneurial success contributed mightily to transforming the local area. It brought in new people as visitors and it brought in new money. Jerry Mitchell believed that the casinos, and the change they brought to the region, contributed to the willingness of white Neshobans to press for a new trial for the 1964 killers. Just as important was the object lesson Choctaw economic success revealed to Neshoba's white business leaders. The very colorful Choctaw resorts demonstrated what could be accomplished financially even in rural east central Mississippi when development was detached from the general opprobrium visited on the county because of the racial violence of the past. Choctaws provided a living model of what success could look like in Neshoba. It was a case of people of the First Nation bringing modern development to an area harnessed to the memory of a premodern past. Because the Choctaws were distanced from Neshoba's legacy of the murders and black racial discrimination, they were not tainted by the experience of white supremacist history that blighted the area. The implicit message of Choctaw achievement was that if east central Mississippi could overcome its racist past, it could become an entrepreneurial zone, and for industries besides casino gambling.

The Smoking Gun

The most damaging glimpse into Neshoba's hidden past came in 1998, in a column written by Jerry Mitchell in the *Clarion-Ledger*. In it Mitchell revealed the contents of a sealed interview Sam Bowers had given to an interviewer after he had been convicted in the Neshoba conspiracy trial in 1967, and Preacher Killen had walked free. Mitchell fortuitously gained access to the Klan chief's secret comments at the Mississippi Department of Archives and History. He reported to his readers that Bowers named Edgar Ray Killen as "the main instigator in the entire affair" in 1964, although it was Bowers himself who had approved the "elimination" of Mickey Schwerner.[49] Bowers, the two-time imprisoned head of the Mississippi Klan, had fingered Killen as the planner of "the entire affair," that is, the full conspiracy.

It was not Bowers's intention to violate the Neshoba code of silence about the murders, directing that his interview be sealed until after his death. Mitchell, however, as a good journalist, identified Killen in his column and tied him to other Klan activities. Most Neshobans already knew, or at least suspected, that Edgar Ray Killen was a Klan leader, but most were probably not ready to see him singled out as the lead conspirator of the murder and beatings. Because of Bowers's own former role as Klan head, he made a credible witness about who participated in the murders and the related widespread Klan violence.

When it became known that Bowers had named Killen, Mickey Schwerner's widow, Rita Schwerner Bender, observed that a case against Killen must be about more than just the "indictment of one old man," but must also include examination of "state-sponsored violence."[50] Bender's charge related to the web of segregationist connections, from the Mississippi State Sovereignty Commission to the Klan, that, unchecked, had promoted violence not only against civil rights workers like her husband, but black residents in every community. There were the Neshoba murders and there was the historic and persistent violence against blacks, and what tied them together was state political support, an injustice far greater than the term "systemic racism" would suggest. Killen's actions needed to be understood within a climate of generalized violence against blacks. Another relative of one of the victims in 1964, Ben Chaney, the brother of James, had been making the same argument for some time, and he, too, called for reopening the case.

By the time Mitchell's column on Bowers appeared, he had already achieved national recognition for his dogged work in a number of civil rights cold cases. He had contributed to the case against Bowers in the death by fire of Vernon Dahmer, as well as to the case against Byron de la Beckwith. He had gained access to the Sovereignty Commission files before they became generally available, and learned that the commission had actively abetted segregationist activists like Beckwith, individuals who undermined federal law. He had also gathered evidence about Bobby Cherry, convicted as a participant in the Birmingham church bombing that had killed four little girls. Mitchell's thorough investigations had helped lead to convictions, and his column became credible evidence against Killen. A Baptist like Killen himself, Mitchell was once described by Killen as "the re-headed Jew" who he would surely like to see gone from the scene.

Gathering the Evidence

The families of the murder victims—Rita Bender, Ben Chaney, Fannie Lee Chaney, and Carolyn Goodman—thought Mitchell's column introduced important new evidence to the thirty-five-year-old case. They contacted Mississippi's attorney general, Mike Moore, and Neshoba's district attorney, Ken Turner, to say that Mitchell's column provided irrefutable new evidence for a new trial. Turner was of the opinion that Bowers's interview did not rise to the test of new evidence warranting reopening the case, although Moore, perhaps feeling empowered following his victory against the country's big tobacco companies, believed they did, and in 1999 he authorized the state to reopen the investigation.[51] The FBI shared its voluminous MIBURN file with the state, files that included additional evidence of the lack of justice for black residents of Neshoba.

Even more startling was the emergence of Cecil Price, deputy sheriff of the county in 1964, as a potential witness in a new trial. Price was one of the leading figures in the murder case, a former Klan member, and a known torment to local blacks. He had been one of those sent to prison in 1967 for violating the civil rights of the three men, and once returned to Philadelphia, he seemed to those who knew him a changed man. The residents of Longdale, who had suffered under his watch, agreed that he appeared to be a new person.[52] Freddie Grady of Longdale had worked with Price for the county and was convinced that his change of heart was genuine.[53] He worshipped at the First Methodist Church in Philadelphia, worked at odd jobs, and landed a position with the county working on the roads. In meetings with investigators from the attorney general's office beginning in 1999, Price laid out a description of the murders that conformed to a confession given in 1964 by Horace Doyle Barnett, another participant. In both accounts Killen figured prominently, as the organizer, chief planner, and contact person with the Meridian Klan.[54] Price took a lie-detector test and signed a statement indicating his role in the murders, "pursuant to a proffer."[55]

Another potential witness for the prosecution if the state were to bring a murder case was a man named Bob Stringer, who many years earlier had worked for Sam Bowers. Stringer lacked the personal association with the events of June 21, 1964 that Cecil Price possessed, but he knew from his own experience that Bowers and Killen were friends and that they had talked together about the "elimination" of Mickey Schwerner.[56] Jerry Mitchell included yet another contact in one of his columns, this one with a former reporter-lawman named George Metz, a long-time friend of Killen's, who reported that Killen had told him he had gone back to the murder site to clean up any remains on the ground or in the surrounding area after the killings.[57]

But then the unthinkable happened. In May 2001, Cecil Price fell fifteen feet from a cherry picker to the ground. Critically injured, he died soon after. The attorney general had been counting on Price as the key witness for the prosecution if the state brought a murder case. It appeared that with Price's death the case had collapsed. Rumors had been circulating in Neshoba County that Price had been talking to the attorney general, a conversation that had come to the attention of the county district attorney and probably many others. To those knowledgeable about the case, his death—alone, and from a cherry picker—seemed ominously ill-timed: his would have been the most vital new testimony since the 1967 federal trial. A few suggested suicide, and others—including Dick Molpus—considered something more sinister, with Molpus wondering aloud, "was it murder or was it suicide? They are not to be toyed with."[58] Jerry Mitchell said the autopsy report noted simply that Price died of head injuries.[59] Molpus's dark allusion to "they" pointed to the possibility that Killen's supporters were still around, armed with staying power and ingenuity. Stanley Dearman thought the development showed the imponderable quality of

Neshoba, which he framed as a question that reflected on the area: "Can you believe that this town produced [both] Dick Molpus and Edgar Ray Killen."[60] Few people, in fact, seemed to believe that Price had fallen accidentally, with Killen partisans lining up behind suicide as the cause, and advocates for a new trial surmising it was murder.

Not only did Cecil Price disappear from the case, in 2004 Bob Stringer committed suicide. What had looked like an accumulation of credible new evidence for a murder trial was gone. Florence Mars said that Attorney General Moore was reported to have decided he no longer had enough evidence to reopen the case, that legal avenues had been closed. The decision was a commentary on the unresolved troubles of the town.

For the residents of Longdale, experienced with justice denied, this turn of events came as no surprise. Most assumed that the state of Mississippi would likely never hold a trial for the murders of the civil rights activists, and their own devastations—burning and beatings—would go unacknowledged, just as all the other abuse had. They would continue their annual commemorative celebrations as testimony to the victims and their own values.[61] The outlook of Mt. Zion Church members was forward-looking, and called for continued witnessing of their faith to the world.

Addressing Unfinished Business

THE PHILADELPHIA COALITION

> *The state of Mississippi has never brought criminal indictments against anyone for the murders of the three young men—an act of omission of historic significance.*
> RESOLUTION OF PHILADELPHIA COALITION, 2004

> *This is going to be a whitewash.*
> STATEMENT OF BEN CHANEY, 2004

> *This is an extraordinary church.*
> DAVID GOODMAN, BROTHER OF ANDREW, 2014

Mt. Zion and the Vanguard of Change

If the gubernatorial defeat was a personal loss for Dick Molpus, the campaign outcome was a gift for the people of Longdale, political moderates, and advocates of civil rights in the state, who could now count on his commitment to racial justice without the distractions of partisan politics. In his race against Fordice, Molpus had shown himself a friend to civil rights. He was a voice of moderation, and once out of politics and returned to private life, he could invest in the causes that interested him most, namely educational reform and racial justice. Families of the civil rights victims, who had been trying to reopen the murder case since the unsatisfactory outcome of the 1967 trials, were encouraged by Molpus's 1989 apology to believe a new trial could happen. Molpus was an engaged activist whose principles didn't quite fit with the Old South values of mainstream Mississippi. In the 1989 speech, he had asked for a new trial along with a re-commitment to the goals of the martyred men, essentially a global definition of the need for justice. And in the years between 1995 and 2005 two new organizations appeared on the scene regionally and statewide to work on such issues: the Philadelphia Coalition and the William Winter Institute for Racial Reconciliation. The Philadelphia Coalition was a pioneering triracial organization in Neshoba County, that made reopening the 1964 case a priority. The William Winter Institute for Racial Reconciliation was located at Ole Miss, with a statewide program to help communities repair the bridges that divided them. The two groups represented, along with Dick Molpus, an alternate Mississippi, committed to inclusiveness, moderation, modernity, and openness. Mt. Zion's commemorative services, which had been providing an almost singular witness to such values since 1965, was an integral part of this moderate coalition.

The people of Mt. Zion learned from the 1967 trial testimony that their community had been targeted in the 1964 Klan conspiracy. The plans Edgar Ray Killen and the other Klan members had devised for the nighttime attacks involved more than just getting rid of the three civil rights activists; they intended to trap Schwerner and the others at the church, then burn the church and attack any of its defenders who got in their way. Mt. Zion Church had given its permission for the voting rights school and a raid would both eliminate the outsiders and end local agitation for the vote. Freedom Schools held the potential to produce a bloc of black voters, whose political choices might well upend Old South values. As the conspiracy plans unfolded, it was apparent that Klan racism disrespected the inviolability of Mt. Zion Church and the rights of its people. A new trial for the killers would draw attention to the connection between the murders and the black vote. Among some white Neshobans, though hardly friends of the Philadelphia Coalition, there was also a dawning recognition that the tarnished image of their town was the result of the legacy of the murders; for them, too, perhaps the time had come to take action on the unresolved case.

However, a new trial, the objective of most white Philadelphians and all black Longdale residents. White Neshobans wanted "closure," meaning that in some relatively benign way the killers of the three movement activists would be made to pay for their crime, thereby freeing the town to rebuild its image. For the people at Mt. Zion, the conspiracy had produced not just one crime but two, the first was the brutal murders of three men, and the second was the death of their mission to increase the black vote. Dick Molpus alluded to such a connection between the two sets of crimes in his speech at Mt. Zion, and though it failed to catch on with many beyond the Longdale people, it generated conversation about the unresolved murders.

Another opportunity to press for a new trial came in January 2004 when Molpus was again a keynote speaker in the county, this time at a gathering of business people and bankers, people Molpus considered old friends. His comments to the two hundred people at the Lake Tia'Khatta setting—well received, he thought—called for a "reexamination" of the county's past, which would be a step in reordering, and perhaps rewriting, its past as fact rather than legend.[1] Most people in the audience knew that Mt. Zion was planning for its fortieth commemorative service, and that public forum could provide an opportunity to combine celebrating the memories of the victims with a call for a new trial.[2] Mt. Zion's services, it was generally agreed, called up memories of suffering and death, but also focused on the work still to be done to foster redemption and reconciliation. Talk of a joint community/church service, therefore, gathered support over the following months, envisioned as a large celebration with the potential to draw in those with little or no familiarity with the events of 1964. Some of those at the lake event, including Molpus himself, were included in the preparations for the fortieth-anniversary commemoration.

Mt. Zion and the Philadelphia Coalition

Active planning for the June service began not long after the meeting at Lake Tia'Khatta, when Susan Glisson, the director of the Institute for Racial Reconciliation, arrived from Ole Miss to discuss with local people in Philadelphia an agenda for the commemoration.[3] The planning group agreed to meet weekly through the spring, its members already of a single mind when it came to the matter of a new trial. By late spring the group had taken as its name the Philadelphia Coalition, a multiracial collection of local people who turned to Glisson and the Winter Institute to advise them on how best to move forward toward their goal of a new trial. Mt. Zion was well represented on the coalition by three of the congregation's active members; Jewel McDonald, Jennifer Riley Hathorn, and Elsie Kirksey.

Glisson filled the role of outside adviser, invited by members who were familiar with her work at the Winter Institute.[4] She was a trained historian, and she brought to the meetings not only her experience from the Institute, but the perspective she had acquired previously when she worked with President Clinton's One America project

in 1998, the president's initiative on racial reconciliation. Her analysis
of a meeting of representatives on Clinton's panel held at Ole Miss was
instrumental in the decision to make the university a permanent center for examining racial issues. Former Governor Winter had served on
Clinton's panel, and with his help, and assistance from the university
chancellor Robert Khayat, the institute was opened on campus in August
1999. It was a privately funded think tank, and counted Dick Molpus
as one of its founding board members.[5] An important dimension of
the institute's mission was to work with local communities, such as
Philadelphia, Molpus's hometown. The Philadelphia Coalition became
an extension of the program of the institute.[6]

The Philadelphia Coalition presented a radically different face to the
local community. A collection of whites, blacks, and Choctaws, it was
the first truly interracial community organization since Reconstruction.
In addition to Glisson as adviser, and the three people from Mt. Zion
Church, there were three representatives from the Choctaw reservation;
Tim Tubby, Bea Carson, and Cyrus Ben. LeRoy Clemons, local head of the
NAACP, was a member, as was a close friend of Dick Molpus who was
also a descendant of a lumber family, Fent DeWeese, a vocal yellow dog
Democrat. DeWeese had a counterpart at a number of meetings in Jim
Prince, the conservative editor of *The Neshoba Democrat*, who remained on
the margins of the organization. The former editor of the paper, Stanley
Dearman, on the other hand, became an active member of the coalition.
Molpus was considered an honorary chairperson. Jim Prince offered to
publish an announcement in *The Neshoba Democrat* inviting anyone in
the area interested in participating in the work to come to a meeting at the
First United Methodist Church. In addition to this published announcement, Glisson and Molpus spoke directly to individuals, and the result
was the twenty-eight member Philadelphia Coalition.

Inspiration for the coalition had come from a variety of sources. It had
been influenced by the modestly improved racial conditions in Neshoba
County, by the efforts of the victims' families, by the persistent reminder
afforded by Mt. Zion's services, and by the concern of white local moderates like Dick Molpus and former lumberman Fent DeWeese. These local
interests coalesced around the Winter Institute. Such a culturally diverse
make-up of the coalition was unique for Neshoba County, making it a kind
of Rainbow Coalition of the area's people, its members more progressive
and more socially involved than many in town. The spirit of its patron,
the Winter Institute, pervaded the discussions. The initial challenge facing

the group faced was simply how to talk to each other across old historical divides, a matter that first showed itself when the group began considering ways to disseminate its message throughout the city and the county. LeRoy Clemons proposed the coalition sponsor a dedicated march up Beacon Street in the city center. Others thought a more cautious approach would be more appropriate, such as writing a letter to the editor of the paper.[7] Clemons suggested that before moving ahead with any program, the members needed to learn how to talk to each other. Soon at the top of the agenda was not only planning for the fortieth-anniversary service, but also reconsideration of the 1964 case, the latter pegged to a recognition that any trial had to include the devastation that had occurred to the people of Longdale.

The Role of the Winter Institute

To outsiders familiar with only the Old South image of Mississippi, the Winter Institute for Racial Reconciliation could sound like an oxymoron, at best a cosmetic effort by wealthy business people to polish the image of the state. But the founders were committed people, individuals like former Governor Winter, Susan Glisson, Chancellor Khayat, historian John Hope Franklin, and Dick Molpus, activists and scholars who had shown a longstanding concern for racial justice, as well as the goals of President Clinton's One America Project: An Initiative on Race. Located at the University of Mississippi, the institute was independent on the contributions of individual donors, corporations, and philanthropies like the Kellogg Foundation.[8] It became another example of the "other" Mississippi, a small but energized minority in the state that few outsiders knew about, one that poked holes in the caricature of the state as home only to rednecks, racists, and demagogues. It remained the case, however, that the Old South image of Mississippi was perpetuated in popular media outlets featuring comedians and talk-show hosts seemingly unaware of an ongoing struggle for racial justice being waged by small groups of blacks and whites. Mississippi itself contributed to its enduring Old South stereotype by its repeated lopsided voting results in national elections. The institute seems to understand that it has a heavy workload. The Clinton initiative was a formative influence on the creation of the institute, as was the collaborative efforts of Chancellor Khayat and former Governor Winter.[9] Perhaps the most decisive influence came from a meeting in February 1998 planned by Susan Glisson, at which 1,000 Mississippians, black and white, met in small group sessions to discuss ways to remove the vestiges of discrimination in the state.

Once settled in at Ole Miss, the institute undertook a study of global models of reconciliation in societies that have been previously broken internally. At the time, in 1999, the South African Truth and Reconciliation Commission (TRC) enjoyed worldwide acclaim, its hearings regarded as the inspiration for the Rainbow Nation, rather than a feared bloodbath after years of apartheid. The institute established contact with the TRC, and later with others involved in reconciliation programs, such as in Belfast.[10] The connection with the TRC expanded to include exchange visits between staff at Ole Miss and Cape Town, and familiarity with former TRC participants like Peter Storey. The leadership of the institute realized that its historical circumstances were vastly different from South Africa's, the most obvious being that it lacked a government mandate for its work, and it was not the designated voice of a persecuted majority. Nevertheless, there were similarities in its quest for justice and reconciliation, procedures that were common to the process in Mississippi and elsewhere. Chief among them was a need to come to terms with the past; in its simplest terms, it meant victim storytelling about a past dominated by persecution. At TRC hearings, transgressors had been able to seek forgiveness from those whom they had harmed. In addition, the South African Commission created a program of restitution for those who had suffered, its funds designed to come from contributions by the government, business, and individuals. The TRC had functioned well as a transitional vehicle for South Africa, preventing large-scale violence. Ultimately, however, it lacked the resources to implement its goals for the country as a whole, and that created resentment among those who believed their needs were being neglected. The important message the TRC gave to the world was that reconciliation demanded open communication between former adversaries, a principle that the Winter Institute has attempted to follow, especially in its community bridge-building program. In a period of just over fifteen years, the institute counted about sixteen interracial community groups similar to the Philadelphia Coalition.[11]

The Winter Institute and the Philadelphia Coalition were therefore bound in a kind of symbiotic relationship; they exchanged information and staff around a common goal. The coalition had an abundance of critics in the local community who saw no need for the organization and were openly opposed. Mindful of the discontent, the Neshoba County district attorney, Mark Duncan, urged coalition members to proceed with their agendas with care to avoid antagonizing those not inclined to reopen the murder case. But next to planning for the fortieth anniversary, a new trial was high the on coalition agenda. Ben Chaney, brother to James, had his own reservations about the coalition. He worried that combining the community's interest in the coalition with the traditional services at Mt. Zion Church would diminish black control over an historical event the church had created and maintained for many years. Other veterans of the civil rights movement agreed with him.

After several meetings and considerable debate, the coalition produced a resolution drafted by Stanley Dearman that called on the state to seek justice in the 1964 case. It said in part:

> The state of Mississippi has never brought criminal indictments against anyone for the murders of the three young men—an act of omission of historic significance. . . . With firm resolve and strong belief in the rule of law, we call on the Neshoba County District Attorney, the state Attorney General and the U.S. Department of Justice to make every effort to seek justice in this case.[12]

The resolution put the coalition on record as favoring the reopening of the case, and making it part of Mt. Zion's fortieth-anniversary memorial.

Molpus: "Our Enemies Are Not Each Other"

Coalition members agreed that the collaborative church/community memorial service in 2004 would be held at the large Coliseum in Philadelphia rather than at the church. The traditional service would remain at Mt. Zion, just celebrated later in the day. Using a large arena like the Coliseum for the occasion and inviting a host of notable speakers were meant to signify the momentous nature of the event. The suggestion of one planner that Republican Governor Haley Barbour be an invited speaker—presumably his presence a sign of state backing for their agenda—became a divisive issue. Some participants thought Barbour would be a red herring: he played the race card in politics, including endorsing the controversial new state flag that still flaunted a miniature version of the old Confederate symbol. There was also that contingent within the coalition concerned with the preservation of black control, and those people eventually withdrew from the planning.

The compromise arranged by the planners was to separate the two events scheduled for June 20, 2004, with the first one at the Coliseum, bolstered by a heavy political presence, and the second at the church the same afternoon. It was the Coliseum event that, as expected, drew the larger crowd, said to number over 2,000, with a collection of speakers known locally and throughout the state. Governor Barbour's presence on the platform captured the attention of liberals in the audience such as Donna Ladd, editor of the progressive *Jackson Free Press*, who was overheard to say, "What the hell is he doing here?"[13] It did not seem a likely political venue for him. The keynoter for the event was former Governor Winter, one of an assemblage of speakers who represented both politics and the civil rights movement.

But the person who stirred the crowd was Dick Molpus. According to Donna Ladd, he roused the crowd to cheers and tears in the best tradition of political oratory. His speech envisioned what was required to reconcile the races, and to bring justice to Philadelphia and Neshoba County. Reminiscent of his 1989 apology, he told the crowd, "Until justice is done, we are all at least somewhat complicit in those deaths." He pointed out again that there were twenty men from the local area who had been involved in the original planning for and carrying out of the murders, and though some likely took their knowledge to the grave, others "certainly told wives, children and buddies of their involvement." A few, old and infirm, could use the present moment to make peace with themselves and with God by standing up and sharing their awful secrets.

Molpus's speech did as the people of Mt. Zion had hoped. It moved beyond the most pressing item, the need to prosecute the surviving killers of Goodman, Chaney, and Schwerner, to include a plea for justice, so lacking for black people. He said essentially what Mt. Zion members had been saying for decades: that the two realities in Neshoba's history could not be separated, that the murders of the three young men were organically connected to justice for the black community. The message was not what anyone from inside or outside of Mississippi had expected to hear from a white former politician. It was essentially a call for reexamination of history and memory. Though not said in his speech, he thought of the men as martyrs. In the tradition of America's earlier martyrs, such as those at the Boston Massacre in 1770, the deaths could not be separated from the cause of liberty and revolution. Neither could the deaths of Goodman, Chaney, and Schwerner be detached from the larger cause of full black freedom. Molpus's words were a sharp public reminder to recognize the significance of how history is remembered.

True justice, Molpus implied, required moving beyond retributive justice to restorative justice, changing the focus from punishment to reconciliation, and a commitment to healing the damages of the past. The most meaningful tribute to the victims, he said, would be to work together to reconcile the differences among people and races. As he concluded, Molpus laid out a hopeful vision: "And finally, we Mississippians must announce to the world what we've learned in forty years. We know today that our enemies are not each other. Our real enemies are ignorance, illiteracy, poverty, racism, disease, unemployment, crime, the high dropout rate, teen pregnancy and lack of support for the public schools. We can defeat all those enemies—not as a divided people—black or white or Indian—but as a united force banded together by our common humanity—by our own desire to lift each other up."[14] He made explicit the connection between the murders and the history of black injustice.

The speech, rousing and amen-ed, got a standing ovation from an excited crowd who did help "lift each other up." Molpus recapitulated the hope of the Philadelphia Coalition, that if Mississippi could undertake this task, and become the "other" Mississippi, it could serve as a model for the rest of the country. Mississippi, long an American joke, could become its brightest example.

In the afternoon after Molpus's speech, the fortieth-anniversary service was held at Mt. Zion Church, with a smaller but no less dedicated crowd. There the featured speakers were not the public dignitaries that had addressed the Coliseum audience, but people with special significance for those gathered: people from the congregation; the Reverend Clay Lee, the minister of the First Methodist Church of Philadelphia in 1964; and many local friends, along with the family members of the victims. Ben Chaney was there with a group of young people he had brought, and there were other former civil rights activists. The smaller facility of the church was soon overcrowded, and there was a brief heated contest for seats that led to serious disagreements. Still, the speakers kept the focus on the victims, the family members, and the cause to which they were committed.

Extensive media coverage of the two ceremonies introduced the Philadelphia Coalition to an audience outside the local area. Although reopening the murder case was the coalition's current objective, most members were also pledged to a program of educational reform, one that would offer a more accurate presentation of past history and create better-informed citizens. The proposal would require major revision of the public school social studies curriculum. Instead of presenting students with images ground through a Southern nostalgia machine, young people would be offered more objective "facts" about Mississippi's past. Coalition members planned for an educational summit in June, especially for social studies teachers, trying to help them get a fuller appreciation of the multicultural past to share with their students. The proposed curriculum revision, including textbook revision, would be overseen by the Winter Institute and its director, Susan Glisson.[15]

Some months later, after the fortieth-anniversary ceremonies at the Coliseum and Mt. Zion, Stanley Dearman of the coalition, proposed inviting Carolyn Goodman to come to Mississippi to meet with the new Attorney General, Jim Hood. Carolyn Goodman was the gracious and aging mother of Andy Goodman, and in recent years she had become a good friend of Dearman's. Mindful of the need for people to know the victims of crimes as individuals, Dearman thought there was much to be learned from a conversation in which Carolyn Goodman personalized her son. She accepted the invitation, and on her visit to Mississippi she met with the attorney general, coalition members, and other invited guests to describe her family's long connection to progressive organizations, as well as her touching memories of her young son. Dearman was right in thinking that her words would have an impact on the attorney general.[16] Carolyn Goodman made Andy more than just a youthful face on an FBI poster.

In addition to Carolyn Goodman's poignant memories of her son, other developments around the state added to the momentum for a new trial. The Mississippi Religious Leadership Conference made a $100,000 contribution to fund a hotline where those with information about the case could leave their comments anonymously.[17] Klansmen who were suspected of being somehow involved with the case were offered immunity if they would testify, although none accepted the offer. While the attorney general and the district attorney expanded their search for new evidence, Edgar Ray Killen, identified as the chief conspirator, remained confident nothing would ever come of it.

To Clear Its Name: Justice or a Whitewash

The concerted efforts of the Philadelphia Coalition and others with a connection to the case finally paid off. On January 4, 2005, the Neshoba County grand jury was empaneled to hear murder charges against Edgar Ray Killen, charges that were now brought by the state. The grand jury considered indictments against others tied to the 1964 events; Jimmy

Arledge, Jimmie Snowden, and Billy Wayne Posey, all of whom had been previously convicted in the 1967 trial for civil rights offenses. But the grand jury concluded that while it had enough information to proceed against Killen, long considered by many locals to be the chief conspirator, more would be needed if they were to try to indict the others.[18]

Prosecutors were aware there had been outward changes in the white community since 1964, a softening of racial lines, but they also understood that Killen had a lot of supporters who still thought as he did. They would need to present hard evidence to a Neshoba County jury to build a case against him. What the prosecution possessed were the records of the 1967 trial, when there was a single holdout against convicting Killen, and not much else that had come to light since that time. But the attorney general reported a kind of revelation when he read the old record; he discovered that in fact he did have a case. "Once I started reading the testimony [I realized] I've got enough here to take a good look at it."[19] The earlier murder trial of Byron de la Beckwith had established the precedent that a new jury was permitted to hear old evidence from a previous trial, material that would be read to them as testimony during the trial in process. The Supreme Court validated that understanding.

Word of a new trial for Killen traveled quickly through Neshoba County, where the various communities processed it differently. Friends of the outspoken segregationist thought it was a show trial and an attack on the Southern way of life. It would be the biggest contradiction yet to the old saying that it was "no crime to kill a nigger." For white business people it appeared as an opportunity to escape the dark shadow that had haunted their community and limited its financial growth. It also appeared likely that a Killen trial would consider only the murders, uncoupled from the long history of black abuse and specific injustices. Longdale people might hope that a trial would bring resolution to the crimes committed in their community, but as realists they were experienced with the process that denied them justice. Rita Schwerner Bender had insisted from the beginning that the murders and black justice were deeply interconnected, and to examine the one was to take on the other, because both were manifestations of racism, and "racism," she said, "is the elephant in the living room of this country."[20] Ben Chaney was even less sanguine that the outcome of a trial for Killen would carry any meaning for the black community. "This is going to be a whitewash," he said. "They are going to use the most unrepentant racist as the scapegoat, leave the others alone because they are more powerful, more wealthy, and more influential—and then move on."[21]

So, while coalition members and black area residents applauded the grand jury's decision, a constituency of white Neshobans came up with a multitude of reasons why a new trial was unnecessary. District Attorney Duncan, who would try the case, had worried about the criticism, and whether there was the solid white citizen base necessary for a trial.[22] Killen's friends pointed to his age—he was eighty years old—and the fact that it had been more than forty years since the murders had occurred. They cited the lack of new evidence and the cost of another trial. A number of critics said the motivation for a new trial was most likely political. Rehashing the events of the past, they said, would only confirm to the public "Neshoba County's a bad place."[23]

The indictment held, though Killen was allowed to go home, released on $250,000 bail, money generated from unknown supporters. Two months later, while he was out cutting trees on his property, Killen was severely injured when a log fell across his legs, damaging them both. He was hospitalized for treatment and the date for a trial was postponed to June 13, 2005, to be held at the courthouse in Neshoba County. Judge Marcus Gordon, a circuit court judge who had grown up in Killen's neighborhood of Union, was named as presiding judge. Both the prosecution and the judge worried about the image of the aging Killen in the courtroom, confined to a wheelchair with a nurse by his side, yet that would be the reality. His defense attorneys would conduct successful challenges to keep members of the Philadelphia Coalition off the jury, mindful that they could be doing battle with the Old South values Killen represented.

14
_____

The Contested Past

BLACK JUSTICE AND THE KILLEN TRIAL

For forty-one years, it's been Edgar Ray Killen and his friends who [have] written the history of Neshoba County.
DISTRICT ATTORNEY MARK DUNCAN,
Killen Trial Record, 2005

We [Americans] congratulate ourselves more on getting rid of a problem than on solving it.
W. E. B. DUBOIS, *Suppression of the African Slave Trade,* 1896[1]

When the trial of Edgar Ray Killen opened in the Neshoba County Courthouse on June 13, 2005, there was, in the statements of the attorneys and the response of the community, a sense that the culture itself was being tried along with the ex-Klansman. Since everyone knew that Killen had been acquitted in the 1967 trial by the vote of a single juror—who "could not convict a preacher"—and virtually no new evidence had come to light, what could have changed since 1967 except the perspective of the jurors? Both the defense and prosecution attorneys were counting on the extent to which jurors would be reflections of the culture. The job of the defense would be to show that nothing significant had changed in the community since the 1967 acquittal, while the prosecution had to argue that much had changed in community values since Killen walked free. In this very limited arena of the courtroom, the trial was also a contest between two Mississippis: one the old, "closed society" of segregationists who memorialized the "Southern way of life," and the other a loose coalition of black and white moderates who accepted integration as an aspect of modernity, morality, and economic progress. This first Mississippi was exclusively white and localistic, and the second was a collection of disparate racial groupings from the churches, business people, corporate life, the civil rights movement, and others with interests beyond the "closed society." Within Mississippi itself, the first group still controlled most of the statewide votes. It remained to be seen whether they also controlled the votes of the jurors in the Killen trial, as the defendant was confident they would. W. E. B. DuBois's perspicacious observation that Americans prefer to get rid of a problem rather than solve it, addressed these differing perspectives aroused by the trial. The defense wanted to get rid of the problem, put the Killen issue to bed for good, whereas the prosecution hoped to expose, and ideally solve, a problem originating in a distant, different past. Local people already knew the basic facts about Killen, that he was an unreconstructed segregationist, a former Klan leader, and a person with many ties to law enforcement, state agencies, and politicians at many levels, all of them quiet supporters of white privilege.

As expected, his trial attracted a vast audience. Interest in the Neshoba case was global, evidenced by the crowd of international media people that camped out around the courthouse, attempting to get access to the locals who turned out daily to see Killen wheeled into court. Killen himself was spirited and feisty, willing to spar with the press or spectators who called out to him. His supporters shouted encouragement, although only one self-identified Klansman showed up. The proceedings were surprisingly brief in such a high-profile case, with everything completed by June 23, just ten days after opening statements. Throughout, Killen gave the impression of someone extremely confident things would go his way.

The official trial record, including the statements of potential jurors, witness testimony, and the comments of the attorneys, serves up an intimate view of Neshoba County, a slice of life as lived in the years between 1964 and 2005. For white Neshobans who had tried to keep their private lives away from public view, it was a time when old secrets, such as Klan support, came out. The majority of the people called by the court were white, whether as potential jurors or witnesses. Their statements lifted the curtain of secrecy and offered a snapshot of how the white supremacist culture had maintained its power during the previous forty years. The bulk of the trial was taken from 1967 testimony, read into the record at the present trial by people recruited for the task, since most of the original witnesses were dead. There were some new witnesses, mainly Killen's friends and family, but there were also a few crucial additions for the prosecution.

The attorneys were also a study in contrasts. Killen's defense relied on Mitchell Moran and James McIntyre, aging lawyers experienced in working for those accused in civil rights cases, their fees for this trial paid by anonymous sources. The state's attorney general now, Jim Hood, led the prosecution, assisted by Mark Duncan, the Neshoba County district attorney, a team that was younger than the defense and possessed of a powerful presence. The lawyers were charged with handling the murder indictment of Edgar Ray Killen for the deaths of the three civil rights workers in 1964, a case narrowly focused on the details of the conspiracy.

The evidence the attorneys would present was essentially about the man, not the local Klan organization he headed, nor the environment in which he operated. Nevertheless, even within those fairly constricted limits, witness testimony would uncover subjects most white Neshobans would have preferred to keep buried. Only indirect reference in the trial—as in the attorney general's reference to "good people who do nothing"—was made about the collective silence that had delayed a murder trial for forty-one years. And there was the continuing concern of Rita Schwerner Bender, expressed outside of court, that there was a historical fallacy in decoupling the murders from the racist culture in which they occurred, creating a separation artificial and inaccurate. The Philadelphia Coalition agreed with her contention that a wide lens was needed to probe Neshoba's past in the course of the trial, yet their primary goal had been to get a new trial and in that they had been successful.

A professional jury consultant, Andy Shelton, helped screen prospective jurors acceptable to both sides.[2] There were a few Choctaws and some blacks included among the mostly white pool of possibilities. In seating the jury, anyone with ties to the Philadelphia Coalition, like Jewel McDonald, was summarily dismissed by the defense. This selection process exposed some of the most revealing aspects of life white residents had kept to themselves. Many potential jurors referred to Killen's extensive white network, as one after another spoke of him as a friend, or kin, or preacher. James McIntyre summarized these comments by noting "everybody in Neshoba County knows Edgar Ray Killen."[3] One man confessed he would find it difficult, if not impossible, to convict Killen. Other people called to serve said they would have to leave their churches, or their jobs, or move to another location if Killen should be found guilty.[4] A number said they knew of a funeral or a wedding Killen had performed for their family, with one man commenting that "they think a lot of the man . . . they think he's an extremely nice, good human man."[5] The judge himself admitted—though out of the courtroom—that Killen had preached the funeral service for both his parents.[6] Two themes predominated during the selection process: one was the extensive nature of Neshoba kinship networks, and the other was the well-developed personal opinions residents held about the case. People had had a long time to talk with family and friends about the events of forty-one years ago and had come to their own conclusions. Mark Duncan made passing reference to the impact of the white kinship connection when he said that Killen and his friends had written the history of Neshoba County for the past forty-one years. After the trial had started, Killen's brother testified that Duncan's "daddy and granddaddy" had belonged to the Klan.[7]

Documentary filmmaker Micki Dickoff gained remarkable access to Killen just a few days before the trial began, and her 2010 film *Neshoba: The Price of Freedom* produced a rich and telling interview with the confident and loquacious defendant. For several days she talked with him in the quiet setting of his trailer home.[8] He referred to the supportive crowds who "mobbed" him everywhere he went, a sure sign, he thought, that no jury would ever convict him. He was as Ben Chaney had described him, an unrepentant segregationist, who believed the murdered men were communists and outsiders who had no business being in Neshoba County, a not uncommon belief among whites. In the days after the disappearance of the men, the community first said it was a hoax, and then after the bodies were found, that they should not have been there to begin with. Killen on camera appeared bright and spirited, a man ready for a fight, anticipating the opportunity to go toe to toe with the attorney general and the district attorney. Although confined to a wheelchair, he proved to be a vital force at all the trial sessions.

He had to have been disappointed as the reality of the trial unfolded. Some of his confidence surely derived from his acquittal in the 1967 case. District Attorney Duncan took pains to remind jurors that times had changed since then: Neshobans, he suggested, now had different values and were more tolerant, commenting that "the fact that those persons that were killed, the fact that they were not from Neshoba County, I think sometimes people who live here have a hard time connecting with people like this."[9] White Neshobans were no longer like that. He implied that in fact the times, and people's perspectives, really had changed since 1967. "Back then" he said, whites denied the vote to black residents, but "no one would dream of denying" the vote today.[10] The past was indeed another country. Duncan was a lifelong resident of Philadelphia, and he knew from his own experience the web of relationships that defined community consciousness. Because the bulk of the evidence both he and the attorney

220   MT. ZION'S WITNESS

general would rely on came from 1967, it was important for them to stress just how much white Neshoba had changed since then, becoming more open to others and accepting of its black neighbors.

The Testimony of Witnesses

Over the course of the trial, jurors heard from witnesses on tape and live in the witness box. Rita Schwerner Bender, a witness for the prosecution and the first to be called, told of the work she and her husband had done in Meridian to support black voting. Following her live testimony was the taped, yet chilling, if occasionally overblown, report of deceased police sergeant Wallace Miller, who made the connection between the murders and Klan policy to intimidate black residents. His 1967 statement was one of the few to provide a clear window into the regional environment where Klan members acted with impunity against blacks living there. Miller said that in 1964 he was a friend of Killen's, and it was at Killen's urging he joined the local Klan, as a number of others in the courtroom that day also had. The Klan was strongly opposed to integration, so it "[applied] pressure" to "control Negroes" who had any notion of challenging the Jim Crow system: that meant "we were to call them up or go to see them and threaten them on their jobs and things of that nature." If those strategies failed to get blacks to conform, then the Klan resorted to "Whippings and beatings." Anyone who still held out would be "eliminated," meaning killed, but that was not the decision of the local Klan alone; approval had to come from the Imperial Wizard of the Klan, Sam Bowers.[11]

Miller told of Killen's relationship with local law enforcement, as well as his involvement in the murder conspiracy. He remembered a time when Killen was opposed to allowing Negroes use the baseball field in Philadelphia, so he called together a small group of men, including Sheriffs Rainey and Price, to consider how to stop them. His comments implied that Killen could influence the lawmen, maybe even control them.[12] Miller said further that he learned of the murders the day after the killings when Killen told him the three men had been shot and buried in a dam, information Miller admitted he had not shared with the FBI. His was an insider's view of the Klan, at the time its definition of itself as a "patriotic Christian" organization, and its long-range mission as explained to him by Killen. Defense attorneys tried to shred his testimony, even questioning whether he had previously lied about the number of marriages he had had.

Ernest Kirkland from Mt. Zion had been one of the few black witnesses called in 1967, the last friendly face the murdered men were to see. His statements were taken at a time when the defense hoped to capitalize on the persistent negative community image of COFO, and the fact that Schwerner was known as an "outsider." Kirkland had been a participant in the secret meetings between the men and their Longdale contacts, and at the trial he continued to be an advocate for them and their COFO Freedom School project. The defense tried to get him to admit that Schwerner was an atheist—his religion, Jewish, or lack thereof, an important issue to local whites—but Kirkland refused and said that in fact Schwerner attended services at Mt. Zion Church.[13] The last time he saw the men, he said, was when they rode together in a car to inspect the ruins of the burned-out church.

Statements from the white officials involved in the capture and arrest of the men in 1964 were among those read into the new trial record. Earl Robert Poe, a highway patrolman, said he was on duty the day the men's car was chased by Deputy Sheriff Price, and he had helped Price carry the men to jail.[14] Minnie Lee Herring, the jailer that day, said speeders—speeding was the charge against Chaney—were not typically arrested, and she had not seen Price give any of them a ticket. She had served the men what would be their final meal.[15]

Several other important prosecution witnesses were physically present for the 2005 trial, namely two FBI agents who had worked on the case, and Carolyn Goodman. FBI Agent Dean Lytle was questioned extensively by the defense about payments to informers, hoping to discredit their statements as the products of government bribes. Lytle admitted that people were paid for information, but he didn't know the source of the money, surmising, "[I]t might be Mr. Hoover."[16] He noted the adversarial relationship with local white residents, particularly their hostility to the FBI and their refusal to talk with agents. He and his colleagues found the Philadelphia environment threatening, even by FBI standards, and he referred to a night when some agents left the courthouse in fear for their lives as they passed through a crowd of angry whites gathered outside.[17] Carolyn Goodman, who was forty-nine when her son was killed, was now ninety, and she was an effective and sympathetic witness for the prosecution despite occasional lapses of memory. She spoke movingly of the now-famous postcard she had received from her son Andy on the day he arrived in Mississippi, describing how "wonderful" Mississippi was and how "fine" his reception had been.[18] Agent Jay Cochran came from retirement to testify at the trial. He had been on the scene at the time the bodies were discovered, and he graphically described the burial site at Olen Burrage's dam. He made no reference to how the FBI found the bodies, nor did either the prosecution or the defense ask him. He had been involved with recovering the car, and then the victims. Agents, he said, dug for the bodies in the red clay at the dam site until flies, and then scavenger birds, appeared. "[A]t that point, we then ceased the use of the bulldozer and began to move the soil using hand implements, garden trowels, and hand rakes . . . [and then] we noticed the heels of a pair of boots."[19] Mickey Schwerner, Cochrane said, was face down in the dirt, identified by a Selective Service card in his pocket, as was Andrew Goodman, who was lying next to Schwerner. Autopsy evidence later showed Goodman was clutching dirt in his hand that appeared to come from another location, raising the possibility that he might have been buried while still alive. The third body was discovered on its back and facing in the opposite direction from the other two; it lacked identification, and shoes, but the agents determined it was a Negro male.[20] James Chaney was the only one of the three who was barefoot. A gunshot wound to the heart had killed Schwerner, Cochran said, and a bullet to the right chest felled Goodman, and two shots, one to the abdomen and the other to the brain, took down Chaney. According to confessions from Klansmen who had been at the scene, Chaney, the last to be killed, had attempted to run and was consequently shot twice. For decades after his death, controversy swirled around how Chaney actually was killed and the reason for the mangled condition of his body. Over the objections of the defense, the district attorney was allowed to show the court a photograph of the grisly murder scene.[21]

The testimonies of Delmar Dennis and James Jordan, two of the most damaging witnesses at the 1967 trial, were read into the new record. Both had become FBI informers and lived in fear for their lives after their court appearances were made public. Delmar Dennis, the Methodist minister who was a close friend to Killen and Sam Bowers, had been a Klan Kludd, or chaplain. James Jordan, also a Klansman, had actually participated in the killings and provided details from the murder scene. Both Dennis and Jordan connected the plan to murder Schwerner with the events at Mt. Zion Church; the beatings and the church burning were designed for entrapment.[22]

The prosecution presented two additional live witnesses at the 2005 trial: the currently imprisoned Mike Winstead, who appeared in his regulation jumpsuit, and Mike Hatcher, another former police officer from

Meridian who had testified at the previous trial as well. Winstead was the more colorful witness of the two. When asked by the defense if he was getting any special treatment as a prisoner in exchange for his testimony, he replied, "I'm sitting in an isolated cell right now with nothing but me and flies, I guess if you call that special treatment."[23] Winstead was the source of the comment that Killen reminded him of Matt Dillon because of his dress and demeanor. In a more relevant statement he told of a visit by Killen to his grandfather's house in the late 1960s, when he overheard Killen tell the older man that he had been involved in the murders and "was proud of it." Winstead said he came forward now because his son was deployed in Iraq, fighting for the "same things these boys were killed for," although he didn't explain what these "things" were.[24] The prosecution named as "hero" of the 2005 trial the former policeman Mike Hatcher. Once a Klansman, Hatcher testified that on the day after the three men had disappeared, Killen had showed up at his station, as he had at Wallace Miller's, to say that "Goatee" and the others had been shot, buried in shallow graves, their bodies covered over with dirt when "Tucker ran the bulldozer" to fill up the space. A lawman, he had not been threatened after his earlier testimony in 1967, but he had been gripped with pangs of conscience, he said, and decided "to become the best policemen [sic] [I] could," which for him included coming to court again to testify.[25] His straightforward comments seemed to remove any doubt about Killen's leading role in the murders.

Killen had his supporters; it was his home territory after all. Friends and relatives attested to his good character and to his whereabouts the day of the murders. One of his taped advocates was former Philadelphia mayor Harlan Majure, who offered a reminder of how potent Southern memory could be for some of the city's white residents. After the prosecution pointed out that Killen had been a member of the Klan, a violent organization, Majure corrected him by saying that "They [Klan members] did a lot of good, too."[26] And, as the trial made clear, it was not a crime at the time to belong to the Klan.

On June 20, after six days of testimony, the attorneys for the state and for the defendant presented their closing arguments.

Deciding Killen's Fate

The fact that the attorney general himself was present at this small-town trial in 2005 indicated how much the state, or at least his office, believed was at stake in the case. Hood noted for the jury the extensive witness testimony connecting Killen to the murders, and made his pointed observation that "Evil flourishes when good people sit idly by and do nothing."[27] They were surely the kind of good people who would not sit idly by any longer.

For the defense attorneys, their argument was based on the claim that nothing of significance had changed in the culture or about the case since the 1967 trial from which Killen had walked free. The prosecution, they noted, with little new evidence, had skewed the argument to emphasize that change had really come to Neshoba County. McIntyre and Moran told the jury that not only did Killen go free in 1967, in that older case even the evidence was tainted, supplied by liars and paid FBI informers. No one had presented testimony that Killen pulled the trigger or was even at the crime scene, said McIntyre. The lawyers, like Killen himself, believed that no Neshoba jury could possibly convict him on a murder charge. But when they learned that the prosecution planned to offer the court the option of a manslaughter conviction, they were quick to object. Said McIntyre, "So they couldn't get him for murder, so they are going to try to get him for manslaughter."[28] He called it a political show trial, conceived for television and media coverage, intending to convince the public that Mississippi was serious about "getting" someone, and that someone was Killen, "the Preacher." There was no need, the defense said, to dig up the past and open old wounds. What about the seven other people out there with ties to the crime who have been ignored, McIntyre wondered, while the state singles out Killen? Presumably modern Neshobans had come to regard the Klan as a dangerous organization, a force to be reigned in, and, given the chance, would regard the rest of the perpetrators as culpable as Killen. Mitch Moran, the other member of the defense, recapitulated in his closing comments much of what McIntyre had said, adding "the truth still hasn't been told to the citizens of the state of Mississippi. The truth is out there."[29] The implication of his statement was vague, although when presented with frequent references to Mississippi's rising crime rate, it hinted at the need to observe an unspoken politically correct standard, lest there be an even greater escalation in crime, even protest in the streets.

The most insightful comments on the grand scope of the case came from District Attorney Duncan, the Philadelphia native, in his summation. Duncan thought it likely that "People have probably told you, well, you know, I know who did this, and I know who did that," comments that were a mixture of truth and folklore.[30] In an appeal to their local pride, he confessed that "When I sat listening to that testimony, I thought, you know, that's not the Neshoba County I know. . . . [T]he question is is a Neshoba County jury going to tell the rest of the world that we are not going to let Edgar Ray Killen get away with murder anymore, not one day longer."[31] Nothing less was at stake in the case, he said, than the "ignoble history" of Neshoba County, and it was in the jury's hands to "either change [that] history for us, or [to] confirm it."[32] His summation constructed for the jury the narrow limit of the case: Edgar Ray Killen should not get away with murder one day more. The prosecutor's strategy kept the historical canvas framed only around the defendant. He focused on Killen (and some of his friends) and less on community denial and the support that had sustained the old Klan. The logic of his argument was that the values of white Neshobans had matured beyond homegrown jurisprudence since 1963, and people were no longer willing to tolerate the lawlessness of the Klan.

The judge's instructions to the jury offered them the options of manslaughter or murder. After only brief deliberations, jury forewoman Shirley Vaughn reported back with a six-six division. The judge told them to reconsider and return in the morning. Overnight, rumors flew around Neshoba County as people attempted to tease out the meaning of the split. Was the jury tied over acquittal or conviction, or was it stuck on deciding for manslaughter or murder? Jury members said after the trial that because the evidence presented by the prosecution was so weak, they were divided between manslaughter and murder: they later explained there was too little evidence for a murder conviction "beyond a reasonable doubt," and acquittal was not an option.[33] The jury split worried members of the Philadelphia Coalition and others who had worked for the new trial.

By the following morning, June 21, the forty-first anniversary of the killings, the jury had reached a verdict; Edgar Ray Killen was guilty of manslaughter. Two days later Judge Gordon sentenced him to twenty years in prison for each of the murders, a total of sixty years in jail, essentially a life sentence for an eighty-year-old man. The verdict was instant world news as the international media group gathered outside the courthouse went to work. In Philadelphia a partisan and celebratory crowd rejoiced at the announcement.

But Rita Schwerner Bender and members of the Philadelphia Coalition were less than enthusiastic about the outcome. They were disappointed that Killen was convicted for manslaughter, not murder. It diminished the significance of the trial and produced the minimal outcome of the

conviction of one man. Was there no relevant social context for the conviction? A Mafia hitman or a renegade soldier would surely be judged within
the context of his surroundings. Some commentators around the country and around the world acknowledged their agreement with the coalition, that this was one more example of Mississippi failing to do the right
thing. Presiding Judge Gordon took umbrage at the extensive criticism of
the manslaughter conviction, and said so at the sentencing hearing: "[I]
watched Court TV the other day, and I saw where the people of Neshoba
County and the jury and even the State of Mississippi was demeaned
because the verdict was manslaughter and not that of murder, and that was
wrong, and that was, again, attacking the integrity of the jury system."[34]

For Dick Molpus, it was an "historic" decision when a Neshoba County
jury in a Neshoba County courthouse pronounced Killen guilty of conspiring to kill a black man and his two activist friends. It was less than
the Philadelphia Coalition wanted, but it was part of a new chapter in the
rewriting of local history.

After the Trial: The Elephant Remains

Killen's attorneys appealed for a new trial almost immediately, noting that
most of the evidence presented against him had come from the 1967 trial,
at which he had been acquitted. The appeal was denied. Before the cameras, Killen, in a yellow jumpsuit, was taken off to prison, a sight that
reportedly caused Rita Schwerner Bender to smile for the first time during
the trial.[35]

Killen's defiant attitude remained even at the jail. Asked by a black
jailer the standard question at admission, that is, did he have any suicidal
thoughts; Killen answered, "I'll kill you before I kill myself."[36] He was
not imprisoned long. In August, after less than two months in jail, he
appealed to the judge to be released for health reasons. He testified that he
had difficulty sleeping, that he had to bribe a convict to get a pillow, that no
one gave him pain medication, that he found it hard to breathe and getting
around was a problem because of his injured legs. Judge Gordon, having
just sentenced him to sixty years, allowed him to go free on August 17
on $600,000 bail, money again provided by unknown sources. To those
Neshobans who hoped that Killen's conviction marked a turning point in
the county's history, his release seemed painful and wrong. Some wanted
to know where the funds raised on his behalf were coming from. What
had the trial actually accomplished?

Although Judge Gordon allowed Killen to return home—because of his age and health he was not considered a flight risk—his freedom proved to be short-lived. On September 7, a deputy sheriff, someone who at an earlier time might have been his protector, reported to the court that he had witnessed Killen driving a car and walking unassisted. The justification for his release had been his poor health, his claim that he "was confined to a wheelchair and in constant pain."[37] He was rearrested and returned to jail, most likely for the rest of his life.

Because of the trial, Neshoba County was once again exposed to extraordinary public attention, this time with mixed responses from different sections of the population. For the most part, the national media agreed that justice had finally been done. Governor Haley Barbour announced that the decision brought "closure" to the forty-year-old civil rights case. Journalist Jerry Mitchell, however, thought it would be better to adopt a cautious "wait and see" response, partly because, as District Attorney Mark Duncan surmised, less than an estimated majority of local white residents approved of the conviction.[38] But the message white leadership in Neshoba wanted to communicate to the world was that the town with the tattered history had changed, that it had rid itself of its bad public image and was, quite literally, open for business.[39] "[T]he decision was historic," even if it had taken forty-one years to achieve.[40]

"We Have only Begun Our Work"

Amid the public rejoicing over a Neshoba County jury finally doing its civic duty, the Philadelphia Coalition called a press conference. Coalition leaders read a statement indicating their gratification with the work the jury had done. In the statement members affirmed that they were pleased Killen was found guilty, although they did not share Governor Barbour's view that the conviction brought "closure." "[W]e have only begun our work here," it said. "Today justice was served," the statement went on, but the unfinished business was as before, to "understand the legacy of the racism that continues to divide us." The task ahead is to "seek the truth, to insure justice for all, and to nurture reconciliation."[41] Coalition members were aware that the Winter Institute would be available with resources for the work of reconciliation.

The "legacy of racism," the message at the heart of the coalition's statement, held different meanings for people in the region. For the residents of Longdale, the legacy of racism went back to slavery days, while for white Philadelphians it was of more recent origin, a consequence of the events that had triggered the civil rights movement. Perhaps similar in their responses to the outcome of the trial, the two groups had memories of a past understood very differently by each of them. Before it would be possible to nurture reconciliation, as the coalition statement said and the Winter Institute desired, it would be necessary for the people in the area to work to come to terms with that past.

In the Mt. Zion Church community the response to the trial was as mixed as the coalition statement. The chief conspirator in the murders had been convicted, and that was a good thing for the families of the victims. Ross Jones, ninety-three at the time and a veteran of the racial struggles of the twentieth century said when he heard about the verdict, "I am happy. I didn't believe it would happen."[42] Jewel McDonald, whose mother and brother had been beaten that memorable night in 1964, was disappointed that the jury had settled on manslaughter, a decision that didn't comprehend the enormity of what happened.[43] Mt. Zion had been invaded by a band of thugs, in the company of law enforcement, and the trial offered the possibility of at least exposing the nature of that crime, if not actually trying it. Like victims' family members Rita Schwerner Bender and Ben Chaney, they could applaud the conviction, while still wondering what impact it would have on black lives in Neshoba to incarcerate one aging Klansman. Some may have quietly agreed with Ben Chaney's view that although Killen was guilty, he was made the scapegoat for those richer, possessed of more powerful friends, who got away. "[W]e're still a long ways from justice," said Chaney.[44]

Just what had the trial accomplished? The basic issue that first caused the crimes, the limited justice and protection for blacks in the region, remained the same. Killen was as guilty of the crime for which he was charged in 1967 as he was in 2005. What had changed since 1967? As skilled as Mark Duncan was at presenting the case, he was not a significantly better lawyer than John Doar had been. What the prosecution in 2005 had to assume was that jury members, who had experienced the cultural changes of the last two decades, now had different attitudes about race. Attitude, however, was as slippery a quality to measure as truth, the stated goal of the trial, and the objective of those who believed truth to be the prelude to racial reconciliation. The Reverend Charles Griffin, a black Baptist minister in Philadelphia, came closer to explaining what was needed for reconciliation by referencing a comment of Archbishop Desmond Tutu of South Africa: what was required for change, Tutu once said, was "a physical transformation, a changing of the quality of life of the most deprived."[45] LeRoy Clemons of the coalition spoke of the community needs similarly: "We don't need an apology. We need jobs and better schools."[46] Clemons knew there had to be an acknowledgment of past wrongdoing, but the thrust of his comment, and that by Charles Griffin, was that discernible change in the quality of life was required to make meaningful progress toward reconciliation, there had to be a physical transformation in life circumstances for black residents.

Yet, the outcome of the trial was indeed historic. When Edgar Ray Killen in his yellow jumpsuit was taken from the courthouse to the jail, Rita Schwerner Bender said she was moved.[47] Neshoba County, by 2005, had changed its racial behavior in important ways. Slavery was long gone. There was no more legal Jim Crow. Most of the time people acted civilly to each other. Equal access, the chance to improve oneself, was presumably open to everyone in this conservative, Bible Belt state. There were also many opportunities open for failure for those who inherited the legacy of racism, the second-generation Jim Crow barriers. The ancestors of those at Mt. Zion Church had learned from early Methodist leaders like James Lynch and A. C. McDonald the moral necessity of an inclusive society, a colorblind social environment that resisted all forms of racial discrimination. And they had maintained their witness to those values by the strength of moral power alone; they possessed no political, no economic, no institutional power, only the power of their convictions. Finally, people in the larger community—younger, better educated, more diverse—were willing to affirm their courage and the rightness of their cause. Neshoba County was not yet an inclusive culture, but a growing number of its residents had hope for a better future.

It would take time and commitment for Mississippi to come to grips with its outsized version of the American Dilemma, to change its ways from an oppressive racist past to an open and tolerant society. The Reverend Jesse Jackson described his thoughts about change in a sermon at Galloway Methodist Church in Jackson, the church once closed to black worshippers: "You can't sow seeds tonight and grow food tomorrow morning," he said. "But if you keep on doing it, you begin to see fruit emerge. I still think Mississippi holds the key for healing in the nation. There's something magic about Mississippi—its pain, its problems, and its possibilities."[48] Willie Morris agreed. After spending considerable time in Philadelphia, he thought he noticed a gradual stirring "in the soul of the town," something that marked the beginning of a pilgrimage potentially instructive to "much of the South and the America of our generation."[49] Former Governor Winter, when asked about continuing evidence of old racial hatreds—like destroying the Goodman, Chaney, Schwerner highway marker, and throwing a lynch rope around the neck of the James Meredith statue on the Ole Miss campus—ascribed it to the work of a "small hand- ful of old haters and bitter enders." They were the people who were "once part of the old massive resistance movement," and though now older, they were not a lot wiser. And some of the culprits were probably undisciplined teenagers, he guessed.[50] For people impatient for change, those unem- ployed or working for low wages at the casinos or denied easy access to the vote, waiting for a generation of segregationists to pass from the scene was not just a difficult task but a regression to the former strategies of delay. While there were poor white people in the state, there were more poor black people, and the feeling among many blacks was that when their young people fell through the cracks in society, they continued to be treated unfairly by law enforcement and the justice system.

Differences between the races persisted and progress was slow. Those who took comfort in the Old South myth looked to the past for their memories and their values. Those who argued, as Mayor James Young of Philadelphia did, that "the fight is not over, the job is not done," looked to the future for redemption.[51] And the brightest future envisioned by those who identify with the "other Mississippi," is one in which reconciliation of the races will be achieved, the inclusive society a step closer. It would be ironic if the state with the most tragic racial history should become the model for resolving the American Dilemma.

Epilogue

The Importance of Remembering

Our country has changed.
CHIEF JUSTICE JOHN G. ROBERTS, June 25, 2013

The legacy of the Rev. Dr. Martin Luther King and the nation's commitment to justice have been "disserved by today's decision.
JUSTICE RUTH BADER GINSBURG, June 25, 2013

Who will help a new generation create a diverse, multiracial society?
JIM WALLIS, *SOJOURNERS*, October 24, 2013

Two Towns, Two Mississippis

This work opened with to Diane McWhorter's characterization of the duality of Mississippi, a quality noted by a host of others, some of them natives of the state, who hold deep affection for the place. When Willie Morris, after twenty years of self-exile in New York City at *Harper's*, returned home in retirement, he said he finally appreciated the significance of Faulkner's comment that "you don't love [Mississippi] because: you love despite."[1] Mississippi historian David Sansing thought his state had "two souls, two hearts, two minds," with the first harboring its racist past, and the second, the "other Mississippi," holding different, even opposing, qualities.[2] This "other" Mississippi was not intolerant, illiterate, impoverished, and nihilistic, but enlightened, humane, literary, and just. A similar variant of this dualism informed editor Stanley Dearman's question about how Neshoba County could produce a Dick Molpus as well as an Edgar Ray Killen.[3] This quality of twoness—the phrase itself borrowed from W. E. B. Dubois—is replicated in the history of Neshoba County, in the experiences of Mt. Zion Church in the Longdale community on the one hand, and in the events that defined the city of Philadelphia on the other. Throughout its past, Longdale has sought and welcomed change, while Philadelphia has yearned after memories of a bygone Southern lifestyle. Martin Luther King called Philadelphia "the worst town I have ever been in," while he commended Mt. Zion for being a witness to moral relevancy.

Change and constancy were integral to the history of both communities. For much of Longdale's 135-year past, however, whenever change took place it was regressive, a retreat from the brief period of social equality that was Reconstruction. Orlando Patterson once wrote about the experience of slavery as a "social death," a social invisibility accompanied by a total lack of rights that too often was passed down for generations.[4] Mt. Zion's members denied the reality of "social death" or social invisibility, because the spiritual inheritance they received from Reconstruction Methodism, a kind of spiritual rebirth, persuaded them that all God's people were entitled to political rights and personal freedom. The harrowing years of Jim Crow closed off their political rights but not their freedom to worship freely. Substantial change of a progressive nature did come to Longdale during the twentieth century, particularly at times when two conditions were in place. One was the convergence of outside forces with local activists. Because segregationist organizations had been sufficiently successful in keeping a critical mass of black citizens from forming into enduring pressure groups and creating powerful leaders, it required outside agencies like the federal government, the Methodist denomination, and social-change agents to provide the additional energy and leadership to stoke the fires kindled by local people. As Jenny Irons has said, it took "[t]he civil rights movement and federal legislation [to change] what it meant to be black in the United States."[5] The second precondition for change was white acceptance, the product of coercion or command, that the demands of black Mississippians for justice and human rights were legitimate. That called for persistent witnessing to their history by blacks who refused to be intimidated by their environment. It also called for white actively listen, for white Neshobans to take seriously the accounts of their black neighbors about injustice and mistreatment. These preliminary steps, recalling the stories of one's history, listening to other recall past injustices, addressing and accepting outside aid, are necessary markers along the road to reconciliation.

Mt. Zion Church has been part of the witnessing Methodist Black Remnant since its founding, but the nature of that witness changed after 1964, when the congregation made a conscious determination to engage with the larger community. It entered the public square by offering its property and its people for a voting rights center. The church also maintained its public presence through the annual commemorative services. The congregation gave its support to the Philadelphia Coalition, which had served as a model and a legacy for other community organizations to emulate. The enduring goal of the church has been an inclusive society, an objective taken up by the Winter Institute, as that organization develops programs for building bridges in a divided society. Mt. Zion's efforts are those of the "other Mississippi," those who share the hope for reconciliation.

In the city of Philadelphia, as in the rest of white Neshoba, change has been slow, largely because many whites change seemed more threatening, than promising. The past, indeed the present status quo, was based on the historic privileges of whiteness and the power that went along with that. Only with struggle, and sometimes grudgingly, did the white community relinquish parts of its past prerogatives. Philadelphia elected a black mayor, James Young, an outcome that required help from some white voters, and the county elected a black alderman, Obbie Riley. The Killen trial turned the light on the two Mississippis; Killen's supporters remained citizens of the Old South, and his accusers were largely representative of the "other Mississippi."

The culturally dominant Mississippi, to which most of white Neshoba and the rest of the state belonged, continued to favor memory over history, constancy over change, privilege over equality. The "other" Mississippi, which a small group of white moderates, Mt. Zion and most black Mississippians supported, courted change, and argued for tolerance, inclusiveness, and equal opportunity. This "other" Mississippi lived on the margin of the culture until the post–Second World War years, when a more assertive group of younger black people began to pound on the doors of privilege and drew the attention of a new generation of educated young whites. The political outcome of their efforts was the implementation of the Civil Rights Act of 1964 and the Voting Rights Act of 1965. By 1980, through this alliance of interests between progressive blacks and moderate whites, Governor William Winter was elected, bringing with him Dick Molpus and Ray Mabus. This "other" Mississippi, in which former politicians are underrepresented, remains an underfunded minority, nevertheless confident that as a rising generation joins them, they can so change the culture of the state that it will serve as the model for racial harmony in America. Susan Glisson of the Winter Institute believes fundamental changes will occur in the state with the next generation, while Dick Molpus thinks it will take less time; perhaps in eight to twelve years, he suspects the state will elect a black governor or lieutenant governor.[6] Neshoba, by the twenty-first century had changed, although as Harvard Law School professor Randall Kennedy said in his 2011 book *The Persistence of the Color Line*, America is still a place where "race matters."[7]

"History Matters"; "Context Matters"

Rita Schwerner Bender, spoke about why history mattered and why context mattered when it came to issues of race at Mt. Zion's fiftieth annual commemoration service in June 2014. While cosmetically and institutionally much has changed for the better in Neshoba County, in contemporary culture it had become "the streets" that take a dreadful toll on young people, a legacy of Jim Crow. And while Mayor James Young, speaking at the same event as Schwerner Bender, declared "this is a new day," he, too, said that much work remained to be done.[8]

Nevertheless, this account of Mt. Zion Church and the cultural environment in which it has existed concludes on an uncertain note. It is a fact of history that Goodwin, Chaney, and Schwerner were killed in Neshoba County because they were trying to assist black people to register to vote. Mt. Zion Church was terrorized and burned because it endorsed the Freedom School. Just a year later, the 1965 federal Voting Rights Act came into being, which enabled black voting to happen. The historical reality and the context must remain connected. The change in local culture to which District Attorney Mark Duncan alluded in the Killen trial—the absence of personal fear, the ability to vote—was largely attributable to the impact of the 1965 federal voting legislation. Absent white obstruction tactics, black voters—when not gerrymandered into insignificance—could impact the direction of Mississippi politics.

The significance of the black vote is the message of Frank R. Parker's *Black Votes Count*, a work that examines voting patterns in the state. In his study, Parker cited the 1989 report of the Joint Center for Political Studies, which noted that of the state's 4,950 elective offices, blacks held 646 positions, or about 13 percent, though they are 35 percent of the state's population.[9] It may seem small, but it is a substantial change from 1965, when just 6 percent of a black electorate had been able to vote. The state has had only one federally elected black official, Representative Bennie Thompson, since Reconstruction, but numerous locally elected black officials for the reason that gerrymandering districts and creating at-large seats has not worked at the local level.

The 2013 decision by the United States Supreme Court to alter the 1965 Voting Rights Act—the culmination of the efforts for which Goodman, Chaney, Schwerner and others gave their lives—threatens to reverse black voting gains. Chief Justice John R. Roberts, writing for the Court's conservative majority, said "our country has changed," and social change had rendered a key provision of the act irrelevant. Section 4 of the act, which had established the formula for preclearance by either the federal government or federal courts before (mostly Southern) states could make changes in their voting regulations, was deemed no longer necessary. Justice Roberts cited as evidence for change the election of Southern black mayors, James Young of Philadelphia among them, and the increase in black voters, who turned out in great numbers to help elect President Obama. Instead of encouraging black voters to go to the polls, the Court with this decision has placed barriers in the way. To many in government—and in black Neshoba County—the decision is regressive. President Obama said he was "deeply disappointed" by the outcome, and Justice Ruth Bader Ginsburg, who voted with the minority, said from the bench that the Court had erred "egregiously," by removing protection from "second generation barriers" to discrimination.

At the time Frank Parker examined Mississippi voting in 1990, he said it remained ambiguous "whether there has been any significant change in white attitudes on racial matters."[10] Parker's observation was a call for continued watchfulness not only in Neshoba, but in all the states affected by the Voting Rights Act. LeRoy Clemons, an early member of the Philadelphia Coalition, commented on the Court's decision by asking, "Why take it [the Voting Rights Act] away now when it is working? Maybe in fifteen years it won't be necessary, but right now it is still needed."[11] The evidence is persuasive: black citizens of Mississippi average half the income of whites, are underrepresented in government, and although roughly 35 percent of the population, represent over 70 percent of prison inmates.[12] These are the people facing what Justice Ginsburg has called "second generation barriers."

Clemons, as well as Jewel McDonald, also of the Philadelphia Coalition—both politically astute—knew what could happen when "crafty politicians" on the local scene saw an opportunity to exploit a legal advantage. They reported that within a week of the Supreme Court decision, Mississippi's legislature had enacted a new voter ID law, requiring some form of "official" identification in order to vote, a measure with potential to disenfranchise many elderly, youthful, immigrant, and minority voters. Neshoba County also took advantage of the Court's decision by ordering redistricting of the school board, likely eliminating any black representation.[13] It is a familiar pattern well known to those citizens of the "other Mississippi", the people in black neighborhoods, in moderate political circles, and involved in work toward reconciliation, as at the Winter Institute and elsewhere. According to Susan Glisson of the institute, a majority of the state's population between ages eighteen and twenty-two is African American, and among children under age six, the clear majority is African American; if they vote like their parents when they come of age, Mississippi could experience significant social improvement in the near future.[14] That reality adds new meaning to Mt. Zion Church's tireless promotion of education. It is also what drives LeRoy Clemons' continuing work with young people, and the Winter Institute's focus on programs for high school–age children. It represents a rate of change tied to the birthrate, one slower than the pace of *One Mississippi, Two Mississippi*, but natural increase has changed voting results in a number of locations in America. Rita Schwerner Bender supports a federally guaranteed right to vote, which would likely call for a constitutional amendment.

Those with ties to the "other" Mississippi remain focused on the future and improving the opportunities for the children of the next generation. Their energy and optimism have much in common with Martin Luther King's conviction that "The arc of the moral universe is long, but it bends toward justice."

Acknowledgments

I AM INDEBTED to the people of Mt. Zion and the Longdale community for their help and hospitality over the decade this work was in process. As is often the case with historical writing, the book has taken longer to complete than I had anticipated; a number of the people I interviewed have died over the course of research and writing. I am grateful to all the members of Mt. Zion who granted me interviews and answered my phone calls. I appreciate, too, the people in Philadelphia, Jackson, and Neshoba County, people of both races, who granted me time and offered new insights.

In the early stages of research I worked extensively in the Methodist General Archives in Madison, New Jersey, where Dale Patterson and his knowledgeable and accommodating colleagues assisted me at every turn. That was true as well when Ann Webster and the other staff librarians at the Mississippi Department of Archives and History in Jackson came to my aid. Deborah McIntosh, the Methodist Archivist at Millsaps College, also in Jackson, expertly guided me though the material on Mississippi Methodism, offered important new insights, and responded swiftly to frantic phone calls. Theresa Ridout, the director of the archives in the Neshoba County Public Library, provided me with access to the archival material, with information about regional history, and equally important, with help using the microfilm readers when they refused to cooperate. In addition, I examined some of the extensive private collection of civil rights material preserved by Jan Hillegas in Jackson, a historically significant body of documents that deserves a new, institutional, home and support. Jan has aided my work in so many other ways, and I could not have finished the project without her assistance. I am grateful as well to the people outside the Philadelphia and Longdale area who shared their ideas with me: in Jackson, Jerry Mitchell, Ed King, Rims Barbour, Owen Brooks, Harry Bowie, Henry Clay, Clay Lee, Governor William Winter, and especially Dick Molpus, who responded to many phone calls; in Oxford, Susan Glisson; and in Washington, DC, Lawrence Guyot. To the many people, noted in the endnotes, who shared their memories with me, I offer my deepest thanks. And to those no longer able to hear my appreciation—Mabel and Mary Wells, Mabel Steele, Ross Jones, Clinton Collier, and Florence Mars—I offer it nevertheless.

Early on in the project I spent the academic year 2006–2007 at the Collegeville Institute for Ecumenical and Cultural Research in Minnesota, one of the most wonderful places I know of to do scholarly work in a community of helpful, caring fellows. I am indebted to the scholars who were in residence with me, for their hard questions and new leads. Much of the smooth functioning and stimulating environment is owed to the resident staff, director Donald Ottenhoff, and his then associates, Elisa Schneider and Carla Durand.

As the work developed along with my interest in collective memory, I have relied heavily on the scholarship of those who write about the role of history and memory, including David Blight, W. Fitzhugh Brundage, James and Lois Horton, and the collective work of Jeffrey K. Olick, Vered Vinitzky-Seroussi, and Daniel Levy. They have made an old field new and relevant again. I have also been appreciative of the recent work of those examining the black church tradition, including Barbara Diane Savage, Curtis J. Evans, Eddie S. Glaude, Jr., and Wallace Best.

I made my first research trip to Mississippi in 2001. Over the intervening years my professional and personal life has taken a new direction. Instead of being a widowed tenured professor, I have become a married research scholar, since 2009 the wife of Alvin J. Poppen, who may not have appreciated the extent to which he was also marrying a manuscript. Al has been a great supporter of my work, taking the photos, priming my thinking and reading each revision of my manuscript with a critical but caring eye. "The book" has been an ever-present partner in our marriage and it is now time for it to be gone from there. Then, too, without support of technological whizzes Lori Landis and Brad McLennan, I would have been a goner. And once again, I thank the tolerance of the rest of my family while I finished this work: Bill and Robin, Zack, Kelsey, and Jake, Rosy, and Glynis, David, Barbara and Ed, Moira and Jeff, Rachael, Nicole, Eric, and Nathan.

Notes

PREFACE

1. Speech of Dick Molpus, fiftieth annual commemoration service, Mt. Zion United Methodist Church, June 15, 2014.
2. *In Search of Another Country* is the title of Crespino's book.
3. "When the Stars Begin To Fall: Imagination and the American South," *New Yorker*, April 14, 2014, 14.

INTRODUCTION

1. TRC Report, Vol. 1, "Chairperson's Report," 22, cited in *After the TRC*, Wilmot James and Linda Van De Vijver, eds., Colin Bundy, "The Beast of the Past: History and the TRC" (Claremont, SA: David Philip, 2000), 15.
2. Speech of David Dennis, fiftieth annual commemoration service, Mt. Zion, June 15, 2014.
3. Interview with former Governor William Winter, May 28, 2014.

CHAPTER 1

1. Quoted in William B. McClain, *Black People in the Methodist Church: Wither Thou Goest?* (Cambridge, MA: Schenkman, 1984).
2. Diane McWhorter, *New York Times*, December 30, 2001.
3. Lewis A. Coser, *Maurice Halbwachs on Collective Memory* (Chicago: University of Chicago Press, 1992), especially 7–13.
4. Richard Aubrey McLemore, *A History of Mississippi* (Jackson: University and College Press of Mississippi, 1973), 1:8, 264–5, 284.

5. Randy J. Sparks, *Religion in Mississippi* (Jackson: University Press of Mississippi, 2001), 50; also McLemore, *History of Mississippi*, 1:325. In 1810 there were 17,088 slaves in Mississippi, and by 1820 there were 32,814, an increase of 92 percent.

6. McLemore, *History of Mississippi*, 1:325–7.

7. Ted Ownby, *American Dreams in Mississippi: Consumers, Poverty, and Culture, 1830–1998* (Chapel Hill: University of North Carolina Press, 1999), 37–41. As Ownby explains, some planters and their wives went to Europe themselves to pick out their goods, the purpose being to impress their friends and not poor whites or impoverished blacks.

8. *The Neshoba Democrat*, March 30, 2011.

9. John H. Graham, *Mississippi Circuit Riders, 1865–1965* (Nashville: Parthenon, 1967), 59, 91.

10. McLemore, *History of Mississippi*, 1:587.

11. McLemore, *History of Mississippi*, 1:586–9.

12. See W. E. B. DuBois, *Black Reconstruction in America, 1860–1880* (New York: Free Press, ca. 1935), for a progressive black man's view of Reconstruction. John Hope Franklin has also written importantly about the achievements of Reconstruction. Also Eric Foner, *Reconstruction: America's Unfinished Revolution* (New York: Harper Collins, 1988), 426–36; McLemore, *History of Mississippi*: 1:575–89, on Congressional Reconstruction; 1:590–600, on Redemption.

13. See "Registration of Voters in Riley's Election District," pamphlet, 1891; and "Election District of Supervisor's District No. 2," 1892 on. Provided by Janelle Yates, MS, Philadelphia; copy in author's possession.

14. Ralph E. Morrow, *Northern Methodism and Reconstruction* (East Lansing: Michigan State University Press, 1956), 213–14.

15. McLemore, *History of Mississippi*, 1:614, 615.

16. See "Registration of Voters in Riley's Election District," 1891; and "Election District of Supervisor's District No. 2," 1892 on. Provided by Janelle Yates, copy in author's possession.

17. Neil R. McMillen, *Dark Journey: Black Mississippians in the Age of Jim Crow* (Urbana: University of Illinois Press, 1990), 186–90.

18. Booker T. Washington, Atlanta Exposition Speech, Cotton States and International Exposition, September 18, 1895.

19. Nathan O. Hatch and John H. Wigger, eds., *Methodism and the Shaping of American Culture* (Nashville: Kingswood, 2001), 11. The editors explain that between the Revolution and the Civil War, the Methodist Church had experienced "a meteoric rise" in membership, which enabled it to have great influence over the "character of American life."

20. Quoted in Graham, *Mississippi Circuit Riders*, 117.

21. Graham, *Mississippi Circuit Riders*, 58, 59, 130, 131.

CHAPTER 2

1. Interview with Ross and Wilbur Jones, July 14, 2002. In an interview on July 9, 2005, Ross Jones said his grandfather's old master gave him some land and a mule. He again alluded to the first version in an interview on October 2, 2009.

2. According to the database of the Neshoba County Court Records, one Thomas Jones is listed as a resident on June 1, 1870. He is described as a mulatto farmer, age thirty-two, with sons James, seven, Robert, six, and William, two. Records compiled by Janelle Yates.

3. No record of their marriage exists. See Janelle B. Yates and Theresa Ridout, *Red Clay Hills of Neshoba since 1833* (Philadelphia, MS: Neshoba County Historical Society, 1992), 62.

4. See Neshoba County records, 317A–317B, compiled by Janelle Yates. See also Edward Royce, *The Origins of Southern Sharecropping* (Philadelphia, PA: Temple University Press, 1993), 17ff.

5. Neshoba County records, 317A–317B. The first name of "D" Wilson is difficult to read in these handwritten records.

6. Neshoba County Deed Record Book, Q, 616; also Florence Mars, *Witness in Philadelphia* (Baton Rouge: Louisiana State University Press, 1977), 153.

7. See Roy L. Brooks, *Atonement and Forgiveness: A New Model for Black Reparations* (Berkeley: University of California Press, 2004), 21; Manning Marable, *The Great Wells of Democracy* (New York: Basic Books, 2002), 223–53. The authors make the case that because of the lack of "basic capital," which includes "life, liberty, and human dignity," as well as financial, social, and human capital, a strong case can be made for forms of black reparations for the unpaid labor of slavery.

8. See compilation by Janelle Yates of "Registration of Voters in Riley's Election District," 1891; "Election District of Supervisor's District No. 2," 1892 on.

9. Morrow, *Northern Methodism and Reconstruction*, 211.

10. McLemore, *History of Mississippi*, 1:590–95.

11. "Election District of Supervisor's District No. 1," 1892; copy in author's possession.

12. Mars, 154; Land Roll, 1887, Neshoba County, MS, compiled by Janelle Yates. See also Inez Calloway Johnson, "History of Longdale High School, 1949–1963," pamphlet, 1999, written for the thirty-fifth reunion celebration in 2005. Mabel Steele once shared a drawing that represented the first log church. July 21, 2001.

13. Interview with Mabel Steele, July 21, 2001.

14. Ross Jones, interview, July 14, 2002.

15. Foner, *Reconstruction*, 70, 71.

16. See DuBois, *Black Reconstruction in America*, 1935.

17. Ross Jones and Wilbur Jones, interview, July 14, 2002.

18. See Charles C. Bolton, *The Hardest Deal of All: The Battle over School Integration in Mississippi, 1870–1980* (Jackson: University of Mississippi Press, 2005),

19–22. Also Yates and Ridout, *Red Clay Hills of Neshoba*, 172; and Inez Calloway Johnson, "History of Longdale High School," 1999 (pamphlet).

19. Christopher M. Span, *From Cotton Field to Schoolhouse: African American Education in Mississippi, 1862–1875* (Chapel Hill: University of North Carolina Press, 2009), 8, 18.

20. Interviews with Ross Jones, July 14, 2002; Jewel McDonald, July 12, 2005; Evelyn Cole Calloway, October 8, 2009.

21. Ross Jones, interview, July 14, 2002. Ross Jones did not assign a date to the $25 a bale price for cotton.

22. Ross Jones, interview, July 14, 2002.

23. Ross Jones, interview, July 10, 2005; interview with Rev. Clinton Collier, July 12, 2005.

24. Ross Jones, interview, October 2, 2009.

25. Collier, interview, May 21, 2002.

26. Ross Jones, interview, July 14, 2002.

27. [27] Interview with Clarence Hill, July 16, 2002.

28. Mars, *Witness in Philadelphia*.

29. Willie Morris, *My Mississippi* (Jackson: University Press of Mississippi, 2000), 105.

30. Mars, *Witness in Philadelphia*, 1.

31. Mars, *Witness in Philadelphia*, 1.

32. Florence Mars, interview, May 17, 2002.

33. Florence Mars, interview, May 17, 2002.

34. This appears as an epigraph in Mars, *Witness in Philadelphia*. The quote, often attributed to Faulkner, does not appear in any of his work. Willie Morris cites it in a number of places, suggesting that the origin is in a private conversation between the two; see Morris, *My Mississippi*, xi.

35. Morris, in *My Mississippi*, xi, references "two souls, two minds." That his home state had these two sides, more different than complementary, has been a significant theme in the writings of Morris. Morris retired to the Magnolia State after decades of residence and writing in New York City.

36. Mars, *Witness in Philadelphia*, 16.

37. Mars, *Witness in Philadelphia*. 16.

38. Mars, *Witness in Philadelphia*, 5.

39. Bishop Clay Lee, interview, May 23, 2002.

40. Mars, interview; Mabel Wells, interview, July 16, 2002. Mabel Wells said "moonshine was made here." Florence Mars said you knew who kept stills by the number of pop bottles and caps lying about a property. Hill, interview, Philadelphia resident Fenton DeWeese was amused when he recalled that as a sixteen-year old he had to show an ID card to buy moonshine; interview with Fenton DeWeese, July 5, 2005.

41. Mars, 39; Yates and Ridout, 72.

CHAPTER 3

1. Rayford W. Logan, *The Negro in American Life and Thought: The Nadir, 1877–1901* (New York: Basic Books); republished as *The Betrayal of the Negro: From Rutherford B. Hayes to Woodrow Wilson* (New York: Collier, 1965).

2. Christopher Lasch, *Haven in a Heartless World* (New York: Basic Books, 1977). Lasch's book studies the idea of family as haven. The annual Minutes of the black Mississippi Methodist Conferences during these years support the argument that Mississippi black Methodists who departed the state did so earlier than blacks in other Southern states. Black membership in Methodist churches actually grew in the years prior to 1916. The Minutes of the black conferences are housed in the archives at Millsaps College in Jackson. I am indebted to Debra McIntosh, archivist, for helping me work through these sources.

3. Eric Foner, *Reconstruction: America's Unfinished Revolution*, 29, 69–72. See also Ralph Morrow, *Northern Methodism and Reconstruction.*

4. The issues of "retreat" and "sanctuary," important to Lasch, he relates to matters of identity and collective consciousness. For discussion of this see work by Pierre Nora and Christopher Lasch. See article on Nora, "Building a Collective Consciousness on a National Scale," *Forward*, July 8, 2011. For Nora, a French-Jewish historian, his massive study on Places of Memory is an effort to link his French and Jewish identities. On Lasch, see Norman Birnbaum, "Gratitude and Forbearance: On Christopher Lasch," *The Nation*, September 13, 2011.

5. See *Journal of (the black) Mississippi Annual Conference of the Methodist Episcopal Church*, 1900.

6. *Journal of (the black) Mississippi Annual Conference of the Methodist Episcopal Church*, 1898. This same injunction is raised at virtually all annual conferences in Mississippi.

7. See David L. Chappell, *Prophetic Religion and the Death of Jim Crow* (Chapel Hill: University of North Carolina Press, 2004), especially his introduction, pp. 1–8. Chappell addresses the question of how the "masses of poor, disfranchised protesters" endured and persevered during the years of both Jim Crow and the civil rights movement. He finds an answer in their commitment to the prophetic tradition, "rooted in the Christian and Jewish myth," and extending from "David and Isaiah in the Old Testament through Augustine and Martin Luther to Reinhold Niebuhr." Also, sermons at Mt. Zion Church by Rev. Gary Hampton, July 14, 2002; Rev. A. J. Murray, October 9, 2009; and Obbie Riley, June 21, 2011.

8. Henry Bullock, *A History of Negro Education in the South* (New York: Praeger, 1970), 149.

9. The local sheriff was probably not among the mob the night the Klan gathered in 1964 to assault five church members and burn the church, but evidence that

appeared later—at the trial of Edgar Ray Killen—indicates that he was aware of the plot and of the complicity of his deputy.

10. Isabel Wilkerson, *The Warmth of Other Suns: The Epic Story of America's Great Migration* (New York: Random House, 2010), 45, 46.

11. Wilkerson, *Warmth of Other Suns*, 437, 528.

12. *Official Journal of the Upper Mississippi Conference of the Methodist Episcopal Church, 1916–1919*, Millsaps College Library.

13. Roy Lawrence, "A Brief History of Black Methodists in Mississippi," in *Mississippi United Methodist Advocate*, November 17, 1974, 6.

14. Wilkerson, *Warmth of Other Suns*, 437.

15. Interview with Rev. Clinton Collier, July 5, 2002.

16. Neil McMillen, quoted in Wilkerson, *Warmth of Other Suns*, 11.

17. Stewart E. Tolnay and E. M. Beck, *A Festival of Violence: An Analysis of Southern Lynchings, 1882–1930* (Chicago: University of Illinois Press, 1995), 40. See Jan Hillegas, "Preliminary List of Mississippi Lynchings by County," ms., 1994, Hillegas COFO [Council of Federated Organizations] collection, Jackson, MS. Three of the seven were not identified by name; one was a white male, another an Indian male, and another a black male under eighteen. There were other victims of assault by law enforcement, like Luther Jackson, shot by Lawrence Rainey, the man who became sheriff.

18. Tolnay and Beck, *Festival of Violence*, 50.

19. Charles Payne, *I've Got the Light of Freedom* (Berkeley: University of California Press, 1997), 7.

20. Foner, *Reconstruction*, 93.

21. Foner, *Reconstruction*, 93; also interview with Mabel Wells, July 16, 2002.

22. This information was gathered from Steele family members: Arecia, July 10, 2005; Mabel, May 12, 2002; John, May 12, 2002; and Mrs. William H. Steele. Also Wilkerson, *Warmth of Other Suns*.

23. Interview with LeRoy Clemons, October 9, 2009. Clemons himself is a person with significant community influence. He was often a speaker at local events, served in an executive position at the casino, was president of the local NAACP, and was a member of the Philadelphia Coalition and its liaison with the William Winter Institute at Ole Miss.

24. Interview with John Steele, May 12, 2002.

25. Most people in Longdale knew about this absurd question, which apparently was used by other registrars to deny the vote. Florence Mars delighted in telling the story, a sign of the folly of white bureaucrats.

26. See Jenny Irons, *Reconstituting Whiteness* (Nashville: Vanderbilt University Press, 2011), xv, xvi, for the role of the Mississippi State Sovereignty Commission in redefining whiteness.

27. Sparks, *Religion in Mississippi*, 162–3.

28. Quoted in Roy L. Brooks, ed., *When Sorry Isn't Enough* (New York: New York University Press, 1999), 395.

29. See Irons, *Reconstituting Whiteness.*
30. Interview with Ross Jones, October 9, 2009.
31. Ross Jones, interview, October 9, 2009.
32. Ross Jones, interview, October 9, 2009.
33. McLemore, *History of Mississippi,* 2:91–2, 75.
34. McLemore, *History of Mississippi,* 2:34. C. Vann Woodward, *The Strange Career of Jim Crow* (New York: Oxford University Press, 1955), 88, contended that this extremely virulent nature of white supremacy was something entirely new, that prior to the codification of Jim Crow laws in the 1890s, interactions between races had a measure of fluidity and variety. James C. Cobb terms this a "redneck-centric" interpretation of the origins of Jim Crow, saying that Woodward did not see Jim Crow racism as existing in the minds of all Southerners, but rather the creation of a group of ill-educated hooligan politicians. Woodward's view is thus itself a significant commentary on white Southern memory. See James C. Cobb, *The Brown Decision: Jim Crow and Southern Identity* (Athens: University of Georgia Press, 2005), 12.
35. McLemore, *History of Mississippi,* 2:37.
36. McLemore, *History of Mississippi,* 2:137.
37. The classic study of lynching is by Arthur F. Raper, *The Tragedy of Lynching* (Chapel Hill: University of North Carolina Press, 1938). Historian Leon Litwack's figure for the number of blacks murdered by lynch mobs is 4,742; see James Allen et al., eds., *Without Sanctuary: Lynching Photography in America* (Twin Palms, 2000). The numbers, though atrocious, actually have less meaning than the constant threat that lynching posed and the climate of fear it was intended to create. Neil McMillen says that between 1889 and 1945, 3,786 people were lynched nationwide, with Mississippi accounting for 13 percent, or 476. See McMillen, *Dark Journey,* 229. Payne, *I've Got the Light of Freedom,* says 539 were lynched between the end of Reconstruction and the beginning of the civil rights movement.
38. Tolnay and Beck, *Festival of Violence,* 214, 221.
39. Interview with Arecia Steele, July 8, 2005.
40. Interview with Mabel Wells and daughter, Mary Wells, May 22, 2002. Mabel Wells was a Sunday school teacher and a highly regarded member of the Longdale community. She was also known in the community for her fondness for chewing tobacco. According to Longdale resident Jewel McDonald, Mabel chewed in the nursing home until she died.
41. See Kathryn Stockett, *The Help* (New York: Amy Einhorn and G. P. Putnam's Sons, 2009), for a perspective on this relationship by a white novelist.
42. Arecia Steele, interview; interview with Edna Hunt, May 28, 2002.
43. Ross Jones, interview, July 14, 2002.
44. Christopher M. Span, *From Cotton Field to Schoolhouse: African American Education in Mississippi, 1862–1875* (Chapel Hill: University of North Carolina Press, 2009), 88; quoted from Michael Wayne, *The Reshaping of Plantation*

Society: The Natchez District, 1860–1880 (Baton Rouge: Louisiana State University Press, 1983), 10.

45. McMillen, *Dark Journey*, 113. See also James C. Cobb, *The Most Southern Place on Earth: The Mississippi Delta and the Roots of Regional Identity* (New York: Oxford University Press, 1992), 91–2, which discusses a similar development in the Delta region.

46. McMillen, *Dark Journey*, 112.

47. McMillen, *Dark Journey*, 114, 115.

48. McMillen, *Dark Journey*, 118.

49. See Mars, *Witness in Philadelphia*, 156, 181.

50. Interview with Eva Tisdale, May 18, 2002. Eva Tisdale was an activist in black community affairs since the 1960s, and worked as a child welfare worker. She said the burning of Mt. Zion Church in 1964 was "misconstrued." Although black residents of Philadelphia and those of Longdale worked together on projects of common concern, there were differences that characterized the residents of the two areas, urban and rural being only the most obvious. Most church-going blacks in town attended either Mt. Nebo Baptist Church, or the large Jerusalem Church, which is Pentecostal.

51. The population of Choctaw Indians does not appear in this US census tally. See Yates and Ridout, *Red Clay Hills of Neshoba*, 91, 92.

52. See Neshoba County Land Deed Book, RR, 537; 2B 534; RR, 523, 538.

53. Nollie W. Hickman, *Mississippi Harvest: Lumbering in the Longleaf Pine Belt, 1840–1915* (Jackson: University Press of Mississippi, 1962). Neshoba grew short-leaf pine. Hickman observes: "There is little evidence to indicate that lumbermen ever greatly abused the enormous power that was theirs in the sawmill towns." This appears to be the case in Neshoba, where the dependence of the owners on black labor contributed to a more favorable relationship than existed, say, for the men who worked in turpentine.

54. Neshoba County Land Deed Books—see for example RR, 537, 538, 523. Interpreting these Land Deed Books is a tedious task, requiring lining up owners with range markers for the county in the record books.

55. Interview with Clarence Hill, July 16, 2002.

56. McLemore, *History of Mississippi*, 2:97.

57. Ross Jones, interview, October 9, 2009.

58. McLemore, *History of Mississippi*, 2:75, 94.

59. McLemore, *History of Mississippi*, 2:93, 94.

60. Inez Calloway Johnson, "History of Longdale High School, 1949–1963 (n.p., 1999) (Jackson, MS: I. C. Johnson).

61. Interview with Ross and Wilbur Jones, July 14, 2002.

62. Clinton Collier, interview, July 5, 2002.

63. Clinton Collier, interview, July 5, 2002.

64. Clinton Collier, interview, July 5, 2002; Ross Jones, interview, July 12, 2002.

65. Inez Calloway Johnson, "History of Longdale High School, 1949–1963."

CHAPTER 4

1. Interview with Rev. Harry Bowie, July 13, 2001.
2. James F. Findlay, Jr., *Church People in the Struggle: The National Council of Churches and the Black Freedom Movement, 1950–1970* (New York: Oxford University Press, 1993), 76ff. Findlay's book is a closely researched, essentially sympathetic, though not uncritical, account of the Delta Ministry.
3. Grant S. Shockley, ed., *Heritage and Hope: The African American Presence in United Methodism* (Nashville, TN: Abingdon, 1991), 18, 19.
4. Bowie, interview. Bowie himself had been subjected to Mississippi racism, under constant scrutiny by the Mississippi State Sovereignty Commission (MSSC) from the time of his arrival. Investigators checked his sources of income, suspecting he might have pocketed money meant for the Ministry's McComb Community Center. One investigator noted that "Bowie had caused nothing but trouble since he came to McComb and we are looking forward to the possibility that this [a search of his income] may be just the thing to stop him." An effort to prove he had an arrest record was fruitless, and an investigator was forced to concede that this salary really was $8,000 annually, paid by the National Council of Churches. MSSC Report, November 21, 1966, L. E. Cole, Investigator, 1-116-10; MSSC Memorandum, written by Erle Johnston, Jr., October 26, 1966, 1-116-6. Credit worthiness and financial status were items well scrutinized by the commission, seeking to find ways to embarrass or even arrest civil rights workers.
5. Bowie, interview.
6. Bowie, interview.
7. Bowie, interview.
8. Bowie, interview. See also Joseph Crespino, *In Search of Another Country: Mississippi and the Conservative Counterrevolution* (Princeton, NJ: Princeton University Press, 2007), 167–71.
9. W. Astor Kirk, *Desegregation of the Methodist Church Polity* (Pittsburgh: RoseDog, 2005), 3. See Russell E. Richey, *The Methodist Conference in America: A History* (Nashville, TN: Abingdon, 1996), 177–8.
10. David Goldfield et al., *The American Journey* (Upper Saddle River, NJ: Prentice Hall, 1998), 760.
11. Goldfield et al., *American Journey*, 772.
12. *Journal of the [Black] Mississippi Annual Conference* (MEC), 1920.
13. Henry Nathaniel Oakes, "The Struggle for Racial Equality in the Methodist Episcopal Church: The Career of Robert E. Jones, 1904–1944," PhD diss., University of Iowa, 1973, 40. See also Carol V. R. George, *Segregated Sabbaths: Richard Allen and the Rise of Independent Black Churches, 1760–1840* (New York: Oxford University Press, 1973), for a discussion of Richard Allen, who was the first black bishop of an African Methodist denomination.

14. Oakes, "Struggle for Racial Equality," 44. His biographer makes note of Jones's light skin, but said he achieved his professional status because of his "ability and promise," not because of his appearance. See also Morris L. Davis, *The Methodist Unification: Christianity and the Politics of Race in the Jim Crow Era* (New York: New York University Press, 2008), 100–102.

15. See Richey, *Methodist Conference in America*, 178; also Dwight M. Culver, *Negro Segregation in the Methodist Church* (New Haven, CT: Yale University Press, 1953), 72–6.

16. Quoted in Richey, *Methodist Conference in America*, 177.

17. Richey, *Methodist Conference in America*, 294.

18. See Davis, *Methodist Unification*; and Richey, *Methodist Conference in America*.

19. Cobb, *Most Southern Place on Earth*, 333.

20. Cobb, *Most Southern Place on Earth*, 333.

21. Reinhold Niebuhr, "Meditations from Mississippi," *Christian Century*, February 10, 1937, 183–4; quoted in Sparks, *Religion in Mississippi*, 186. Also Ronald H. Stone, *Professor Reinhold Niebuhr: A Mentor to the Twentieth Century* (Louisville, KY: Westminster/John Knox, 1992), 111–15.

22. Kirk, *Desegregation of the Methodist Church Polity*, 3.

23. Kirk, *Desegregation of the Methodist Church Polity*, 7.

24. See Richey, *Methodist Conference in America*, 180–81.

25. Davis, *Methodist Unification*, 1–2.

26. Oakes, "Struggle for Racial Equality," 418.

27. Culver, *Negro Segregation in the Methodist Church*, 75.

28. *Christian Century*, February 17, 1937, 204.

29. Oakes, "Struggle for Racial Equality," 432.

30. See Oakes, "Struggle for Racial Equality," who seems certain that Jones did not support the Central Jurisdiction.

31. *Christian Advocate*, August 8, 1940.

32. *Christian Advocate*, May 30, 1940.

33. Culver, *Negro Segregation in the Methodist Church*, 6. Culver attempted to give an objective analysis of the Central Jurisdiction and its implications for black Methodists. The work is a product of the time in which Culver was writing.

34. Culver, *Negro Segregation in the Methodist Church*, 88.

35. Ramsey Bridges, "Can the Central Jurisdiction be Abolished?" *Central Christian Advocate*, March 4, 1948, quoted in William Edge Dixon, "Ministerial Leadership in the Central Jurisdiction of the Methodist Church," PhD diss., Boston University, 1955, 110, 111, 50.

36. Ralph A. Felton, *The Ministry of the Central Jurisdiction of the Methodist Church* (New York: Division of National Missions, Methodist Board of Missions, n.d. [ca. 1953]), 10–12. Official Methodist records at the time indicated that black giving was proportionally on a par with or higher than white giving. See also Emory Stevens Bucke, ed., *The History of American Methodism*, 3 vols.

(New York and Nashville, TN: Abingdon, 1964); Murray H. Leiffer, "The Central Jurisdiction," 485–95, in Chapter 33, "United Methodist." "The Central Jurisdiction does not suffer disproportionately in comparison with the rest of the church in the matter of the support of the benevolence program, especially when the difference in economic status of the majority of its membership is taken into account," 479.

37. Felton, *Ministry of the Central Jurisdiction of the Methodist Church*, 10–12.
38. Dixon, "Ministerial Leadership in the Central Jurisdiction of the Methodist Church," 82, 71; Oakes, "Struggle for Racial Equality."
39. Dixon, "Ministerial Leadership in the Central Jurisdiction of the Methodist Church," 47, 48.
40. *Official Journal of the Mississippi Annual Conference of the Methodist Episcopal Church* 1911, 1931. After 1939 the minutes of the black Methodist Conference in Mississippi are known as the *Official Journal of the Mississippi Annual Conference Methodist Church CJ*, 1941.
41. Oakes, "Struggle for Racial Equality," 388.

CHAPTER 5

1. William B. McClain, *Black People in the Methodist Church: Whither Thou Goest?* (Cambridge, MA: Schenkman, 1984), 83.
2. Minutes of the Mississippi Methodist Conference, CJ, 1940, 1942. The drop in the Philadelphia Circuit was temporary, perhaps the result of an error in reporting. The number went from 64 in 1942 to 175 two years later.
3. Shockley, *Heritage and Hope*, 18.
4. Shockley, *Heritage and Hope*, 19.
5. McClain, *Black People in the Methodist Church*, 33, 35.
6. Matthews says he borrowed the term "liminal self" from the anthropologist Victor Turner in *The Ritual Process: Structure and Anti-Structure* (Chicago: Aldine Transaction, 1995), 94–120; see Donald G. Matthews, "Evangelical America—The Methodist Ideology," in *Perspectives on American Methodism: Interpretive Essays*, ed. Russell E. Richey, Kenneth E. Rowe, and Jean Miller Schmidt, 17–30 (Nashville, TN: Abingdon, 1993), 29, 23–28.
7. Charles H. Long, "Perspective for a Study of African-American Religion in the United States," originally published in 1971; in *African-American Religion: Interpretive Essays in History and Culture*, ed. Timothy E. Fulop and Albert J. Raboteau, 21–36 (New York: Routledge, 1997), 25. Long's basic argument gets expressed by others, and in many ways. Barbara Dianne Savage, *Your Spirits Walk Beside Us: The Politics of Black Religion* (Cambridge, MA: Harvard University Press, 2008), 13, has noted it is a misnomer to speak of "the Black Church," since there are many black churches and a multiplicity of forms of spiritual experiences that African Americans pursued in the past and continue

to seek out in recent times, from Black Jews to Pentecostals, to a wide variety of independent groups.

8. See Long, "Perspective for a Study of African-American Religion in the United States."

9. A library of church and Sunday school material at Mt. Zion holds some of these Methodist tracts.

10. Donald K. Gorrell, "The Social Creed and Methodism through Eighty Years," in *Perspectives on American Methodism: Interpretive Essays*, ed. Russell E. Richey, Kenneth E. Rowe, and Jean Miller Schmidt, 386–99 (Nashville, TN: Abingdon, 1993).

11. Gorrell, "The Social Creed and Methodism through Eighty Years," 395.

12. Gorrell, "The Social Creed and Methodism through Eighty Years," 398.

13. Ellis Ray Branch, "'Born of Conviction': Racial Conflict and Change in Mississippi Methodism," PhD diss., Mississippi State University, 1984, 36, 37. A Methodist minister as well as a doctoral student, Branch wrote a careful history of the Methodist struggle in Mississippi. Branch discusses Satterfield at length.

14. Crespino, *In Search of Another Country*, 167–74. Crespino has observed that "no denomination faced greater challenges from the social upheaval of the 1960s than Mississippi Methodists."

15. Branch, "Born of Conviction," 95.

16. Charles Parlin was Chair of the Committee on Inter-Jurisdictional Relations, the committee to oversee the future of the Central Jurisdiction. He served from 1960–1968. See Parlin Collection, Methodist archives, Madison, NJ.

17. Payne, *I've Got the Light of Freedom*, 25.

18. Payne, *I've Got the Light of Freedom*, 13–15. See also Jan Hillegas, "Preliminary List of Mississippi Lynchings," manuscript, Hillegas COFO collection, Jackson, Mississippi.

19. Payne, *I've Got the Light of Freedom*; Hillegas, "Preliminary List of Mississippi Lynchings."

20. John Dittmer, *Local People: The Struggle for Civil Rights in Mississippi* (Champaign: University of Illinois Press, 1995), 1–5.

21. Raper, *Tragedy of Lynching*, 9n.

22. See comment in McMillen, *Dark Journey*, 399n84.

23. McMillen, *Dark Journey*, 399n84.

24. *Journal of the Mississippi Annual Conference of the Methodist Church*, CJ, 1942.

25. Interview with Ross Jones, July 14, 2002.

26. Felton, *Ministry of the Central Jurisdiction of the Methodist Church*, 10.

27. *Journal of the Mississippi Annual Conference of the Methodist Church*, CJ, 1942.

28. *Journal of the Mississippi Annual Conference of the Methodist Church*, CJ, 1942.

29. *Journal of the Mississippi Annual Conference of the Methodist Church*, CJ, 1946.

30. *Journal of the Mississippi Annual Conference of the Methodist Church*, CJ, 1946.

31. *Christian Advocate*, April 1, 1948.
32. *Christian Advocate*, January 25, 1945.
33. *Christian Advocate*, July 1, 1948.
34. *Christian Advocate*, February 5, 1948.
35. *Journal of the Southeastern Jurisdictional Conference* (MC), 1960, 122, 124.
36. McClain, *Black People in the Methodist Church*, 59.
37. See Crespino, *In Search of Another Country*, 170.
38. Crespino, *In Search of Another Country*, 277.
39. Ellis Ray Branch, "Born of Conviction," 59, 98–9.
40. *Bulletin of the Mississippi Association of Methodist Ministers and Laymen*, pamphlet, published irregularly, 1955–1966. Copies of the bulletin are housed in the archives of MDAH, Jackson.
41. See Dittmer, *Local People*, 37.
42. Cobb, *Brown Decision*, 44.

CHAPTER 6

1. Interview with Jewel McDonald, July 5, 2005; phone interview, March 20, 2013; see also *Journal of the Mississippi Annual Conference of the Methodist Church* CJ, 1955.
2. McDonald, interview.
3. Cobb, *Brown Decision*, 31ff. For the revisionist view critical of *Brown*, see Michael J. Klarman, *From Jim Crow to Civil Rights* (New York: Oxford University Press, 2004).
4. Tomiko Brown-Nagin, *The Courage to Dissent* (New York: Oxford University Press, 2011), 440.
5. Ray Holder, *The Mississippi Methodists, 1799–1983: A Moral People "Born of Conviction"* (Jackson, MS: Maverick Prints, 1984), 145.
6. See Cobb, *Brown Decision*, who argues that in 1930 Georgia was spending on average $45 on each white pupil and $8 on each black pupil.
7. Robert A. Margo, *Race and Schooling in the South, 1880–1950: An Economic History* (Chicago: University of Chicago Press, 1990), 64.
8. *Mississippi School Survey, County Public Schools, Neshoba County*, cited in Mars, *Witness in Philadelphia*, 57.
9. *Mississippi State Sovereignty Commission Report*, from Zack Van Landingham, January 26, 1960.
10. Hodding Carter, *The South Strikes Back* (Garden City, NY: Doubleday, 1959), 54; also cited in Mars, 64.
11. Kirk, *Desegregation of the Methodist Church Polity*, 33–4; see also *Central Christian Advocate*, June 1 and June 5, 1954.
12. *Central Christian Advocate*, June 1 and June 5, 1954.
13. Russell E. Richey, Kenneth E. Rowe, and Jean Miller Schmidt, eds., *The Methodist Experience in America: A Sourcebook* (Nashville, TN: Abingdon, 2000), 2;589.

14. *MAMML Information Bulletin*, March 1963. Rev. Dr. J. Philip Wogamon, in his doctoral dissertation, "A Strategy for Racial Desegregation in the Methodist Church," noted that, "According to one observer, 'the best-organized' lay resistance to church integration in the South appears to be in The Methodist Church. The Mississippi Association of Methodist Ministers and Laymen . . . is undoubtedly the strongest of these."

15. *MAMML Information Bulletin*, June 1960.

16. Ellis Ray Branch, "Born of Conviction," 59.

17. See McMillan, *Dark Journey*, 253, and Cobb, *Most Southern Place on Earth*, 216.

18. Mars, *Witness in Philadelphia*, 59.

19. Cobb, *Brown Decision*, 42. Cobb says Faulkner later claimed that he was drunk at the time he made the statement, as if that made a difference.

20. There are many accounts of Till's murder. See Mars, *Witness in Philadelphia*, 67; Cobb, *Most Southern Place on Earth*, 220–21; Howard Ball, *Justice in Mississippi: The Murder Trial of Edgar Ray Killen* (Lawrence: University of Kansas Press, 2006), 38, 39; Seth Cagin and Philip Dray, *We Are Not Afraid: The Story of Goodman, Schwerner, and Chaney, and the Civil Rights Campaign for Mississippi* (New York: Nation, 2006), 54, 348, 349; also interview with Florence Mars, May 17, 2002.

21. Hugh Stephen Whitaker, "A Case Study in Southern Justice: The Emmett Till Case," MA thesis, Florida State University, 1963, 162; cited in Cobb, *Brown Decision*, 221.

22. Reportedly 12 percent of NAACP meetings were held at black churches, although the figure takes account of only those that were known. Most meetings were small, secret, and informal. See McMillan, *Dark Journey*, 315–16; also Mars, *Witness in Philadelphia*, 162–3.

23. Mars, *Witness in Philadelphia*, 162, 163.

CHAPTER 7

1. Gunnar Myrdal, *An American Dilemma: The Negro Problem and Modern Democracy* (New York: Harper and Sons, 1944). I am indebted to W. Astor Kirk, in *Desegregation of the Methodist Church Polity*, for pointing out the relevance of Myrdal's work to the Methodist situation.

2. Methodist historian Murray H. Leiffer noted that by 1956, "many Methodists"— an estimate presumably based on Conference records—have been troubled as to the symbolic significance of this type of structure (the CJ) in a church which boasts of the inclusiveness of all peoples, irrespective of race or nationality"; Leiffer, *History of Methodism* (New York: Abingdon, 1964), 3:494.

3. Kirk, *Desegregation of the Methodist Church Polity*, 58–9; Branch, "Born of Conviction," 56–7. Branch quotes *The Advocate*, which noted that Amendment IX passed the conference "like greased lightning," since it contained something

for both regions: merger, for the Northern church, and voluntarism for the Southern.

4. *Journal of the 1956 General Conference of the Methodist Church* (Nashville, TN: The Methodist Publishing House, 1956), 1693.

5. *Journal of the 1956 General Conference*, 1693.

6. Dittmer, *Local People*, 94–5; Raymond Arsenault, *Freedom Riders: 1961 and the Struggle for Racial Justice* (New York: Oxford University Press, 2006), 266–7.

7. Interview with James Farmer, August, 1993; see also Arsenault, *Freedom Riders*, 267.

8. See Dittmer, *Local People*; Arsenault, *Freedom Riders*.

9. Crespino, *In Search of Another Country*, 170, 171. Crespino argues that extremist segregationist groups—of which MAMML would be one—joined the Methodist exodus to "organizations such as Oral Roberts, Bob Jones, Jim Bakker, Jimmy Swaggert, Jerry Falwell, and many others."

10. Crespino, *In Search of Another Country*, 71, 72; phone interview with Bishop Clay Lee, October 18, 2006. Bishop Lee said that some Methodist moderates believed the signers did the rest of them a disservice by stirring up controversy and then leaving the state.

11. Irons, *Reconstituting Whiteness*, 15.

12. See Branch, "Born of Conviction," 78–85.

13. Branch, "Born of Conviction," 85.

14. Satterfield was also secretary-treasurer of a Washington lobby, the Coordinating Committee for Fundamental American Freedoms, which opposed any civil rights bill. He reportedly earned $2,000 a month for his services. He also maintained a lucrative private practice for Mississippi Chemical Corporation. See Satterfield Papers in MDAH. Jackson. The Satterfield file is a small, but revealing, commentary on the most active public figure in Mississippi Methodism at the time. Satterfield (John Creighton) Papers.

15. Kirk, *Desegregation of the Methodist Church Polity*, 56–65.

16. To some in the church, Parlin and Satterfield appeared to represent polar opposites on most issues the denomination faced. They became good friends, and likely were not so removed from each other's position as first appeared. Both were successful private attorneys, and both were active laymen in the church on the national—and in Parlin's case, international—scene.

17. Major J. Jones, "The Central Jurisdiction: Passive Resistance," in *Heritage and Hope: The African American Presence in United Methodism*, ed. Grant S. Shockley (Nashville: Abingdon, 1991), 202.

18. Kirk, *Desegregation of the Methodist Church Polity*, 58–63.

19. Kirk, *Desegregation of the Methodist Church Polity*, 203.

20. Branch, "Born of Conviction," 87.

21. Interview with Arecia Steele, July 18, 2002.

22. Interview with Ross Jones, July 9, 2005.

23. Interview with Jennifer Riley Hathorn, May 28, 2002.

24. James F. Findley, *Church People in the Struggle: The National Council of Churches and the Black Freedom Movement, 1950–1970* (New York: Oxford University Press, 1991).

25. Steele, interview July 8, 2002.

26. Dittmer, *Local People*, 79.

27. "Mississippi Eyewitness," pamphlet, n.a., n.d. The MIBURN files also report police brutality against blacks.

28. Dittmer, *Local People*, 79.

29. Dittmer, *Local People*, 87.

30. Interview with Jerry Mitchell, July 12, 2005. Jerry Mitchell of the Jackson *Clarion-Ledger* first exposed the MSSC support for Beckwith, including financially. Beckwith was a virulent segregationist, eventually brought to trial in 1994, his defense costs over the years secretly supplemented by funds from the MSSC. Jerry Mitchell had located the evidence which led to his conviction. Beckwith died in prison.

31. W. J. Cunningham, *Agony at Galloway* (Jackson: University Press of Mississippi, 1980), 3, 4; Branch, "Born of Conviction," 91; Minutes of Galloway Church Board, June 21, 1961, MDAH, ms.

32. Interview with Rev. Ed King, July 20, 2001.

33. Charles W. Eagles, *The Price of Defiance: James Meredith and the Integration of Ole Miss* (Chapel Hill: University of North Carolina Press, 2009); Araminta Stone Johnston, *And One was a Priest: The Life and Times of Duncan M. Gray, Jr.* (Jackson: University Press of Mississippi, 2011); Crespino, 43.

34. Branch, "Born of Conviction," 94; *Advocate*, September 1962.

35. Minutes of the Galloway Church Board, Oct. 1963, MDAH, ms.

36. King, interview, July 20, 2001.

37. King, interview, July 5, 2004.

38. Cunningham, *Agony at Galloway*, 3. Selah's response to his board was "Now, gentlemen, let me reiterate this Christian principle—there can be no color bar before the cross of Christ."

39. Branch, "Born of Conviction," 110.

40. Cunningham, *Agony at Galloway*. Cunningham's book is a deeply personal and painful account of his years at Galloway, where he felt abandoned by his bishop and thwarted by the Citizens' Council members who controlled the official board.

41. This account appears in Branch, "Born of Conviction," 145. There are also letters to and from Cunningham about the incident. See Galloway Church Records, MDAH, ms.

42. Branch, "Born of Conviction," 149.

43. Kirk, *Desegregation of the Methodist Church Polity*, 145.

44. *MAMML Information Bulletin*, June, 1965.

45. *MAMML Information Bulletin*, June, 1965.

46. Cunningham, *Agony at Galloway*, 62–7.

47. Dennis became a sad, haunted man after the trial. His career was mentioned in an interview with Bishop Clay Lee, October 18, 2006, and in Branch, "Born of Conviction," 91 ff. See also Cunningham, *Agony at Galloway*, 62–7.
48. Silver, *The Closed Society*, 50.
49. *Meridian Star*, June 19, 1964.
50. See *MAMML Information Bulletin*, June 1964.

CHAPTER 8

1. Sparks, *Religion in Mississippi*, 220.
2. Cited in *MAMML Information Bulletin*, February 1964.
3. Cunningham, *Agony at Galloway*, 93; Minutes of the Board of Galloway Church, March 1965, MDAH, ms.
4. *MAMML Information Bulletin*, January 1965.
5. *In Search of Another Country* is the brilliant title of Joseph Crespino's analysis of modern Mississippi. He quotes the line from the Phil Ochs's folk song, "Mississippi find yourself another country to be part of," 3.
6. These figures come from a report to the NCC on behalf of the Delta ministry. Cited in *MAMML Information Bulletin*, October 1964: "The main problem at this point is the concentration of wealth among the few; e.g., on an average 5% of the farmers control 50% of all farmland."
7. Cagin and Dray, *We Are Not Afraid*, 218.
8. Cagin and Dray, *We Are Not Afraid*, 251.
9. Cagin and Dray, *We Are Not Afraid*, 251, 252. The *Meridian Star* at that time had an extremely racist editorial policy.
10. Cagin and Dray, *We Are Not Afraid*, 260.
11. Cagin and Dray, *We Are Not Afraid*, 261.
12. See the MSSC Report for March 19–20, 1964, for Agent A. L. Hopkins's investigative report on the Schwerners.
13. Don Whitehead, *Attack on Terror: The FBI against the Ku Klux Klan in Mississippi* (New York: Funk and Wagnalls, 1970), 38, says that there was no resolution at the end of the conversation on May 31, and that it required a return visit by James Chaney "to one of the community's leaders" to get final approval. Members of the congregation do not remember it that way.
14. Interview with Jennifer Riley Hathorn, May 13, 2002.
15. Whitehead, *Attack on Terror*, 38, 39; Cagin and Dray, *We Are Not Afraid*, 38.
16. Interview with Jewel McDonald, daughter of Georgia Rush, May 14, 2002. Jewel McDonald, who had two members of her family attacked that night, diligently gathered information about the event over the years. It was her impression that the mob was unusually well armed, prepared with heavy guns. The most extensive account of the attack as well as the murders appears in Cagin and Dray, *We Are Not Afraid*.

17. Interview with Mabel Steele, May 12, 2002.

18. Cagin and Dray, *We Are Not Afraid*, 3.

19. Mabel Steele, interview May 12, 2002. Beddie Cole's prayer appears in all accounts of the attack on the church.

20. A similar account appears in Cagin and Dray, *We Are Not Afraid*, 5.

21. Cagin and Dray, *We Are Not Afraid*, 31–2; Whitehead, *Attack on Terror*, 43.

22. Cagin and Dray, *We Are Not Afraid*, 30–31.

23. Whitehead, *Attack on Terror*, 44; Cagin and Dray, *We Are Not Afraid*, 28–9.

24. Quoted in Cagin and Dray, *We Are Not Afraid*, 30.

25. Interview with Florence Mars, July 8, 2005. Also Mars, *Witness in Philadelphia*, 84–5.

26. *State of Mississippi vs. Edgar Ray Killen* (hereafter cited as *Killen Trial Record*), No. 05-CR-0006-NS-G, 2005 (Circuit Court of Neshoba County, Mississippi; Philadelphia, MS: 2005), 3:765. This is from testimony by Delmar Dennis, but other participants agreed with the essential part of his report.

27. *Killen Trial Record*, 3:765.

28. *Killen Trial Record*, 4:767.

29. An alternate version of the church fire explains it as an inside job, started by someone from Mt. Zion who feared the operation of a Freedom School in their community. Some names have been tossed around, even Cornelius Steele himself, a suggestion that seems inconsistent with his later public role in the commemoration of the event. Comments come from members of the community, including Clint Collier, Clarence Hill, and Ross Jones, as well as the Sovereignty Commission records. The editor of *The Neshoba Democrat* at that time, Jack Long Tannehill, told Florence Mars he was skeptical that "night riders" caused the beatings and burning and he was reluctant to publish the story. According to Mars, "He seemed to be implying that the Mt. Zion community had been a party to the burning"; Mars, *Witness in Philadelphia*, 85. She did not believe him. See also Taylor Branch, *Pillar of Fire: America in the King Years, 1963–65* (New York: Simon and Schuster, 1998), 363. Branch has Tannehill telling Mars that he "was finding Negro members who were so deeply troubled by the idea of civil rights work at Mount Zion that they might have destroyed their own church in protest." Branch doesn't identify the source for this information, other than the allusion to Tannehill. White Neshobans obviously did not want to come forward and admit that some of their white neighbors could have committed the crime. More convincing is Carlton Wallace Miller, the policeman-turned-informant, who said Killen told him the following day that "they [the Klan] burned the Church to get the Civil Rights workers up-there"; *Killen Trial Record*, 3:630. If there was complicity of a Mt. Zion member in the events that transpired in June 1964, it was most likely not in the burning of the church. The lack of proper investigation of what transpired has allowed these and other theories to thrive.

30. See Whitehead, *Attack on Terror*, 51, who says there was also an agent in Meridian.

31. These events are reported in accounts by Florence Mars, William Bradford Huie, Seth Cagin and Philip Dray. With slight variations, Mt. Zion residents confirm the accounts: interviews with Mabel Wells, Mabel Steele, Ross Jones, Clarence Hill, Jennifer Riley Hathorn, Jewel McDonald, and others.

32. Crespino, *In Search of Another Country*, 106.

33. Interview with Evelyn Cole Calloway, daughter of Bud and Beddie Cole, October 9, 2009. Bud, said his daughter, was a man not much given to sentiment; if he had had his hunting gun with him the night of the attack, he would have shot at the mob.

34. This appears in *Killen Trial Record*, 4:955; it is also quoted in Cagin and Dray, *We Are Not Afraid*, 365.

35. MSSC on Agent X. The Sovereignty Commission had many paid informers who infiltrated civil rights meetings, including the one in Ohio. A black agent— and there were several of them—would be less conspicuous. There has been much speculation about who Agent X was, with many suggesting it was Robert L. "R. L." Bolden. Bolden was a black man, at one time very active in MFDP and many other community activities in Jackson and around the state as a vendor to Head Start programs.

36. Quoted in William Bradford Huie, *Three Lives for Mississippi* (Jackson: University Press of Mississippi, 1965), 96.

37. Kirkland's recollection is in the trial testimony; *Killen Trial Record*, 3:685.

38. See Whitehead, *Attack on Terror*, 47; Cagin and Dray, *We Are Not Afraid*, 12.

39. Interview with Jennifer Riley Hathorn, May 28, 2002. Seemingly everyone in the community knew the men were there, their car visible, and their bodies sagging as they viewed the ruined church. It was described as a poignant sight.

40. This is one of the questions writers about the murders raise. Why did the men choose the longer route? Did they suspect the Klan was looking for Schwerner and the busier thoroughfare would offer more protection? See Cagin and Dray, *We Are Not Afraid*; also Huie, *Three Lives for Mississippi*.

41. *Killen Trial Record*, 3:694–700.

42. Cagin and Dray, *We Are Not Afraid*, 11, taken from MIBURN file. At the First National Conference on Civil Rights, held in Philadelphia, MS, June 16–21, 2011, one of the speakers (Linden Ratliff) referred to the possibility that someone from Longdale—part of the bootleg whiskey trade—informed Sheriffs Rainey and Price of the visit of the three civil rights workers. The speaker suggested that people from Mt. Zion Church think it is likely someone from their community was involved in some way with the event, perhaps to keep the trade in whiskey going. Again, without a proper investigation of what happened in and at Mt. Zion, rumors replace information. If a person from the community was involved in some way, that person has never been ostracized. Anyone

in Longdale could have seen their car the day of their visit, as well as other residents in the area and in Philadelphia.

43. *Killen Trial Record,* 3:699.

44. Huie, *Three Lives for Mississippi,* 102.

45. This material comes from the four-volume *Killen Trial Record.* Various witnesses testified to the events of that day and night.

46. *Killen Trial Record,* 4:948.

47. Cagin and Dray summarize what is known about how James Chaney died: "While his [Dr. David Span, the private pathologist's] conclusions cannot be disproved, there has never been any corroborating evidence that Chaney was physically abused before being shot"; *We Are Not Afraid,* 407.

48. It was Jordan who placed Price at the scene of the crime; *Killen Trial Record,* 4:806.

49. Whitehead, *Attack on Terror,* 276–7.

50. Ball, *Murder in Mississippi,* 80.

51. See chapter 10, note 11.

52. Seale trial, June 11, 2007. James Ford Seale was convicted in 2007, due in part to evidence uncovered by Jerry Mitchell in this cold case.

CHAPTER 9

1. Taped interview between Dave Dennis and Tom Dent, October 8, 1983, Tougaloo College library.

2. Dennis and Dent, interview.

3. *Mississippi Free Press,* July 4, 1964.

4. *Killen Trial Record,* 4:929.

5. W. Fitzhugh Brundage, ed., *Where These Memories Grow: History, Memory, and Southern Identity* (Chapel Hill: University of North Carolina Press, 2000), 11.

6. W. Fitzhugh Brundage, *The Southern Past: A Clash of Race and Memory* (Cambridge, MA: Harvard University Press, 2009), 63.

7. Interview with Florence Mars, July 5, 2005.

8. Timothy Naftali, ed., *Lyndon B. Johnson: The Presidential Recordings* [Mississippi Burning and the Passage of the Civil Rights Act], 8:59.

9. Naftali, *Lyndon B. Johnson,* 8:59.

10. See *The New York Times,* October 1, 2010, for the decision by Boston Judge William G. Young, which ordered the Justice Department to pay a fine to families who said they had been bullied by the department when they sued the government, claiming the FBI was responsible for the murders of their relatives.

11. Olen Burrage was one of the Klansmen initially charged in the conspiracy to murder the men. Although he was acquitted, most civil rights activists, as well as the distinguished investigative reporter Jerry Mitchell, believed he was involved in the conspiracy. On March 17, 2013, after Burrage died, Mitchell wrote that a

few years earlier he had phoned the wealthy owner of a trucking company to ask him again about the case. Mitchell said he had asked Burrage, "How could a bunch of Klansmen have slipped onto your property in the dead of night, run a bulldozer and buried three bodies 15 feet down without you hearing or knowing something." Burrage hung up. And with his death went the last chance to prosecute one suspected of being involved in the case. Although Burrage's obituary in *The Neshoba Democrat* said nothing about the 1964 case, it did mention that Burrage had been a Marine, had built a successful trucking business, and was a Baptist deacon. More extensive obituaries in the national press, including *The New York Times* and the *Los Angeles Times*, as well as others, focused instead on Burrage's role in the civil rights murders. Social amnesia, or forgetting, can last a very long time and be highly selective. Mitchell has a number of online sites: see his blog: http://clarionledger.com/jmitchell/2013/03/17. See also http://www.nytimes.com/2013/03/19/us/olen-burrage-dies-at-82-linked-to-killings-in-1964.html?r=O.

12. See Howard Ball, *Murder in Mississippi: United States vs. Price and the Struggle for Civil Rights* (Lawrence: University Press of Kansas, 2004), 77. Ball provides an extensive discussion of the trials of the perpetrators and the role of the FBI. The redacted FBI files on MIBURN provide little help.

13. Both before and during the trial of Edgar Ray Killen, the question of who might have talked to the FBI was addressed by numerous witnesses. Also see Micki Dickoff's documentary *Neshoba: The Price of Freedom* (2010), which pictures a defiant and confident Killen on the eve of his 2005 trial. See also *Killen Trial Records*, 2005.

14. Naftali, *Lyndon B. Johnson*, 8:401, 446–8. Governor Johnson of Mississippi had told the people of his state they did not have to obey the Civil Rights Act "until it was tested in court," 401. President Johnson, the Southerner, and the Democrats as well, became the new "outsiders" to Mississippians. The president allegedly once told close friends and intimates of another scheme he had, one for penetrating the Klan. Even before the start of Freedom Summer, he said he had developed a plan to send "FBI men and put them in every place they anticipate they can as informers and put them in the Klan and infiltrate it." Few investigators since then have found evidence of the plan—though he could have sent specially qualified deep-cover moles—and the president continued to own the case as "my problem." See also Naftali, *Lyndon B. Johnson*, 7:11, 22, 23.

15. Fredric Dannen, "The G-Man and the Hit Man," *New Yorker*, December 16, 1996. There are other studies on Mafia involvement with the FBI in civil rights–related cases, including Sandra Harmon, *Mafia Son: The Scarpa Family, the FBI, and a Story of Betrayal* (New York: St. Martin's Press, 2009); Anthony Villano, with Gerald Astor, *Brick Agent: Inside the Mafia for the FBI* (New York: Quadrangle, New York Times Books, 1977), and Jerry Mitchell, investigative reporter, the

Jackson *Clarion-Ledger* at http://clarionledger.com/jmitchell/2013/03/17. See also http://www.nytimes.com/2013/03/19/us/olen-burrage-dies-at-82-linked-to-killings-in-1964.html?r=0.

16. Villano, *Brick Agent*, 89–93. The techniques used by Villano's Mafia contact to extract information from a Mississippi source replicate almost exactly those described in the Neshoba case, with the important exception that the source was being grilled about the shooter of Medgar Evers.

17. Telephone interview with Lin DeVecchio, November 23, 2010. As in the film *Mississippi Burning*, Scarpa was allegedly briefed by agents before driving to an electronics store run by "a Klansman named Byrd"; see Harmon, *Mafia Son*, 61–63. In her testimony, Schiro may have confused the details of two different civil rights cases: the Neshoba case from 1964 and the Klan killing in 1966 of Vernon Dahmer. Lawrence Byrd was one of the men accused in the death of Dahmer. Schiro claimed that Scarpa kidnapped Byrd, took him to a remote shack where he beat him and probably threatened him with castration, until the thoroughly intimidated Byrd provided details of the murders and the location of the bodies on the farm of Olen Burrage. Dahmer had been burned to death and was buried in a cemetery, not on Burrage's farm. In 2007, Schiro's testimony was discredited because of inconsistencies in her account, and FBI Agent DeVechhio was acquitted; see Mitchell, http://clarionledger.com/jmitchell/2013/03/17, August 31, 2010. Lawrence Byrd, who ran an electronics store in Laurel, was identified as an informer in the Dahmer case. The intelligence Mitchell gathered is detailed in Naftali, *Lyndon B. Johnson*, 8:455n31. Schiro's memory, if not her veracity, was called into question and therefore her testimony was considered not relevant to the Neshoba case. Despite that, the possibility of a Mafia connection in the Neshoba case had gained wide currency because of the movie. Jerry Mitchell, an acknowledged expert on civil rights cold cases, also questioned Schiro's memory, but not her linking of Scarpa to bureau investigations into Klan activities, just not the Neshoba case. Agent DeVecchio was Scarpa's second bureau handler, and the two likely spoke frequently about cases of mutual interest. Although Scarpa told DeVecchio that he had participated in the bureau's work in Mississippi on past civil rights cases, neither man presumably pursued the subject nor Scarpa's role. So while DeVecchio did not believe Schiro's testimony, he did confirm that Scarpa had gone to Mississippi to assist the bureau in its struggle against the Klan. In a letter to the author from Gregory Scarpa's son, Greg Jr., currently incarcerated in the maximum security prison in Florence, CO, the younger Scarpa wrote, "I do remember clearly of what went down with the 3 civil rights workers—I guess because of the action (so to speak) on how he learned exactly where the workers were buried—from what I understand it if wasn't for him they never would've been found. . . . The details of my father finding the location of the 3 c.r. bodies is well known. . . . My father was proud of finding the bodies. He told me everything in detail." November 21, 2006, ms., letter in author's possession.

18. Ball, *Murder in Mississippi*, 74–6.

19. Branch, *Pillar of Fire*, 529.

20. Ball, *Murder in Mississippi*, 76.

21. *Clarion-Ledger*, December 3, 2007; February 15, 2010. See also Naftali, *Lyndon B. Johnson*, 8:455n31, where Mitchell is cited as naming Klansman Pete Jordan as the original informant who talked to Maynard King. Florence Mars also believed Maynard King was "Mr. X." This is not, however, the same so-called Mr. X who worked for the MSSC.

22. Durkheim's work is cited in Coser, *Maurice Halwachs on Collective Memory*, 24–5.

23. Coser, *Maurice Halwachs on Collective Memory*, 24–5.

24. http://www.southernliving.com/travel/south-central/neshoba-county-fair-mississippi.

25. Morris, *My Mississippi*, 53.

26. Mars, *Witness in Philadelphia*, 31.

27. Morris, *My Mississippi*, 53.

28. Quoted in Mars, *Witness in Philadelphia*, 108–9; also Steven H. Stubbs, *Mississippi's Giant Houseparty: The History of the Neshoba County Fair; 115 Years (and Counting) of Politicking, Pacing, Partaking, and Partying* (Philadelphia, MS: Dancing Rabbit, 2005). Stubbs's work, a large volume of 873 pages, represents in photos and prose a kind of "official" history of the fair. There are no black people pictured in any of the many photographs.

29. Drake Hokanson and Carol Kratz, *Purebred and Homegrown: America's County Fairs* (Madison, WI: Terrace, 2008), 14, 15. In this popular study of American fairs, the authors astonishingly omitted the Neshoba County Fair, convinced there were only a "small number of fairs in the Deep South." Southern states and counties, the writers believed, were not eager to absorb the Northeastern model of the fair as it emerged in the nineteenth century to display a region's harvest. Relying on a very different cultural type, the authors observed that "Just as it's hard to find a crayfish festival in Minnesota . . . it's harder to find a county fair in Mississippi."

30. Interviews with Florence Mars, July 10, 2005; Fent DeWeese, July 5, 2005; Dick Molpus, March 3, 2010.

31. Fent DeWeese, interview, July 5, 2005.

32. *Jackson Free Press*, August 5, 2010.

33. *Jackson Free Press*, August 5, 2010.

34. Ferdinand Tönnies, *Community and Civil Society*, trans. Jose Harris and Margaret Hollis (Cambridge: Cambridge University Press, 2001).

35. Toby Glen Bates, *The Reagan Rhetoric: History and Memory in 1980s America* (DeKalb: Northern Illinois University Press, 2011), 41. The photo of Reagan and his wife Nancy at the fair is ubiquitous in the state. The picture shows a broadly smiling candidate in a rocking chair on a fair platform, with Nancy about to take

her place on his lap. A large blown-up version of the picture has hung on the wall behind the editor's desk at *The Neshoba Democrat* since Stanley Dearman retired. It is also half the book jacket of Joseph Crespino's book *In Search of Another Country*.

36. Bates, *Reagan Rhetoric*, 29–30.

CHAPTER 10

1. Edward T. Linenthal, "Epilogue: Reflections," in *Slavery and Public History: The Tough Stuff of American Memory*, ed. James Oliver Horton and Lois E. Horton, 213–24 (Chapel Hill: University of North Carolina Press, 2006), 216.

2. Mars, *Witness in Philadelphia*, 113.

3. *Mississippi Statistical Summary of Population, 1800–1980*, Economic Research Department, Mississippi Power and Light Company, Jackson, MS, February 1983.

4. Mars, *Witness in Philadelphia*, 108.

5. Cagin and Dray, *We Are Not Afraid*, 181.

6. Mars, *Witness in Philadelphia*, 210.

7. Daniel Jonah Goldhagen, *Hitler's Willing Executioners: Ordinary Germans and the Holocaust* (New York: Random House, 1996).

8. John Paul Lederach, *Building Peace: Sustainable Reconciliation in Divided Societies* (Washington, DC: United States Institute of Peace, 1997), 18. There is an extensive body of literature on the political and/or moral responsibility of individuals in divided societies. Two of the most studied deal with Nazi Germany and apartheid South Africa. See, for example, François Du Bois and Antje Du Bois-Pedain, eds., *Justice and Reconciliation in Post-Apartheid South Africa* (Cambridge: Cambridge University Press, 2008), particularly the chapter by Antje Du Bois-Pedain, "Communicating Criminal and Political Responsibility in the TRC Process," 62–89. A somewhat different perspective on the responsibility of "ordinary people" is described by Geoff Eley, "Ordinary Germans, Nazism, and Judeocide," in *The "Goldhagen Effect": History, Memory, Nazism—Facing the German Past*, ed. Geoff Eley (Ann Arbor: University of Michigan Press, 2003), 1–32. Yet another perspective on individual culpability comes from the white liberal editor and publisher in Pascagoula of *The Chronicle*, Ira Harkey. Threatened and assailed for his antisegregation columns in the 1960s, Harkey asserted, "The gathering of mobs . . . is not spontaneous. It is provoked and it happens only when the mobs know that their presence will not be punished . . . [M]obs are artfully called up by demagogues." Ultimate responsibility for racial violence in Mississippi, Harkey said, belongs to abusive "political monsters" who have played the race card in the state for so long; Ira Harkey, *The Smell of Burning Crosses: A White Integrationist Editor in Mississippi* (Jacksonville, IL: Harris-Wolfe, 1967), 193, 189.

9. Du Bois and Du Bois-Pedain, *Justice and Reconciliation in Post-Apartheid South Africa*, 89.

10. Goldhagen, *Hitler's Willing Executioners*, 463–6.

11. Goldhagen, *Hitler's Willing Executioners*, 55.

12. Goldhagen, *Hitler's Willing Executioners*, 398–9.

13. Goldhagen, *Hitler's Willing Executioners*, 107.

14. Susannah Heschel, *The Aryan Jesus: Christian Theologians and the Bible in Nazi Germany* (Princeton, NJ: Princeton University Press, 2008).

15. Atina Grossmann, "The Goldhagen Effect: Memory, Repetition, and Responsibility in the New Germany," in *The "Goldhagen Effect": History, Memory, Nazism—Facing the German Past*, ed. Geoff Eley (Ann Arbor: University of Michigan Press, 2003), 89–129.

16. Grossmann, *"Goldhagen Effect."*

17. See article by David Nevin, *Life*, December 18, 1964.

18. Interview with Florence Mars, July 5, 2005.

19. Ball, *Murder in Mississippi*, 87.

20. Memo of Joe T. Patterson, attorney general, November 9, 1964, ms., MDAH.

21. Ball, *Murder in Mississippi*, 62; Mars, *Witness in Philadelphia*, 95; Cagin and Dray, *We Are Not Afraid*, 345–7.

22. Mars, *Witness in Philadelphia*, 136. The charges against the aging Burkes were dropped, Willis was acquitted at trial, and a jury could not reach a verdict on Barnett. Ball, *Murder in Mississippi*, 94.

23. Ball 109; Mars, interview, July 5, 2005.

24. Ball, *Murder in Mississippi*, 124–5.

25. 1967 Trial Records; also in *Killen Trial Records*; and Ball, *Murder in Mississippi*, 134–5. Cox also referred to a group of black witnesses on another case as "a bunch of chimpanzees." Cagin and Dray, *We Are Not Afraid*, 309.

26. Ball, *Justice in Mississippi*, 135. The sealed interview at MDAH was once inadvertently given to me, then quickly retrieved as soon as the error was discovered.

27. *Times-Picayune*, October 21, 1967

28. Cagin and Dray, *We Are Not Afraid*, 391.

29. Interview with Rev. Clay Lee, May 28, 2002.

30. Mars, *Witness in Philadelphia*, 180.

CHAPTER 11

1. Quoted in Jere Nash and Andy Taggart, *Mississippi Politics: The Struggle for Power, 1976–2008* (Jackson: University Press of Mississippi, 2009), 14–15.

2. Nash and Taggart, *Mississippi Politics*, 20.

3. See Bolton, *Hardest Deal of All*.

4. Interview with Ross Jones, July 9, 2005.

5. Bolton, *Hardest Deal of All*, 45.

6. David W. Blight, "If You Can't Tell It Like It Was, It Can Never Be as It Ought to Be," in *Slavery and Public History: The Tough Stuff of American Memory*, ed. James Oliver Horton and Lois E. Horton, 19–33 (Chapel Hill: University of North Carolina Press, 2006), 24.

7. Bolton, *Hardest Deal of All*, xii.

8. Interviews with Bernard Johnson, October 6, 2009; LeRoy Clemons, October 7, 2009; James Young, October 7, 2009; Obbie Riley, March 5, 2012.

9. James Young, interview Oct. 7, 2009.

10. Interview with unnamed office staff member, *Neshoba Democrat* office, March 5, 2012.

11. Interview with Fent DeWeese, July 5, 2005.

12. *Neshoba Democrat*, September 12, 1968.

13. Interview with Patsy McWilliams, March 5, 2012.

14. McWilliams, interview March 5, 2012.

15. Interview with Rev. Henry Clay, June 5, 2007.

16. *Methodist Daily Christian Advocate*, May 2, 1956.

17. *Methodist Daily Christian Advocate*, May 3, 1956.

18. Letter of Floyd H. Coffman to Bishop Matthew W. Clair, Jr., February 14, 1965, ms., Methodist Archives, Madison, NJ.

19. *Journal of the 1966 Adjourned Session of the 1964 General Conference of the Methodist Church*, III (Nashville, TN: The Methodist Publishing House, 1966).

20. *Journal of the 1966 Adjourned Session of the 1964 General Conference*, III.

21. Methodist Church, Commission on Public Relations and Methodist Information, June 24–27, 1964, copy in archives, Drew University, Madison, NJ.

22. See Findlay, *Church People in the Struggle*. See also Chris Myers Asch, *The Senator and the Sharecropper: The Freedom Struggles of James O. Eastland and Fannie Lou Hamer* (Chapel Hill: University of North Carolina Press, 2011), which effectively argues that white racists were able to link segregation with anticommunism.

23. Branch, "Born of Conviction," 212.

24. Branch, "Born of Conviction," 232, passim.

25. Branch, "Born of Conviction," 293.

26. Branch, "Born of Conviction," 193–6.

27. Interview with Rev. Henry Clay, June 9, 2007.

28. Clay, interview, June 9, 2007.

29. Interview with Rev. W. B. Crump, Methodist Annual Conference, Jackson, June 9, 2007.

30. See Minutes of the two white Mississippi conferences and the two black Mississippi conferences to 1970. Membership declined after 1970, with white Methodists going to independent churches and black members leaving for Baptist and Pentecostal churches. Membership figures between 1965 and 1975 show the trend. In 1965, there were 186,772 white Methodists and 36,349 black; in 1970 the figures were 181,408 white and 32,489 black. In 1975, when the conferences were

merged and figures were no longer reported separately, the combined total was 205,365, or an approximate total decline of 8,000 members from 1970. Records of black conferences in Millsaps College archives. White conference records in Methodist archives, Drew University, Madison, NJ.

31. Interview with Methodist bishop Clay Lee, October 18, 2006. Bishop Lee remembered of his hospital visit with Satterfield that "his mind was not functioning right . . . He was very upset . . . Three weeks later he shot himself." Rev. Henry Clay, a black Methodist who in 1980 was appointed district superintendent for the area that included Galloway Church, said of Satterfield, "He was sharp as a whip." Before Satterfield died, Clay heard that Satterfield wanted to talk to him. Said the Rev. Clay, "The story is that before he died, he changed"; Clay, interview, June 9, 2007.

32. Interview with Arecia Steele, July 10, 2005.

CHAPTER 12

1. *Mississippi Statistical Summary of Population, 1800–1980,* Economic Research Department, Mississippi Power and Light Company, Jackson, MS, February 1983.

2. Nash and Taggart, *Mississippi Politics,* 144–45

3. Nash and Taggart, *Mississippi Politics,* 160–61.

4. *Jackson Free Press,* September 10, 2008.

5. Interview with Dick Molpus, March 3, 2011.

6. Comments from an interview with Lloyd Gray, March 9, 2011. Gray, the son of Rev. Duncan Gray, who had boldly challenged the mob at the Oxford riots, had been communications adviser to Molpus in 1989.

7. Molpus, interview March 3, 2011.

8. Molpus speech, copy in author's possession. See also Mark Lawrence McPhail, "The Price of an Apology: Honesty and Honor in Richard Molpus' Rhetoric of Reconciliation," paper presented at the November 2008 National Communication Association Convention, San Diego.

9. Gray, interview March 9, 2011.

10. Gray, interview March 9, 2011.

11. Interview with Florence Mars, July 8, 2005.

12. Molpus, interview, March 3, 2011.

13. Gray, interview March 9, 2011.

14. Interview with Constance Slaughter-Harvey, March 2, 2011. Like Florence Mars, she too believed the state was not ready for his apology in 1989.

15. Interview with Molpus staff member Bob Lyle, March 2, 2011.

16. *Clarion-Ledger,* Jackson, August 4, 1995.

17. *Clarion-Ledger,* August 4, 1995.

18. *Clarion-Ledger,* August 4, 1995.

19. *Clarion-Ledger,* August 4, 1995.

20. *Clarion-Ledger*, August 4, 1995.

21. *The Carthaginian*, Carthage, August 17, 1995.

22. *Clarion-Ledger*, August 4, 1995.

23. *Clarion-Ledger*, August 4, 1995.

24. *Clarion-Ledger*, August 4, 1995.

25. Cited in Stubbs, *Mississippi's Giant Houseparty*, 563–5.

26. Cited in Nash and Taggart, *Mississippi Politics*, 252–3.

27. Bob Lyle, interview March 2, 2011.

28. Quoted in Willie Morris, *The Courting of Marcus Dupree* (Jackson: University Press of Mississippi, 1992), 34.

29. Morris, *Courting of Marcus Dupree*, 35.

30. Morris, *Courting of Marcus Dupree*, 304.

31. Mars, interview July 5, 2005.

32. Morris, *Courting of Marcus Dupree*, 33.

33. Morris, *Courting of Marcus Dupree*, 304.

34. http://espn.go.com/30for30/film?page=the-best-that-never-was.

35. The belief in "generational change" continued to be expressed by many, including Fent DeWeese, LeRoy Clemons, and Dick Molpus, as well as by an older group that included Florence Mars and Clint Collier.

36. Interview with Jerry Mitchell, July 12, 2005.

37. Morris, *Courting of Marcus Dupree*, 64.

38. Morris, *Courting of Marcus Dupree*, 64, 65.

39. Morris, *Courting of Marcus Dupree*, 18.

40. Interview with Stanley Dearman, May 14, 2002; *Neshoba Democrat*, 1945 and passim.

41. Philip Martin, *Chief* (Brandon, MS: Quail Ridge, 2009), 15.

42. Deanne Stephens Nuwer and Greg O'Brien, "Mississippi's Oldest Pastime," in *Resorting to Casinos: The Mississippi Gambling Industry*, ed. Denise von Hermann, 11–25 (Jackson: University Press of Mississippi, 2006), 11, passim; *Resorting to Casinos* is a collection of essays by academics at educational institutions in Mississippi and adjacent states.

43. Nuwer and O'Brien, "Mississippi's Oldest Pastime," 11.

44. Cited in Denise von Hermannn, "Were Casinos a Solution for State Economic Growth?" in *Resorting to Casinos*, ed. Denise von Hermann, 67–80, at 79.

45. Martin, *Chief*, 193.

46. Molpus, interview, March 10, 2011.

47. Interview with Rev. Ed Howard, First Baptist Church, Philadelphia, July 5, 2005.

48. Dearman, interview May 14, 2002.

49. Jerry Mitchell, Jackson *Clarion-Ledger*, December 1998, quoted in Ball, *Justice in Mississippi*, 59. Since Bowers stipulated that his interview was not to be unsealed until after his death, he had not given it to curry favor with a judge to get his sentence reduced.

50. Rita Schwerner Bender, quoted in Ball, *Justice in Mississippi*, 60.

51. Ball, *Justice in Mississippi*, 62, 63.

52. Interview with Jennifer Riley Hathorn and Freddie Grady, July 6, 2002.

53. Interview with Freddie Grady, May 28, 2002.

54. Barnett's confession appears in the Killen trial records; Price's statement, given to the state investigators, is cited in Ball, *Justice in Mississippi*, 65–70.

55. Ball, *Justice in Mississippi*, 67.

56. *Clarion-Ledger*, July 19, 2001.

57. *Clarion-Ledger*, July 19, 2001.

58. Molpus, interview, November 24, 2009.

59. E-mail from Jerry Mitchell to the author, August 2010.

60. Ball, *Justice in Mississippi*, 73.

61. Interviews with Florence Mars, July 5, 2002; Arecia Steele and Edna Hunt, July 5, 2002.

CHAPTER 13

1. Interview with Dick Molpus, May 22, 2014.

2. Molpus, interview, March 3, 2011; Ball, *Justice in Mississippi*, 78; interview with Constance Slaughter-Harvey, March 3, 2011.

3. Interview with Susan Glisson, June 2, 2014.

4. Glisson, interview, June 2, 2014; Glisson said, "We only go where we are invited."

5. Glisson, interview June 2, 2014.

6. Glisson, interview, June 2, 2014.

7. Interview with LeRoy Clemons, October 9, 2009; Molpus, interview, March 3, 2011.

8. Glisson, interview, June 2, 2014; interview with former Governor William Winter, May 27, 2014.

9. Winter, interview, May 27, 2014.

10. Glisson, interview, June 2, 2014.

11. Glisson, interview, June 2, 2014. Former Governor Winter estimates that there could be as many as twenty, depending on how one identifies a community group; Winter, interview, May 27, 2014.

12. Cited in Ball, *Justice in Mississippi*, 83, 84.

13. *Jackson Free Press*, June 21, 2004.

14. Copy of speech in author's possession; also in *Jackson Free Press*, June 21, 2004.

15. Interview with Fent DeWeese, July 5, 2005.

16. Interview with Stanley Dearman, May 14, 2002.

17. Ball, *Justice in Mississippi*, 95.

18. Cagin and Dray, *We Are Not Afraid*, 450; Ball, *Justice in Mississippi*, 102.

19. Hood's comment was about the 1967 trial records. Cited in Ball, *Justice in Mississippi*, 97, based on a taped interview between Hood and Ball.

20. Ball, *Justice in Mississippi*, 103.

21. Ball, *Justice in Mississippi*, 104.

22. *Killen Trial Record*, passim.

23. *Killen Trial Record*, 2:249.

CHAPTER 14

1. Blight, "If You Don't Tell It Like It Was," 23.

2. Interview with Fent DeWeese, July 5, 2005.

3. *Killen Trial Record*, 1:30.

4. *Killen Trial Record*, 1:30, passim.

5. *Killen Trial Record*, 1:218.

6. *Killen Trial Record*, 4:996.

7. *Killen Trial Record*, 4:873.

8. Dickoff was allowed to interview Killen at his home, where he spoke openly to the camera about his segregationist views and his confidence in his acquittal.

9. *Killen Trial Record*, 2:491.

10. *Killen Trial Record*, 4:975.

11. *Killen Trial Record*, 3:626.

12. *Killen Trial Record*, 3:627.

13. *Killen Trial Record*, 3:692.

14. *Killen Trial Record*, 3:694–709.

15. *Killen Trial Record*, 3:710–717.

16. *Killen Trial Record*, 3:726.

17. *Killen Trial Record*, 3:728.

18. *Killen Trial Record*, 3:734.

19. *Killen Trial Record*, 3:744.

20. *Killen Trial Record*, 3:746.

21. *Killen Trial Record*, 3:747.

22. *Killen Trial Record*, 3:752–74, 4:792–811.

23. *Killen Trial Record*, 4:790.

24. *Killen Trial Record*, 3:789.

25. *Killen Trial Record*, 4:834.

26. *Killen Trial Record*, 4:908.

27. *Killen Trial Record*, 4:941.

28. *Killen Trial Record*, 4:961.

29. *Killen Trial Record*, 4:968.

30. *Killen Trial Record*, 4:974.

31. *Killen Trial Record*, 4:980.

32. *Killen Trial Record*, 4:981.

33. See Ball, *Justice in Mississippi*, 173–5; DeWeese, interview, July 5, 2005.

34. *Killen Trial Record*, 4:1000.

35. Ball, *Justice in Mississippi*, 177.

36. Ball, *Justice in Mississippi*, 177.

37. *Neshoba Democrat*, September 7, 2005.

38. Duncan's concerns actually related to the trial, not the conviction.

39. DeWeese, interview, July 5, 2005. DeWeese asked rhetorically, "Don't you know merchants?"

40. Interview with Dick Molpus, March 10, 2010.

41. Ball, *Justice in Mississippi*, 180.

42. Interview with Ross Jones, July 5, 2005.

43. Interview with Jewel McDonald, July 5, 2005.

44. Ball, *Justice in Mississippi*, 103, 189, 195.

45. Ball, *Justice in Mississippi*, 203.

46. Interview with LeRoy Clemons, October 9, 2009.

47. Ball, *Justice in Mississippi*, 179.

48. Quoted in Morris, *My Mississippi*, 102.

49. Morris, *Courting of Marcus Dupree*, 18.

50. Interview with William Winter, May 27, 2014.

51. Speech of James Young, fiftieth annual commemoration service, Mt. Zion Church, June 15, 2014.

EPILOGUE

1. Morris, *My Mississippi*, 103.

2. Morris, *My Mississippi*. Quoted in introduction.

3. Interview with Stanley Dearman, May 14, 2002. Dearman repeated the comment at the fiftieth annual commemoration service, June 15, 2014.

4. See Orlando Patterson, *Slavery and Social Death: A Comparative Study* (Cambridge, MA: Harvard University Press, 1982).

5. Irons, *Reconstituting Whiteness*, 198.

6. Interviews with Susan Glisson, June 2, 2014; Dick Molpus, June 20, 2014.

7. Randall Kennedy, *The Persistence of the Color Line: Racial Politics and the Obama Presidency* (New York: Pantheon, 2011), 248.

8. Speeches of Rita Schwerner Bender and James Young at the fiftieth annual commemoration service, June 15, 2014. Excerpts from the many speeches given that day can be found in the *Clarion Ledger* for June 16, and *The Neshoba Democrat* for June 18.

9. Frank R. Parker, *Black Votes Count: Political Empowerment in Mississippi after 1965* (Chapel Hill: University of North Carolina Press, 1990), 195.

10. Parker, *Black Votes Count*, 202.

11. Interview with LeRoy Clemons, October 31, 2013.

12. Robert McDuff, "The Voting Rights Act and Mississippi: 1965–2006," *Southern California Review of Law and Social Justice*, 17(2), 475–99, at 476.

13. Interview with LeRoy Clemons, October 11, 2013.

14. Glisson, interview, June 2, 2014.

Bibliography

Alexander, Grove. *A History of the Methodist Church, South, in the United States.* New York: Christian Literature, 1894.

Arsenault, Raymond. *Freedom Riders: 1961 and the Struggle for Racial Justice.* New York: Oxford University Press, 2006.

Ball, Howard. *Murder in Mississippi: United States vs. Price and the Struggle for Civil Rights.* Lawrence: University Press of Kansas, 2004.

———. *Justice in Mississippi: The Murder Trial of Edgar Ray Killen.* Lawrence: University Press of Kansas, 2006.

Bates, Toby Glenn. *The Reagan Rhetoric: History and Memory in 1980s America.* DeKalb: Northern Illinois University Press, 2011.

Blight, David W. "If You Can't Tell It Like It Was, It Can Never Be as It Ought to Be." In *Slavery and Public History: The Tough Stuff of American Memory*, edited by James Oliver Horton and Lois E. Horton, 19–33. Chapel Hill: University of North Carolina Press, 2006.

Branch, Ellis Ray. "'Born of Conviction': Racial Conflict and Change in Mississippi Methodism." PhD diss., Mississippi State University, 1984.

Branch, Taylor. *Pillar of Fire: America in the King Years, 1963–65.* New York: Simon and Schuster, 1998.

Brooks, Roy L. *Atonement and Forgiveness: A New Model for Black Reconciliation.* Berkeley: University of California Press, 2004.

———, ed., *When Sorry Isn't Enough.* New York: New York University Press, 1999.

Bolton, Charles C. *The Hardest Deal of All: The Battle over School Integration in Mississippi, 1870–1980.* Jackson: University Press of Mississippi, 2005.

Boraine, Alex. *A Country Unmasked.* Oxford: Oxford University Press, 2000.

Brown-Nagin, Tomiko. *The Courage to Dissent.* New York: Oxford University Press, 2011.

Brundage, W. Fitzhugh. *The Southern Past: A Clash of Race and Memory.* Cambridge, MA: Harvard University Press, 2009.

Brundage, W. Fitzhugh, ed. *Where These Memories Grow: History, Memory, and Southern Identity*. Chapel Hill: University of North Carolina Press, 2000.

Bucke, Emory Stevens, ed. *The History of American Methodism*. 3 volumes. New York: Abingdon, 1964.

Bullock, Henry Allen. *A History of Negro Education in the South*. New York: Praeger, 1970.

Cagin, Seth, and Philip Dray. *We Are Not Afraid: The Story of Goodman, Schwerner, and Chaney, and the Civil Rights Campaign for Mississippi*. New York: Nation, 2006.

Chappell, David L. *Prophetic Religion and the Death of Jim Crow*. Chapel Hill: University of North Carolina Press, 2004.

Cobb, James C. *The Most Southern Place on Earth: The Mississippi Delta and the Roots of Regional Identity*. New York: Oxford University Press, 1992.

———. *The Brown Decision: Jim Crow and Southern Identity*. Athens: University of Georgia Press, 2005.

Coser, Lewis A. *Maurice Halbwachs on Collective Memory*. Chicago: University of Chicago Press, 1992.

Crespino, Joseph. *In Search of Another Country: Mississippi and the Conservative Counterrevolution*. Princeton, NJ: Princeton University Press, 2007.

Culver, Dwight W. *Negro Segregation in the Methodist Church*. New Haven, CT: Yale University Press, 1953.

Cunningham, W. J. *Agony at Galloway*. Jackson: University Press of Mississippi, 1980.

Dannen, Fredric. "The G-Man and the Hit Man," *New Yorker*, December 16, 1966.

Davis, David R., ed. *The Press and Race: Mississippi Journalists Confront the Movement*. Jackson: University Press of Mississippi, 2001.

Davis, Morris L. *The Methodist Unification: Christianity and the Politics of Race in the Jim Crow Era*. New York: New York University Press, 2008.

DeVecchio, Lin, and Curtis Brandt. *We're Going to Win This Thing: The Shocking Frame-up of a Mafia Crime Buster*. New York: Berkley, 2011.

Dickoff, Micki. *Neshoba: The Price of Freedom*. First Run Features, 2010 [documentary film].

Dittmer, John. *Local People: The Struggle for Civil Rights in Mississippi*. Champaign: University of Illinois Press, 1995.

Dixon, William Edge. "Ministerial Leadership in the Central Jurisdiction of the Methodist Church." PhD diss., Boston University, 1955.

Du Bois, François, and Antje Du Bois-Pedain, eds. *Justice and Reconciliation in Post-Apartheid South Africa*. Cambridge: Cambridge University Press, 2008.

DuBois, W. E. B. *Black Reconstruction in America, 1860–1880*. New York: Free Press, ca. 1935.

Eagles, Charles W. *The Price of Defiance: James Meredith and the Integration of Ole Miss*. Chapel Hill: University of North Carolina Press, 2009.

Edelstein, Julian. *Trust and Lies: Stories from the Truth and Reconciliation Commission in South Africa*. New York: New Press, 2001.

Eley, Geoff, ed. *The Goldhagen Effect: History, Memory, Nazism—Facing the German Past*. Ann Arbor: University of Michigan Press, 2003.

Elkins, Stanley. *Slavery: A Problem in American Institutional and Intellectual Life*. Chicago: University of Chicago Press, 1969.

Erenrich, Susie, ed. *Freedom is a Constant Struggle: An Anthology of the Mississippi Civil Rights Movement*. Montgomery, AL: Black Belt, 1990.

Evans, Curtis J. *The Burden of Black Religion*. New York: Oxford University Press, 2008.

Felton, Ralph A. *The Ministry of the Central Jurisdiction of the Methodist Church*. New York: Division of National Missions, Methodist Board of Missions, n.d. [ca. 1953].

Findlay, James F., Jr. *Church People in the Struggle: The National Council of Churches and the Black Freedom Movement, 1950–1970*. New York: Oxford University Press, 1991.

Foner, Eric. *Reconstruction: America's Unfinished Revolution*. New York: Harper Collins, 1988.

Fredrickson, George. *White Supremacy: A Comparative Study of American and South African History*. New York: Oxford University Press, 1981.

Fulop, Timothy E., and Albert J. Raboteau, eds. *African-American Religion: Interpretive Essays in History and Culture*. New York: Routledge, 1997.

George, Carol V. R. *Segregated Sabbaths: Richard Allen and the Rise of Independent Black Churches, 1760–1840*. New York: Oxford University Press, 1973.

Glaude, Eddie S., Jr. *Exodus! Religion, Race, and Nation in Early Nineteenth-Century Black America*. Chicago: University of Chicago Press, 2000.

Goldfield, David, et al. *The American Journey: A History of the United States*. Upper Saddle River: Prentice-Hall, 1988.

Goldhagen, Daniel Jonah. *Hitler's Willing Executioners: Ordinary Germans and the Holocaust*. New York: Random House, 1996.

Graham, John H. *Mississippi Circuit Riders, 1865–1965*. Nashville, TN: Parthenon, 1967.

Halbwachs, Maurice. *Our Collective Memory*. Chicago: University of Chicago Press, 1992.

Harkley, Ira. *The Smell of Burning Crosses: A White Integrationist Editor in Mississippi*. Philadelphia: Xlibris, 1967.

Harmon, Sandra. *Mafia Son: The Scarpa Mob Family, the FBI, and a Story of Betrayal*. New York: St. Martin's, 2009.

Harvey, Paul. *Freedom's Coming: Religious Culture and the Shaping of the South from the Civil War to the Civil Rights Era*. Chapel Hill: University of North Carolina Press, 2005.

Hatch, Nathan O., and John H. Wigger, eds. *Methodism and the Shaping of American Culture*. Nashville: Kingswood, 2001.

Heschel, Susannah. *The Aryan Jesus: Christian Theologians and the Bible in Nazi Germany*. Princeton, NJ: Princeton University Press, 2008.

Hickman, Nollie W. *Mississippi Harvest: Lumbering in the Longleaf Pine Belt, 1840–1915.* Jackson: University Press of Mississippi, 1962.

Highsaw, Robert, and Charles Fortenberry. *The Government and Administration of Mississippi.* New York: Thomas Y. Crowell, 1954.

Hillegas, Jan. "Preliminary List of Mississippi Lynchings by County," manuscript, 1994. Hillegas COFO [Council of Federated Organizations] Collection, Jackson, Mississippi.

Hockanson, Drake, and Carol Kratz. *Purebred and Homegrown: America's County Fairs.* Madison, WI: Terrace, 2008.

Holder, Ray. *The Mississippi Methodists, 1799–1983: A Moral People "Born of Conviction."* Jackson, MS: Maverick Prints, 1984.

Horton, James Oliver, and Lois E. Horton, eds. *Slavery and Public History: The Tough Stuff of American History.* Chapel Hill: University of North Carolina Press, 2006.

Huie, William Bradford. *Three Lives for Mississippi.* Jackson: University Press of Mississippi, 1965.

Irons, Jenny. *Reconstituting Whiteness.* Nashville, TN: Vanderbilt University Press, 2011.

James, Wilmot, and Linda Van De Vijver, eds. *After the TRC: Reflections on Reconciliation in South Africa.* Athens: Ohio University Press, 2001.

Johnson, Inez Calloway. "The History of Longdale School." Printed for thirty-fifth reunion celebration in 2005.

Kammen, Michael. *Mystic Chords of Memory: The Transformation of Tradition in American Culture.* New York: Vintage, 1991.

Kennedy, Randall. *The Persistence of the Color Line: Racial Politics and the Obama Presidency.* New York: Pantheon, 2011.

King, Edwin. "Memoirs," manuscript, Tougaloo College archives, Jackson, MS, 1963.

Kirk, W. Astor. *Desegregation of the Methodist Church Polity: Reform Movements that Ended Racial Segregation.* Pittsburgh: RoseDog, 2005.

Klarman, Michael J. *From Jim Crow to Civil Rights.* New York: Oxford University Press, 2004.

Lawrence, Roy. "A Brief History of Black Methodists in Mississippi," in *Mississippi United Methodist Advocate,* November 17, 1974.

Lederach, John Paul. *Building Peace: Sustainable Reconciliation in Divided Societies.* Washington, DC: United States Institute of Peace, 1997.

———. *The Little Book of Conflict Transformation.* Intercourse, PA: Good Books, 2003.

———. *The Moral Imagination: The Art and Soul of Building Peace.* New York: Oxford University Press, 2005.

Leiffer, Murray H. "The Central Jurisdiction." In *History of American Methodism,* vol. 3, edited by Emory Stevens Bucke, 485–95. New York: Abingdon, 1964.

Logan, Rayford W. *The Negro in American Life and Thought: The Nadir, 1877–1901.* New York: Basic Books; republished as *The Betrayal of the Negro: From Rutherford B. Hayes to Woodrow Wilson.* New York: Collier, 1965.

Long, Charles H. "Perspectives for a Study of African-American Religion in the United States." In *African-American Religion: Interpretive Essays in History and Culture*, edited by Timothy E. Fulop and Albert J. Raboteau, 21–36. New York: Routledge, 1997.

Marable, Manning. *The Great Wells of Democracy*. New York: Basic Books, 2002.

Margo, Robert A. *Race and Schooling in the South, 1880–1950: An Economic History*. Chicago: University of Chicago Press, 1990.

Mars, Florence. *Witness in Philadelphia*. Baton Rouge: Louisiana State University Press, 1977.

Marsh, Charles. *The Beloved Community: How Faith Shapes Social Justice, from the Civil Rights Movement to Today*. New York: Basic Books, 2005.

Marsh, Charles, and John Perkins. *Welcoming Justice: God's Movement toward Beloved Community*. Downers Grove, IL: InterVarsity Press, 2009.

Martin, Philip. *Chief*. Brandon, MS: Quail Ridge, 2009.

McClain, William B., *Black People in the Methodist Church: Whither Thou Goest?* Cambridge, MA: Schenkman, 1984.

———. *Come Sunday: The Liturgy of Zion*. Nashville, TN: Abingdon, 1990.

McLaren, Brian, Elisa Pedilla, and Ashley Bunting Seeber, eds. *The Justice Project*. Grand Rapids, MI: Baker, 2009.

McLaughlin, William C. *Revivals, Awakenings, and Reform*. Chicago: University of Chicago Press, 1978.

McLemore, Richard Aubrey. *A History of Mississippi*. 2 volumes. Jackson: University and College Press of Mississippi, 1973.

McMillen, Neil R. *Dark Journey: Black Mississippians in the Age of Jim Crow*. Urbana: University of Illinois Press, 1990.

McWhorter, Diane. "The Lives They Lived: 60's: Byron de la Beckwith, b. 1921 Cecil Ray Price, b. 1938; Mississippi Gothic." *New York Times*, December 30, 2001.

Methodist Episcopal Church. Central Jurisdiction, *Southwestern Christian Advocate*, 1908.

———. *Christian Advocate*, 1945, 1946, 1948.

———. *Journal of the General Conference*, 1904, 1908.

———. Records of Committee on Interjurisdictional Relations, manuscripts, Drew University Archives.

Middleton, Mabel P. "The Development of Black Methodist Churches in Mississippi." n.p.: n.d. [pamphlet].

Mississippi Association of Methodist Ministers and Laymen (MAMML). *Bulletin*, Archives MDAH, Jackson, and Millsaps College.

Mississippi Methodist Conference, Central Jurisdiction. *Annual Conference Records*, 1878–1920.

Mississippi State Sovereignty Commission Reports (MSSC), 1958–1977.

Morris, Willie. *The Courting of Marcus Depree*. Jackson: University Press of Mississippi, 1982.

Morris, Willie. *My Mississippi*. Jackson: University Press of Mississippi, 2000.

Morrison, Toni. *Home*. New York: Alfred A. Knopf, 2012.

Morrow, Ralph E. *Northern Methodism and Reconstruction*. East Lansing: Michigan State University Press, 1956.

Myrdal, Gunnar. *An American Dilemma: The Negro Problem and Modern Democracy*. New York: Harper and Sons, 1944.

Naftali, Timothy, ed. *Lyndon B. Johnson: The Presidential Recordings* [Mississippi Burning and the Passage of the Civil Rights Act], vol. 7, *June 1, 1964–June 22, 1964*, and vol. 8, *June 23, 1964–July 1, 1964*. New York: W. W. Norton, 2011.

Nash, Jere, and Andy Taggart. *Mississippi Politics: The Struggle for Power, 1976–2008*. Jackson: University Press of Mississippi, 2009.

Nelson, Jack. *Terror in the Night: The Klan's Campaign against the Jews*. Jackson: University Press of Mississippi, 1996.

Neshoba County. Neshoba County Land Deeds Book. #RR, 537:2B; RR, 523.

Neshoba Democrat, 1885–, passim.

Niebuhr, Reinhold. "Meditations from Mississippi," *Christian Century*, February 10, 1937.

Nuwer, Deanne Stephens, and Greg O'Brien. "Mississippi's Oldest Pastime." In *Resorting to Casinos: The Mississippi Gambling Industry*, edited by Denise von Hermann, 11–25. Jackson: University Press of Mississippi, 2006.

Oakes, Henry Nathaniel. "The Struggle for Racial Equality in the Methodist Episcopal Church: The Career of Robert E. Jones, 1904–1944," PhD diss., University of Iowa, 1973.

Olick, Jeffrey K., Vered Vintzky-Seroussi, and Daniel Levy, eds. *The Collective Memory Reader*. New York: Oxford University Press, 2011.

Ownby, Ted. *American Dreams in Mississippi: Consumers, Poverty, and Culture, 1830–1998*. Chapel Hill: University of North Carolina Press, 1999.

Parker, Frank R. *Black Votes Count: Political Empowerment in Mississippi after 1965*. Chapel Hill: University of North Carolina Press, 1990.

Payne, Charles. *I've Got the Light of Freedom*. Berkeley: University of California Press, 1995.

Raper, Arthur F. *The Tragedy of Lynching*. Chapel Hill: University of North Carolina Press, 1988.

Richey, Russell E. *The Methodist Conference in America: A History*. Nashville, TN: Abingdon, 1996.

Richey, Russell E., Kenneth E. Rowe, and Jean Miller Schmidt, eds. *Perspectives on American Methodism: Interpretive Essays*. Nashville, TN: Abingdon, 1993.

———, eds. *The Methodist Experience in America: A Sourcebook*. Nashville, TN: Abingdon, 2000.

Ricoeur, Paul. *Memory, History, and Forgetting*. Chicago: University of Chicago Press, 2004.

Royce, Edward. *The Origins of Southern Sharecropping*. Philadelphia, PA: Temple University Press, 1993.

Savage, Barbara Diane. *Your Spirits Walk beside Us: The Politics of Black Religion.* Cambridge, MA: Harvard University Press, 2008.

Shockley, Grant S., ed. *Heritage and Hope: The African American Presence in United Methodism.* Nashville, TN: Abingdon, 1991.

Silver, James W. *Mississippi: The Closed Society.* New York: Harcourt, Brace and World, 1963.

Span, Christopher M. *From Cotton Field to Schoolhouse: African American Education in Mississippi, 1862–1875.* Chapel Hill: University of North Carolina Press, 2009.

Sparks, Randy J. *Religion in Mississippi.* Jackson: University Press of Mississippi, 2001.

State of Mississippi vs. Edgar Ray Killen (*Killen Trial Record*). No. 05-CR-0006-NS-G, 2005. 4 volumes. Circuit Court of Neshoba County, Mississippi. Philadelphia, MS: 2005.

Stevens, Francis B. "Splinter Group Develops in ms." n.p.: n.d. [probably June 1965].

Stockett, Kathryn. *The Help.* New York: Amy Einhorn and G. P. Putnam's Sons, 2009.

Stone, Ronald H. *Professor Reinhold Niebuhr: A Mentor to the Twentieth Century.* Louisville, KY: Westminster and John Knox, 1992.

Stout, Harry S. *Upon the Altar of the Nation: A Moral History of the Civil War.* New York: Viking, 2006.

Stout, Harry S., and D. G. Hart, eds. *New Directions in American Religious History.* New York: Oxford University Press, 1997.

Stubbs, Steven H. *Mississippi's Giant Houseparty: The History of the Neshoba County Fair; 115 Years (and Counting) of Politicking, Pacing, Partaking, and Partying.* Philadelphia, MS: Dancing Rabbit, 2005.

Tolnay, Stewart E., and E. M. Beck, *A Festival of Violence: An Analysis of Southern Lynchings, 1882–1930.* Chicago: University of Illinois Press, 1995.

TRC Report, Vol. 1, "Chairperson's Report," 22, cited in *After the TRC*, Wilmot James and Linda Van De Vijver, eds., Colin Bundy, "The Beast of the Past: History and the TRC," 15. Claremont, SA: David Philip, 2000.

Tyson, Timothy B. *Blood Done Sign My Name.* New York: Three Rivers, 2004.

Villano, Anthony, with Gerald Astor. *Brick Agent: Inside the Mafia for the FBI.* New York: Quadrangle, New York Times Books, 1977.

Von Hermannn, Denise. "Were Casinos a Solution for State Economic Growth?" In *Resorting to Casinos: The Mississippi Gambling Industry*, edited by Denise von Hermann, 67–80. Jackson: University Press of Mississippi, 2006.

———, ed. *Resorting to Casinos: The Mississippi Gambling Industry.* Jackson: University Press of Mississippi, 2006.

Wharton, Vernon Lane. *The Negro in Mississippi, 1865–1890.* Westport, CT: Greenwood, 1947, reprint 1984.

Whitehead, Don. *Attack on Terror: The FBI against the Ku Klux Klan in Mississippi.* New York: Funk and Wagnalls, 1970.

Wigger, John H. *Taking Heaven by Storm: Methodism and the Rise of Popular Christianity in America.* New York: Oxford University Press, 2001.

Wikipedia. "Lynching in the United States." Last modified September 15, 2014. http://en.wikipedia.org/wiki/Lynching_in_the_United_States.

Wilkerson, Isabel. *The Warmth of Other Suns: The Epic Story of America's Great Migration.* New York: Random House, 2010.

Winstead, Mary. *Back to Mississippi: A Personal Journey through the Events that Changed America in 1964.* New York: Hyperion, 2002.

Woodman, Harold. "Sequel to Slavery: The New History Views the Postbellum South." *Journal of Southern History,* 43 (November 1977), 523–54.

Woodward, C. Vann. *The Strange Career of Jim Crow.* New York: Oxford University Press, 1955.

Yates, Janelle B., and Theresa T. Ridout. *Red Clay Hills of Neshoba since 1833.* Philadelphia, MS: Neshoba County Historical Society, 1992.

Index

Property Bill of Mississippi and,
107; Circuit Riders, Inc. and,
98; Coordinating Committee
for Fundamental American
Freedoms and, 253n14; Galloway
Methodist Church and, 82, 111;
General Conference and, 82, 88,
107–108, 175–176; as legal advisor to
Governor Barnett, 169; Methodist
Federation for Social Action
opposed by, 81, 88, 98; Mississippi
Association of Methodist Ministers
and Laymen and, 98–99, 107;
Parlin and, 253n16; segregation
and, 81–82, 88, 98–100, 107–108,
113–114, 167–168, 170–171, 175–178,
180; Southeastern Jurisdiction
and, 115, 167, 177; suicide of, 179,
265n31; White Citizens' Council
and, 82, 107
Scarpa, Gregory, 149, 193, 260n17
Scarpa, Gregory Jr., 260n17
Schiro, Linda, 149, 260n17
Schwerner, Michael "Mickey": jailing
of, 135–137, 221; Mt. Zion United
Methodist Church and, 126,
130–131, 133, 221, 257–258n42;
murder of, ix, 9, 32–33, 127,
131–132, 135–137, 143–144, 146, 200,
202, 205, 211, 220–223, 234–235;
nonviolent philosophy of, 135;
religious identity of, 221
Schwerner, Rita Bender: Freedom
Summer campaigns and, 124–125,
130–131; on Freedom Summer
murder conspiracy trial (1967), 165;
Killen murder trial (2005) and,
200–201, 214, 218, 220, 225–226,
228–229; Mt. Zion fiftieth
anniversary commemoration
of Freedom Summer murders
(2014) and, 234; Mt. Zion United

Methodist Church and, 130;
proposed federal right to vote
and, 236
Seale, W.J., 14, 26
segregation: black landowership and,
51; *Brown* decision overturning
educational forms of, 50, 88–102,
167; campaigns against, 84, 93–95,
103–106, 111–114, 117–119, 121–122,
128, 144, 220; cattle industry and,
56; Civil Rights Act of 1964 and,
148–149; Great Migration and,
40, 43; interracial sex and, 34; of
interstate travel, 105; Methodist
Church and, 3, 17, 36–39, 61–99,
101–108, 110–117, 119–122, 165,
167–169, 173–178, 232; military
ban on, 84; Mississippi laws and
customs supporting, 3, 15–17, 21,
24, 30, 35–37, 40–52, 56, 64–66,
69, 89–90, 95–100, 103, 105–106,
108–114, 117–123, 133–134, 136–138,
141, 151, 153, 165, 167–170, 178,
181–182, 214, 216; of public schools,
48–49, 66, 95–96, 167–172;
"voluntary" forms of, 17; white
supremacy ideology behind, 1,
8, 24–25, 37, 46–49, 62, 64, 121,
165, 181
Selah, W.B., 89, 111–114, 254n38
Senate Internal Security
Subcommittee, 90
sharecropping, 27, 51, 53–55
Sharpe, Jerry McGrew, 138, 163
Shaw, Alexander P., 67, 73
Shelton, Andy, 218
Sherman, William Tecumseh, 25–26
Shockley, Grant S., 78
Shuttlesworth, Fred, 93
Silver, James, 116, 152
Silver Star Hotel casino, 198
Simmons, Isaac, 83